New
Life Begins

What Can Happen When We Pray

What Can Happen When We Pray

Daily Devotional

Foreword by Rev. Dr. Jeremiah A. Wright Jr.

Augsburg Fortress
Minneapolis

WHAT CAN HAPPEN WHEN WE PRAY
Daily Devotional

The hymns listed under the "Today's Song" heading at the end of each daily devotion are referenced to the book *This Far by Faith: An African American Resource for Worship* (Minneapolis: Augsburg Fortress, 1999.)

Editor: Ronald S. Bonner
Cover illustration: *Visions,* by Synthia Saint James, Los Angeles, California. Used by permission of the artist.
Cover design and pattern: Shalette Cauley-Wandrick
Interior text design: James Satter

ISBN 0-7394-2557-9

Manufactured in the U.S.A.

Contents

Foreword

The Word of God teaches over and over again that prayer is the most powerful weapon in a believer's arsenal. From the awesome challenge that God gives in 2 Chronicles 7:14 through the words of Jesus encouraging us to "always pray," the biblical principle of the importance of prayer is quite clear.

God says in the Old Testament that if we humble ourselves and pray, God will hear us from heaven, forgive our sins, and heal the land. Jesus says that if we ask what we need in God's name, if it is in accord with the will of God, it will be done!

These biblical principles come alive in a very different way in the African-American experience. Both James Washington, in his *Conversations with God,* and Harold Carter, in his *The Prayer Tradition of Black People,* discuss these differences and the powerful way that black "prayer life" has made a difference.

Theology is never impersonal, and theological is never "universal." Theology is culture-specific and is always done through the lenses of those who experience God and encounter God in their particularity. It is this theology that has shaped African-American prayer for more than 300 years.

The uniqueness of the African-American experience does not need rehearsing. Five hundred years of white supremacy have shaped the perspectives of Africans on this continent and Africans who live in the diaspora.

A personal encounter with Jesus Christ, however, has produced a theology and an understanding of prayer that is distinctly unique and breathtakingly inspiring! That is what you will experience in this volume. The writers who contribute to this devotional book have come to know God as the sons and daughters of Africa. That means that their forebears have known "the middle passage," white supremacy, racism, segregation, Jim Crow, and the insanity of the "Ham Doctrine."

Through it all, however, the personal relationships that were developed by each of these writers' foreparents and the personal relationship that they have developed with Jesus Christ, have given them not only a different perspective on prayer—they also have a hope that is indestructible!

Their experience of prayer is quite personal. In Howard Thurman's autobiography, *With Head and Heart,* there is a clue to what follows in the devotional. The writers in this volume have a perspective on prayer that is shaped by both head

a. heart. These writers know Jesus for themselves and they also know what it means to be black in America! They know the risen Lord and they serve him.

At the same time, however, they have lived through the Civil Rights movement and have seen the hatred of white Christians who believe that the sons of Canaan were supposed to be "hewers of wood and drawers of water." They have lived in the 20th century—a century that Dr. Martin Luther King Jr. described as the most "segregated hour in America!" King made reference to the eleven o'clock worship hour on Sunday mornings when white-racist Christians thought themselves superior to blacks and forced the creation of the African-American churches.

Because there flows through these writers' veins the blood of Harriet Tubman, Bishop Henry McNeal Turner, Edward Wilmot Blyden, Jarena Lee, Sojourner Truth, Marcus Garvey, and Queen Nzinga, they have a different hermeneutic. Their understanding of "calling on the Lord" to get an answer is a far different understanding than one that was shaped in the drawing rooms of Europe or in the cold, sterile halls of academia in New England in America. The whip, the auction block, the slave patrols, the fire hoses, the German shepherds, the overseers and the "Uncle Toms" have shaped the faith of these writers and it bleeds through very powerfully as they speak of prayer from a very personal, powerful, and painful experience!

The same Jesus who met Africans in the holds of slave ships and in the cane breaks of Mississippi during slavery meets us today. That is the perspective they bring to their meditations, and that is why this volume goes straight to the heart of those of us who know personally the "stony road" that we have trod!

The writers in these pages use images and vignettes of experience from the African-American reality. Because they are like Ezekiel, who sat where his people sat, their meditations will certainly hit home among African-American readers. For readers of this devotional who are not African-American, their writings are just as important. They are important because they will give to the non-African-American audience a glimpse of a people whose faith could not be destroyed no matter how "bitter" the chastening rod. It will give the uninitiated a peek at the "glossary" and the "code language" of those who have known sorrow but who have come out of "the gloomy past" victoriously!

In the words of one of the writers in this volume and in the words of a gospel song, it will help the uninitiated reader to understand why African-Americans are so jubilant when they say, "We are still here!" I commend this volume to you, and I also commend the Christ who makes us more than conquerors to you. As you read this work, may God bless your reading with God's power and God's Spirit.

Jeremiah A. Wright Jr.
Trinity United Church of Christ
Chicago, Illinois

Introduction

I would like to thank you for choosing this volume and adding it to your collection of devotional materials. I trust that you will come to find this an indispensable tool for your daily praise life. Using this book as it is designed will help you develop your spiritual dexterity and strength. I know that while I was editing this resource I was getting stronger as I was being filled with God's word. Once you start reading *What Can Happen When We Pray*, please resist trying to read ahead. If you want more to read, then read the entire Bible chapter that each day's reflection is based on. In fact, as you progress, our hope is that reading the Bible alongside this devotional will become part of your daily devotional period.

Next, try to write a few notes each day as you reflect on what you have read. Think about how God is working in your life and write down your thoughts. Ask yourself how to apply today's lesson to your life. Then, sing and fill your spirit with a Holy song, one based on God's redeeming love for you.

And now, beloved, please know the grace of God that comes through the love and sacrifice of our Lord and Savior Jesus Christ. May you grow in God as you exercise your faith daily, and may your works be blessed by God. In Jesus' name. Amen.

Ronald S. Bonner
Augsburg Fortress, Publishers

365

Daily Devotions

Blessed, Holy Rest

*"So God blessed the seventh day and hallowed it,
because on it God rested from all the work
that he had done in creation."*

GENESIS 2:3

Today's Prayer

God, help us to meet you in the quiet place you have prepared for us. Amen.

Today's Reflection

It is Monday morning, and the week begins. You are so tired, and it's only Monday. This is American life: full, busy, crowded, and chaotic. Swirling, whirling—and the week is not over yet.

God worked hard, too. Spoke the world into existence. God made humankind in God's image and saw the "very goodness" of creation. Then God stopped and took a break. God breathed deeply and enjoyed the scenery. God chilled out. God blessed this day of rest and made it holy and rested. We, created in God's image, are blessed to do the same.

Today's Song: "Blessed Assurance," #118

Journal Notes Be thankful that you're able to open your eyes for another day. Don't take the little things for granted. Always be grateful, no matter how things may appear. Amen

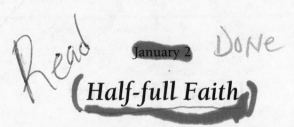

Read **January 2** DoNe

Half-full Faith

"Where you go, I will go; where you lodge, I will lodge;
your people shall be my people, and your God my God."

RUTH 1:16b

Today's Prayer

Holy God, we pray for faith to see rainbows after floods, new life after death, and gifts from you in the midst of our losses. In Jesus' name. Amen.

Today's Reflection

In one of my favorite novels, a little boy is kidnapped while in the care of his big brother. Paralyzed by grief, their mother cannot appreciate what she has left—a son and daughter who need her, and a husband who loves her. Like this fictional mother, Naomi lost so much while in Moab: her husband and two sons were dead. Naomi was unable to appreciate what she has left.

Like Naomi, we may feel bitter, that life has dealt harsh or unfair blows. Let us pray for faith to claim the gifts that come to us even in the midst of our tragedies and losses.

Today's Song: "The Lord Is My Light," #61

Journal Notes *No matter how things seem to appear. Even with the loss of love ones you must trust in Jesus Christ and our Lord God for strength and continue to thank God for what we have. And Ask him to help you through the tragic times as well as the good, times. In Jesus Name Amen*

Next

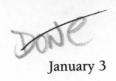

January 3

Well-Watered Trees

"They are like trees planted by streams of water, which yield their fruit it its season, and their leaves do not wither."

PSALM 1:3

Today's Prayer

Lord God, refresh us with the living water, that our faith may be strong. Keep us deeply rooted in your word and in your love. In Jesus' name. Amen.

Today's Reflection

When my parents bought their home in Chicago, it was quite a momentous occasion. The house represented for them security and a place to grow things—children, gardens and plants. What they touch is full life. The plants grew strong, tall, and sturdy, like well-watered trees.

Mom and dad are like well-watered trees—strong and sturdy in their faith and their faithfulness to their family. They, like many of our ancestors who have gone before them, delight in God's law. They read it and pray over it. May we, who come from a strong people, know the love of God expressed in God's commands to us. May we be like trees planted by streams of water.

Today's Song: "Shine, Jesus, Shine," #64

Journal Notes _____

_____

_____

_____

Dove

January 4

. . . And the Living Is Easy

_" . . . but those who listen to me will be secure and will live at ease,
without dread of disaster."_
PROVERBS 1:33

Today's Prayer

Wise and loving God, help me to hear your word, understand its wisdom, heed your instruction, and rest in the security of your grace. When I wander far from your truth, bring me home—to you. In the magnificent name of Christ. Amen.

Today's Reflection

Sometimes our lives feel like perilous journeys, as we seek a place to call home, a place to be known and loved.

We may go down the wrong path; obstacles may confront us. We sometimes confuse our search for courage, love and wisdom with fame, fortune, and status. In fact, we have that which we seek. We have God's wisdom, teaching, guiding, and counseling us toward the desires of our hearts.

Our restless wandering and wondering can be replaced by security and living at ease, when we listen to God's voice.

Today's Song: "Blessed Assurance," #118

Journal Notes _____

_____

_____

_____

January 5

The Kingdom of God Is Near

" . . . the time is fulfilled, and the kingdom of God has come near;
repent and believe in the good news."

MARK 1:15

Today's Prayer

Holy One of God, come near us. Make waves in our lives. Beloved Son of God, may your kingdom come, your will be done in my life and in all the earth. Amen.

Today's Reflection

I love the ocean, especially at high tide. One can see, hear, and feel God's nearness. As the moon and the earth get close, they literally pull on one another.

The nearness of the moon makes waves on the earth. The nearness of God's kingdom makes waves on the earth, as well. The waves crash over, and people's lives are changed. Disciples are called, the sick are healed, unclean spirits are cast out, and sins are forgiven.

Friends, hear the good news of Jesus Christ, the Son of God: the kingdom of God is near, making waves.

Let us pray for strength to turn our lives around and be changed.

Today's Song: "I Want to Be Ready," #41

Journal Notes _____

_____

_____

_____

Faith to Faith

For in it the righteousness of God is revealed through faith for faith;
as it is written, "The one who is righteous will live by faith."
ROMANS 1:17

Today's Prayer

Righteous and merciful God, thank you for your gift of eternal life. Give us faith
to live for you, through Jesus Christ. Amen.

Today's Reflection

I learned early to enjoy the praise of my parents for doing a good job. When my
siblings and I excelled, our parents were very happy. We are all grateful for the confidence our parents have in us, as we live into their vision of our abilities.

We live in a world where what we achieve matters; the works we do really set us
apart. Not so in God's kingdom. Paul reminds us that the good news reveals God's
righteousness, which becomes ours when we receive it by faith. God's faithfulness—
and then our faith in God, saves us.

The righteous one will live by faith to faith, not faith to works. From God's faith
to our faith—this is the way of the cross, this is the way to live.

Today's Song: "Just a Closer Walk with Thee," #253

Journal Notes _____

_____

_____

_____

God Is Light

*"This is the message we have heard from him and proclaim to you,
that God is light and in him is no darkness at all."*
1 JOHN 1:5

Today's Prayer

God of light and life, illumine our path, that we may walk with you. Keep us in the light and in fellowship with you, with your Son, Jesus Christ, and with one another. In the blessed name of Jesus. Amen.

Today's Reflection

God made light, and darkness, both very good. But in John's community, and much of the New Testament world, light and darkness were metaphors for contrasting values. We are invited to walk in wisdom, beauty, purity, and joy!

Walking in truth, we fellowship with Christ and with one another. Walking in grace, our sins are washed away. Let us walk in the light of the world.

Today's Song: "We Are Marching in the Light of God," #63

Journal Notes _____

_____

_____

_____

_____

The Power of Confession

And the LORD *said, "What have you done? Listen;*
your brother's blood is crying out to me from the ground!"

GENESIS 4:10

Today's Prayer

God of grace and truth, every day you call me to come close to you and experience the power of your love. Make me willing to confess to you the sins that trouble me and bring harm to those around me. Release in me the power to bring atonement and reconciliation where it is needed in my life. Let your forgiveness remove the burden of shame from me, that I may truly serve you. Amen.

Today's Reflection

When you confess your sins to God, you must trust that God is listening to you as if you are the only person in the world. God already knows what you have done and what you have left undone. But when you confess your sins and ask for forgiveness in Jesus' name, a wonderful power is released that forgives and restores you and equips you to make amends for any wrong you have done. No matter how great your faults or serious your crimes, God's love for you is greater still. As you receive forgiveness from God, you are empowered to work for reconciliation and atonement with those you may have injured. What have you done? Tell it to Jesus, the elders used to say. Earth has no sorrow that heaven cannot heal!

Today's Song: "Come Ye Disconsolate," #186

Journal Notes _____

_____

_____

_____

Unsung Heroes

But Boaz answered her, "All that you have done for your mother-in-law since the death of your husband has been fully told me."
RUTH 2:11

Today's Prayer

Teach me to trust you with my whole life, Lord. Especially when I need to rest my body and renew my spirit, stay by my side and give me peace. Amen.

Today's Reflection

When the demands of life press down on you, it is hard to stay connected to the healing power of a peaceful rest. Normal stress and worry are not the only things that can disrupt your ability to sleep peacefully. When injustice and human cruelty strike close to home, your outrage and your fear can work together to keep you restless and confused. Faith in God can help you release these fears to the One who made you and who knows all about the troubles you face. Especially as you participate in the struggle against the political and spiritual enemies of our people, you need to trust that at all times God is with you. Let faith teach you how to surrender to God daily and find the rest that is needed for a healthy life.

Seek God's power when life is overwhelming, so that you can stay strong even in the presence of your enemies.

Today's Song: "The Lord Is My Light," #61

Journal Notes _____

_____

_____

_____

Sleep in Heavenly Peace

"I lie down and sleep;
I wake again, for the LORD sustains me."
PSALM 3:5

Today's Prayer

God who watches over me, you know how easily I am disturbed by the stress and struggle of daily living. I am happy to know that you are a God who neither slumbers nor sleeps. Your care for me is constant. Your love for me is boundless. Amen.

Today's Reflection

What a joy when assurances are that we can take to the bank and cash. We expect that with our paychecks, we expect that in vows, we exchange with others. How secure we are in having God, the creator of all that is, to give us an assurance.

God assures us that we are cared for, that we are loved. Oh let us praise and worship this God of divine and holy love.

Today's Song: "Blessed Assurance," #118

Journal Notes _____

_____

_____

_____

The Search for Wisdom

" . . . if you indeed cry out for insight, and raise your voice for
understanding (then you will understand righteousness
and justice and equity, every good path)."

PROVERBS 2:3, 9

Today's Prayer

God of wisdom, I am often confused and disturbed by the ups and downs of life. I cannot always make sense of the struggles that challenge me, nor do I fully appreciate the blessings that I know you send every day. Give me your inspiration so that I may grow wiser and more mature. strengthen my personal discipline as a child of God, so that I may learn from you how to live in peace. Let my faith in Christ renew my mind this day, and teach me to always walk in the way of the good. Amen.

Today's Reflection

The word if usually suggests that something is possible as long as certain conditions are met. God has promised to give wisdom and knowledge and understanding if you are truly seeking these things. Often this means that you must give time and attention to some spiritual discipline such as scripture reading with prayer and meditation. Are you struggling to make sense of the world around you? Many others who felt this same struggle have found peace because their spiritual understanding began to grow. Talk to yourself about your desire for wisdom, and then talk to God. Choose a spiritual discipline and ask God to open up your understanding. If you seek God's wisdom, you will surely find it.

Today's Song: "O Lord, Open My Eyes," #134

Journal Notes

The Uncommon Life

"When his family heard it, they went out to restrain him,
for people were saying, He has gone out of his mind."
MARK 3:21

Today's Prayer

God of Mystery, I know that you have made me in your image. Give me courage today so that I will not allow others to lower my self-esteem or my self-confidence. Make me aware of the people you have placed in my life who are here to support and guide me as I continue to learn the truth about who I am and why you made me this way. Thank you for the gift of life. Keep me secure in your love as I live each day open to self-discovery and available for your service. Amen.

Today's Reflection

Conformity is not always a virtue. There are times when the majority's rules are unfair, and the path of least resistance is not the way of God. You may experience daily pressure to live according to the most popular values and standards of behavior. Are you surprised to discover that the same pressure was applied to Jesus, even by his own family? If Jesus had allowed people to force him to conform to the dominant views of his day, he never would have accomplished his mission. He knew he had to be different, like Moses before him and like Rosa Parks and George Washington Carver and so many after him. Be encouraged today. The children of God are never called to just fit in. By the grace of God we are called to be spiritually outstanding!

Today's Song: "Oh, I Woke Up This Morning," #166

Journal Notes

January 13

Grace Abounds

"All have sinned and fall short of the glory of God."
ROMANS 3:23

Today's Prayer

O Divine Liberator, you have come into my life with a spirit of freedom and love. You have looked beyond my faults and offered me a new life in you. Keep me secure in the faith that is growing in me through Jesus Christ. By your grace, show me how to share this faith with others. Let me never forget that you have freed me from the power of sin, and that your spirit of freedom and love will keep changing my life for the rest of my life. Thank you for this marvelous gift. Amen.

Today's Reflection

When God reaches out to human beings, God does not discriminate. God does not come to one zip code and not another. God does not favor one nation over another. Nor does God choose one language, one culture, or even one gender over another. Regardless of who you are and where you live, you are now part of a new community where love can abound. Everyone struggles with the power of sin, but our new community in Christ shares something that is stronger than sin. Perhaps you are being challenged today to share the love that has made you a child of God.

Trust the power of this love that is working in you right now. God's love does not discriminate, and neither should you.

Today's Song: "Fill My Cup, Let It Overflow," #127

Journal Notes

It Takes a Community

*"I am writing to you fathers, because you know him who is from
the beginning. I am writing to you, young people, because
you have conquered the evil one."*
1 JOHN 2:13

Today's Prayer

Faithful God, you are the God of our ancestors and the God of our children yet
unborn. Continue to open my eyes so that I may recognize the gifts of my spiritual
heritage and the promise of my future in you. Continue to reveal to me the role models and mentors and teachers you have provided to assist me in my spiritual growth.
Continue to make me strong in my faith and confident in the power of your Spirit in
me, so that I may become more spiritually mature and better able to help another
child of God today. Amen.

Today's Reflection

I am not the first, nor am I the last. The walk of faith did not start with me, nor
will it end with me. I am blessed by strong people of faith who show me so much
about living in Christ. Where would I be without the spiritual fathers and mothers
God has sent into my life? It takes a whole village to raise a child of God. The
children, too, are my teachers. The Spirit of God moves in them with beauty and
innocence. They remind me that the power of evil does not rule this world.

Today's Song: "Lift Every Voice and Sing," #296

Journal Notes _____

_____

_____

_____

Regrets

> *"And the Lord was sorry that
> he had made humankind on the earth."*
>
> GENESIS 6:6

Today's Prayer

Lord, take all those who long for shelter from the storms of life into your ark of safety. Surround us with your strong arms—protect us from harm as the great torrential rains of adversity begin to fall all around us. As you gave Noah instruction before hand to prepare and spared him from the wrath which was to come—instruct me Lord. Amen.

Today's Reflection

And God saw things were bad in the land, and God had a plan. Have you ever felt like all was for naught? Have you ever felt like all your good intentions and efforts were completely wasted? This may have been how God felt when God surveyed the earth and found it wanting. Yet God saw amidst the corruption something worth salvaging—redeeming. God saw, and God sees, and God has a plan requiring your participation. God saw, and God sees God's own, and then calls them into service.

Today's Song: "I Can Hear My Savior Calling," #146

Journal Notes _____

_____

_____

_____

January 16

Heaven's Provisions

"My daughter, should I not try to find a home for you,
where you be will provided."
RUTH 3:1, NIV

Today's Prayer

Gracious God, I thank you for this day and the ways that you have cared for me. I ask now that you will continue to bless me as I seek to do your will. Amen.

Today's Reflection

As we search for serenity Jesus calls us to have the spirit of Ruth. Upon hearing the word of God, Ruth received it with a glad heart and let the word of God grow within her until it came forth as humility, obedience, and trust. One of the hardest things in life is to let go of control and trust someone else to guide and lead us, to have our best interest at heart, and to know more than we know. Trusting God is the way of the wise disciple of Christ, the way of a child of God, and it is a way to live life in serenity and the shalom of God.

Today's Song: "God Has Smiled on Me," #190

Journal Notes _____

_____

_____

_____

Safe Haven

*"I will both lie down and sleep in peace; for you alone,
O Lord, make me lie down in safety."*
PSALM 4:8

Today's Prayer

Dear Lord God of Peace, grant that today may be a day of peace within my heart. Grant me the courage to trust you for all I need. Let your *shalom* that surpasses all understanding rest and abide over your people this day and forever. Amen.

Today's Reflection

One night while serving as a hospital chaplain, I received a request from a nurse to come visit a patient. The patient's request was for someone to sit and help him make it through the night. He was despondent over his condition and had talked about committing suicide. We talked, reflected on God's word, and prayed for the shalom of God. Eventually he was led by God's Spirit to lay down in the peace of sleep.

When he awoke, he called for me to come to his room again. He shared his dream. Something indeed had changed. There was the sound of hope in this voice. His attitude had changed. Where there was sadness, now joy and peace seemed to abide. His circumstances were the same but he was different. He had met the Savior and was now trusting in the Lord to grant him God's shalom.

Today's Song: "I Must Tell Jesus," #183

Journal Notes

_____

_____

_____

_____

January 18

Paying Back

*"Honor the LORD with your substance and with
the first fruits of all your produce."*

PROVERBS 3:9

Today's Prayer

Dear God, Blessed Redeemer, teach me to honor thy word. Amen.

Today's Reflection

Do you feel empty, do you feel as if something is missing from your store house of happiness? Then let's journey further along the path of God's word. In today's scripture reflection, we read, "Honor the Lord with your wealth with the first fruits of all your produce" . . . then the Lord says your barns will be filled to overflowing and your vats will brim over with new vine.

Honor the Lord with your wealth. Today seek to discover what your wealth is and then Honor God with it.

Today's Song: "I'm a-Goin'-a Eat at the Welcome Table," #263

Journal Notes _____

_____

_____

_____

Hidden Treasure

*"But where in this remote place can anyone
get enough bread to feed them?"*
MARK 8:4

Today's Prayer

Eternal God, I thank you for waking me this morning and I ask that you will guide me this day. It seems hard sometimes, but I know with you by my side I can do all that you ask. Amen.

Today's Reflection

Earlier this week, our devotion called us to focus on the Old Testament character named Ruth. Hopefully, we will emulate Ruth. The thing I admire most about Ruth is her sense of assurance in the word of a God she had never met but had learned of only from the stories that she heard from others.

Naomi was uncertain of what the future held in store and she wanted to flee back to her native land after the deaths of her providers. Even in the face of uncertainty and adversity, Ruth trusted in God to be her provider. If we but learn to trust and obey, the same. Shalom will be ours for the asking.

Today's Song: "Lead Me, Guide Me," #70

Journal Notes _____

_____

_____

_____

Reborn to Live Free

"For whoever has died is freed from sin."
ROMANS 6:7

Today's Prayer

Holy God, teach me your way so I might be pleasing in your sight. Amen.

Today's Reflection

Thanks be to God! The God of Abraham, Sarah, Isaac, and Rebecca, and now my God. Thanks be to God for the redemption that is mine from sin, shame, fear, desperation, poverty, sadness, grief, and rejection. Thanks be to Jehovah Jirah for providing a way out of darkness, out of sin, out of suffering and shame into God's marvelous light of love, happiness, wholeness, joy, wealth, and abundance. Thanks be to God for the newness I feel as I walk in the light of Christ's love and righteousness. Thanks be to God for my life—my victory over sin and helplessness and for the gift of eternal peace and earthly serenity.

Today's Song: "God Sent His Son," #93

Journal Notes _____

_____

_____

_____

Eternal Hope

"In the hope of eternal life that God, who never lies,
promised before the ages began."
TITUS 1:2

Today's Prayer

Heavenly Father, creator of all that is and is to be, today I surrender my heart to you and reaffirm the vows that I made for my baptism and reclaim the promises that you gave. I recommit myself to be the follower of Christ, now tell me what I have to do, what I have to say, how I have to walk each and every day to be a faithful follower. Teach me Lord that I may teach others. Amen.

Today's Reflection

If there is one thing I want in life, it is to have life and that more abundantly. If there is one thing I want to be in life, it is a child of God. What is godliness? Being like God. Titus looked to Paul for direction and guidance. Who do you look to for spiritual direction? Who do you look to teach you the truth of God's word? In this truth you can believe and never doubt that in all of God's promises to you—"God does not lie."

Whatever God has promised to you—will come to be—for God does not lie!

Today's Song: "All to Jesus I Surrender," #235

Journal Notes _____

_____

_____

_____

I Can Count on God

*"As long as the earth endures, seedtime and harvest, cold and heat,
summer and winter, day and night, shall not cease."*
GENESIS 8:22

Today's Prayer

Eternal and Holy God, I know that storms are a part of life. I am tempted to give in, give out and give up. Thank you for the storms and for the peace that comes after each one. Thank you for remembering me when the world would ignore and push me aside. Grant me the patience to wait on you to move and act in my life. I count on you to see me through. In Christ's name I pray. Amen.

Today's Reflection

Lord, give me patience right now. Sometimes, it is hard to wait. We get restless and anxious—we want to know how things are going to turn out—right now! Noah was commanded by God to build and populate an ark when there was not a cloud in the sky. Although the community laughed at him, Noah did as God commanded. When the heavens opened, it rained and rained and rained and rained! No doubt Noah wondered if the rain would ever stop or if God had simply forgotten about him.

Finally, after 150 days, God remembered Noah! Isn't that just like God? God may not come when we want, but God is always on time. While we wait, we can pray that God will take away doubt, fear, anxiety, and impatience. We are assured that as God remembered Noah, God will remember us. As faithful as the cycle of life and harvest is, that is how faithful God is. We can depend on God to fulfill God's promises.

Today's Song: "Great Is Thy Faithfulness," #283

Journal Notes

_____

_____

_____

_____

January 23

Making a Way

Then the women said to Naomi, "Blessed be the LORD,
who has not left you this day without next-of-kin;
and may his name be renowned in Israel!"
RUTH 4:14

Today's Prayer

Loving God, you are like a parent to me. You provide what I need. Your grace overflows, and I am grateful. Help me, God, to share your love with someone who is lonely and needs a kind word. May I be a sparkle of hope for someone who feels alone this day. In Jesus' name. Amen.

Today's Reflection

Do you have a "play" mother or an "other" mother? Black folks have always experienced creative family systems—the extended family has been a strength of the black community since long before slavery. We know how to take care of one another. You may have grown up in a community where the adults took responsibility for the well-being of all the children in the neighborhood. This kind of caring made for safe and secure communities.

Even though times have changed, we are blessed if we live in caring communities. Naomi was blessed because her daughter-in-law was devoted to her. God opened a way for Naomi to be blessed in her golden years. When she lost hope of ever having a "real" family, God made a way. God brings into our lives, men, women, and children who love us and remind us that we are related to one another through the love of Jesus. God creates a present and a future worth living.

Today's Song: "God Sent His Son," #93

Journal Notes

Never Alone

*"I am weary with my moaning; every night I flood my bed with
tears; I drench my couch with my weeping."*

PSALM 6:6

Today's Prayer

When I cannot utter the words, God, I know you are with me. Your presence is a
comfort to me even in my deepest pain. Thank you for being that One who sticks so
close that your breath is my breath. Be my leaning post and hold me up that I might
be strong of mind and body. Amen.

Today's Reflection

Have you ever been really sick? How did you feel? Were you scared? Did you cry?
Did you pray? Were there family and friends to support you? There are times in life
when we are overcome with emotion. The psalmist gives us an example of raw, honest, and open emotion. He talks about moaning and weeping—to the point of being
worn out and done in.

Sometimes, our hearts are so heavy with sadness that all we can do is weep. We
are assured that even weeping is prayer. God who loves us and cares about us notices
each tear. We are told, "weeping may linger for the night, but joy comes in the morning" (Psalm 30:5b). God never leaves us alone—God sits with us in whatever we are
going through. And God's presence heals us. As people of faith, we are taught a simple truth: if we pray, there is no need to worry. If we are going to worry, there is no
need to pray!

Today's Song: "When I Think of the Goodness of Jesus," #269

Journal Notes _____

_____

_____

_____

January 25

Step by Step

*"I have taught you the way of wisdom; I have led you in the paths
of uprightness. When you walk, your step will not be hampered;
and if you run, you will not stumble."*

PROVERBS 4:11-12

Today's Prayer

Holy One, to give me strength and courage. Continue to use me for your glory.
I ask these blessings in the name of the Christ. Amen.

Today's Reflection

A young, promising athlete was in a terrible accident. His right leg was amputated above the knee. He was lost in a sea of depression and wanted to die. He often was overwhelmed by feelings of uselessness and despair. The man resisted the comfort and reassurance from family and friends that he still had a full life ahead of him. By studying the Bible, he began to think about the stories of courageous women and men and their victories against all odds. He started to believe that he could have a life beyond his accident.

Today, this young man is running and winning track meets all over the world. He even participated in the Special Olympics in Sydney, Australia, a few years ago. He credits his faith in God for his turnaround. He shares his story and faith with all who will listen. He has learned that the beginning of wisdom is faith—faith that God is able to turn a tragedy into a victory!

Whatever you are dealing with, whatever your condition or circumstance, give it over to God and let God work with it and with you. God is able!

Today's Song: "I Want Jesus to Walk with Me," #66

Journal Notes _____

_____

_____

_____

January 26

Just a Little Bit

"For all of them have contributed out of their abundance;
but she out of her poverty has put in everything she had,
all she had to live on."

MARK 12:44

Today's Prayer

Loving God, you don't ask for much and you give us so much in return. Thank you for being generous and giving. Help me to give of my time, talent and treasure. Use my gifts for your work here on earth. When I would hold back, remind me of the poor widow who gave everything she had. I pray for a generous spirit. Amen.

Today's Reflection

The woman was on a fixed income. Before paying her rent and bills, she put aside 10 percent for her tithe to the church. Some months, she ate only beans as the month came to a close. Her pastor suggested that she decrease her tithe so that she could make ends meet better. But she was adamant: "Oh, no, Pastor! I must give my tithe. When I do, I always have everything I need. I love this church and this is my family. I must give my fair share to keep things going."

Such devotion goes beyond money. She has found a home and wants to make a contribution. She may not be rich but she lives in the abundance of joy, love, and community. We all have something to give—no matter how small our gifts may seem, God can take them and multiply them for Kingdom-building. Every gift counts!

Today's Song: "All to Jesus I Surrender," #235

Journal Notes _____

_____

_____

_____

January 27

Blessed Assurance

*"No, in all these things we are more than conquerors
through him who loved us."*
ROMANS 8:37-39

Today's Prayer

Gracious God, we trust that you are working in creation and in history despite outward appearance. When we cannot see a viable future, reassure us that you are near. Let our prayers for justice and peace be heard. Grant to us a vision of hope and vitality that we may withstand the assault of evil, knowing that nothing is too hard for you to overcome. Shape us so that we are part of the solution and not part of the problem. In the name of the Savior. Amen.

Today's Reflection

Life is hard! Forces set to destroy us often hit when we least expect it. The effects of slavery and Jim Crow have left many of us scarred and weary. But we are still here. Discrimination and neglect have left many communities without important resources and services. But we are still here. Drugs are among the latest threats to our survival as they kill a generation of our young people. But we are still here! We are reminded that the forces of evil surround us daily. But we live in the hope that God, who watched over our ancestors, is still watching over us. We live in the hope that not all is lost. Our present circumstances do not seal our fate. God is bigger than any situation we can experience. God still has marvelous things in store for us. Our task is to believe, to work, and to wait to see what will be. God is not through with us yet!

Today's Song: "Blessed Assurance," #118

Journal Notes

January 28

A Clean Heart

*"[Jesus] it is who gave himself for us that he might redeem
us from all iniquity and purify for himself a people out his own
who are zealous for good deeds."*

TITUS 2:14

Today's Prayer

O Redeeming God, you know my faults and shortcomings. I am only human—
this is not an excuse, but a fact. I confess that I indulge my ego and do little things
that hurt others and myself. Please forgive my sins—those I do knowingly and those
I do unconsciously. Search my heart and cast out any wickedness there. Create in
me a clean heart and a pure spirit, so that I may serve you fully. In Jesus' name, your
perfect example and our role model. Amen.

Today's Reflection

An African proverb states: To know is to do. If one fails to behave properly, it is
because one does not truly know. There is something about the life of faith that
changes our behavior toward God's people and world.

We are children of God through our belief and faith in Jesus Christ. As such, we
seek harmony and peace in our interactions and relationships. To be sure, we face
challenges as we try to be good people—clear-headed, self-controlled, forgiving,
kind, generous and loving. Most of the time, we do a great job; every once in a
while, we fail. Our failures are not counted against us if we earnestly repent and
seek forgiveness. In this life, we are not asked to be perfect, but we are asked to try
our best.

Today's Song: "Give Me a Clean Heart," #216

Journal Notes _____

_____

_____

_____

God Hears Our Cries

*"God heard their groaning, and God remembered his covenant
with Abraham, Isaac, and Jacob."*

EXODUS 2:24a

Today's Prayer

Dear God, please help me in my doubt so that I can face life's obstacles with the knowledge that all things are possible with you. Amen.

Today's Reflection

The psalmist believed that everything praises the Lord—the sun, moon, sky, trees, animals—everything. That means then, that the Lord is listening. It is very comforting to know that the Lord listens to us and our praise. However, it is even more comforting to know that the Lord listens to our groaning and our cries. God not only listens to our cries but also remembers the covenant with Abraham, Isaac, and Jacob. The promise is that, as descendants of Abraham, we will be delivered from our cries and given the promised land.

Today's Song: "I, the Lord of Sea and Sky," #230

Journal Notes

God's Love Never Ceases

"The LORD, the LORD, the Compassionate and gracious God,
slow to anger, abounding in love and faithfulness . . ."
EXODUS 34:6b

Today's Prayer

Kind and loving God, thank you for enveloping us in your love. May we always be mindful of the fact that we are loved. Amen.

Today's Reflection

God's words to Moses continues to remind us that the love of God is all encompassing. His love cuts across all barriers. God's love is not limited, hampered, nor bound by human ideals and idiosyncrasies. God's love is always present. We cannot escape God's compassion and forgiveness, for God is compassionate.

Today's Song: "O, How He Loves You and Me," #82

Journal Notes _____

_____

_____

_____

Please Send Someone Else

But he said, "O my LORD, please send someone else."
EXODUS 4:13

Today's Prayer

Our Creator and Sustainer, the very idea that you would call us into service is often overwhelming. It is such a privilege and yet the responsibility is awesome. Help us not to fear those things that you would lead us to do if, we keep our eyes on your divine purpose instead of our human frailties. Lord work through our fears and insecurities so that we may faithfully serve you and be a blessing to others. Amen.

Today's Reflection

Moses was a bit reluctant to say the least. Sound familiar? Has God asked you to go where you would rather not go and do what you would rather not do? Do you feel that you just don't have what it takes to meet the challenge, lead the charge, or answer the call? God not only calls us into service, God equips! The request that we most fear from God, may well be a defining moment, the turning point, the way out of no way, or the ultimate blessing. Be of good courage. This is why God reminds us that what is important is not what we can do, but, what God can and will do through us. Amen.

Today's Song: "When the Storms of Life Are Raging," #198

Journal Notes _____

_____

_____

_____

February 1

Holy Spirit

*"I baptize you with water for repentance. But after me will come one
who is more powerful than I, whose sandals I am not fit to carry.
He will baptize you with the Holy Spirit and with fire."*
MATTHEW 3:11, NIV

Today's Prayer

God, help me not to fear the Holy Spirit. I'm not sure what having the Holy Spirit
means or what having it will make me do! I don't like reaching for what I cannot see,
and I don't understand the Holy Spirit. That's why I am afraid. Help me to trust you
enough to seek Your spirit in my life. Amen.

Today's Reflection

There are three parts of the Holy Trinity: the Father, which is our creator, the Son,
who is our redeemer, and the Holy Spirit, which is our sustainer. The Holy Spirit
enables us to cope and to praise God, in spite of what might be going on in our lives.

But the Holy Spirit is even more. It empowers us and connects us to God in an
almost inexplicable way. It moves us closer to the source of our strength. The more
we ingest and accept the Holy Spirit, the more transformed we become. And repentance, if nothing else, is about transformation. Don't be afraid. Accept the gift of the
Holy Spirit and be changed.

Today's Song: "Spirit of the Living God," #101

Journal Notes _____

_____

_____

_____

Being an Heir

*"In other words, it is not the natural children but it is the children
of the promise who are regarded as Abraham's offspring."*
ROMANS 9:8, NIV

Today's Prayer

Spirit of the living God, fall fresh on me today. I am in need of new ears and a new heart. I feel unworthy of you. When I look back over my life, I see so many mistakes, so many wrong turns. How could you possibly even want me to walk with you? Help me today to forgive myself so that I can experience peace and joy and a relationship with you. Amen.

Today's Reflection

A big stumbling block for many African-Americans is the phrase "the chosen people." That phrase has made members of some religions feel superior, made other people try to define themselves as the chosen people, and generally made a lot of people feel bad and excluded.

The Jews were the so-called "chosen" people because in a polytheistic society, they worshiped just one God. But they took their position for granted and fell out of covenant with God. Who is chosen? The Bible says, "children of the promise," meaning those who follow God and not themselves or any other idol.

You are chosen.

Today's Song: "Come and Go with Me to My Father's House," #141

Journal Notes

_____

_____

_____

_____

No Time for Foolishness

"But avoid foolish controversies and genealogies and arguments and quarrels about the law, because these are unprofitable and useless."

TITUS 3:9, NIV

Today's Prayer

Most loving God, help me today not to get caught up in trying to change someone's beliefs, but instead help me to walk in such a way that anyone who sees me sees you. I don't want to be a clanging cymbal. I want to be a witness as to who you are. I want someone to see in me the love that is you, the empowerment and grace and mercy that come from you. Strengthen my spirit, God, and keep me quiet. Let my life be a light to you. Amen.

Today's Reflection

How many times have you heard people arguing over scriptures, or worse, over denominational doctrine? How many times have you been in arguments like that? It's all fruitless. God didn't make denominations. Neither did Jesus. Denominations are the creation of human beings, and therefore they are full of human frailties. Better that we spend our time opening up to God and receiving the truth. God's truth is hard, as are his requirements. But ultimately, nobody can tell you the truth but God. Leave the polemics alone. That's time wasted. Seek God and let God teach you.

Today's Song: "Precious Lord, Take My Hand," #193

Journal Notes

_____

_____

_____

_____

Set Free

"Woman, you are set free from your ailment."
LUKE 13:14

Today's Prayer

Gracious God, giver and keeper of life, I thank you for this day and for the portion of health that you have given me. Loving God, I pray for those who are in need of healing and for those who suffer. God, I pray that you will continue to share your love and help me to rejoice in all that you do. Amen.

Today's Reflection

Jesus thinks and acts outside of the box. Jesus went against tradition by healing on the Sabbath. When the church leaders protest what Jesus was doing to help this woman, Jesus showed them how they had violated the principle of the Sabbath for their own personal gain. Jesus said there is no time that isn't the right time to help our neighbors.

We are called by Jesus to act outside of the box as well. In a society that promotes the myth of rugged individualism, we are called by Jesus to show concern for others. Who are you able to help today? In Matthew 25:40, Jesus reminds us that we are to care for those who are not able to care for themselves.

Today's Song: "Why Should I Feel Discouraged," #252

Journal Notes

_____

_____

_____

_____

Hold On—God's Coming

But Jacob said, "I will not let you go, unless you bless me."
GENESIS 32:26

Today's Prayer

Dearest Lord, I stand before you an empty vessel. I've tried to do it on my own and failed. Allow me to stand before your presence with patience. Let me wait upon you until the blessings flow. Amen.

Today's Reflection

Sixteen-year-olds know it all. Around age 21, people know that they know it all. It is no wonder that around age 25, no one can tell these know-it-alls anything. Oh, the perils of the young mind. The truth is that like Jacob, our know-it-all attitudes can get us into trouble. We just aren't smart enough to accept the wisdom of God. Jacob made some bad decisions. Yet, standing on the threshold of uncertainty, fearful of his brother's wrath, Jacob knew that he could no longer do it alone. It was why he wrestled that night, tossing and turning his life over in his mind and heart. Jacob realized at that pivotal point in time that he could not go forward without God's intervention. For once in his life he would hold on for dear life to the true God of his ancestors. He would learn from their mistakes and his.

Do you accept that God's wisdom is there for the asking? When we hold on, we are literally holding on for dear life. Only then can we be assured that when day breaks, God's blessings are there for us.

Today's Song: "Will Your Anchor Hold," #255

Journal Notes _____

_____

_____

_____

The Tie That Unbinds

*"But the L*ORD* hardened Pharaoh's heart,
and he would not let the Israelites go."*
EXODUS 10:20

Today's Prayer

We've come a long way, Lord, on this freedom trail. Yet, still on the horizon are those who would take those freedoms away. Let our hearts be troubled until the time comes when all God's children know the true meaning of being free. Amen.

Today's Reflection

"A hard head makes a soft behind" is an important saying in the African-American community. So it seems that Pharaoh was exactly the person our elders would talk about. No matter how much it rained hard times, Pharaoh was big and bad and thought he could stand up to God.

What does that mean for us today? There are still those in our community who are imprisoned by drug and alcohol abuse, lack of education, health concerns, and a myriad of other issues that plague our community. Over and over again, God says, "Let my people go." He says it not only to the drug dealer, but also to each parent, teacher, and minister. When Pharaoh refused to let Israel go, he was, in effect, keeping them bound to a way of life unacceptable to God. Today is the day to reach out and unshackle the chains of destruction in our homes and communities. It means standing up to the enemy and telling him that it is time to let God's people go!

Today's Song: "King of My Life," #87

Journal Notes _____

_____

_____

_____

Choosing Life

"You are a hiding place for me; you preserve me from trouble;
you surround me with glad cries of deliverance."

PSALM 32:7

Today's Prayer

In the midst of chaos and confusion, Dearest Lord, have mercy on me. Even as I look upon my circumstances and surroundings, let me know that you are near. Give me comfort and help me to be of comfort to others. Amen.

Today's Reflection

David knew what side his bread was buttered on. He had flaws, true, and his personal choices often got him in hot water. But he knew that the best part of him came through when he relied on God. David knew that calling on God was always the right choice.

Life can be unbearable at times. add to this our inability to lead perfect lives, and what is unbearable becomes unlivable. A friend once remarked that when she and her brothers were young, they would get into trouble for their childish pranks. Their mother would admonish them with the words "You better choose life." What she gave them was a choice—sometimes between a spanking and straightening up their act. "It was usually an easy choice," the friend remembers.

God brings life to us daily. Choosing life is what God asks of us. With our choice comes God's protection of love, essential in our quest to make it through each day.

Today's Song: "God Sent His Son," #93

Journal Notes

_____

_____

_____

_____

No Justice, No Peace

"The LORD rises to argue his case; he stands to judge the peoples."
ISAIAH 3:13

Today's Prayer

Thank you for our leaders, Father. Their jobs loom large over the daily struggles for justice and peace. Guide the footsteps of those of us who lead and those who follow that we may do so wisely. Amen.

Today's Reflection

Justice issues still loom large in our communities. While issues such as unfairness in the criminal-justice system and unfair business practices are only a few of the issues our brothers and sisters deal with on a daily basis, our hope lies in Jesus. Statistics may show us what we're up against, but the numbers cannot measure up to God's justice. Moreover, we can be assured that God is ever present in our daily struggles. God will have the final say.

As we start each day, acknowledge the men and women in your life and others who make a difference. Thank God for those who lead, teach, and protect. God will strengthen us spiritually and mentally so that we can do our jobs. If we remember to do what God asks of us in our capacity as leaders and as followers, God will take care of the rest.

Today's Song: "Time Is Filled with Transition," #231

Journal Notes _____

_____

_____

_____

Hope Will Not Disappoint

"But the one who endures to the end will be saved."
MATTHEW 24:13

Today's Prayer

Father, give me hope. When I see the pain and sorrow of others, help me to hold on. Help me to be ready. Lord, keep me faithful and help me endure to the end. Amen.

Today's Reflection

The little girl sat in the pew next to her grandmother. She listened intently to the words of the minister. Later, at dinner while her parents, aunts, and uncles laughed, it seemed, without a care in the world, the girl questioned her grandmother. How could they be so carefree? Wasn't the end near? After all, that was what she heard.

Like the forecasts of the stock exchange, many predictions come saying they know the truth. Over and over again, forecasts fall short of the reality. Like the little girl, we must ask the question, but not out of fear. God calls us to be faithful. God wants us to believe in him.

Here is what the grandmother said to the little girl: "We don't know the time or place, child, but Jesus is coming back. We know only that we must love God and love each other and do what is right. If you do that, my little one, God will always be there for you."

Today's Song: "Soon and Very Soon," #38

Journal Notes

_____

_____

_____

_____

The Blessing of Life

"But thanks be to God, who in Christ always leads us in triumphal procession, and through us spreads in every place the fragrance that comes from knowing him."

2 CORINTHIANS 2:14

Today's Prayer

Knowing you, Lord, has been the blessing of life. Without you, my life would have no meaning. Reaffirm your love for me as only you can. Place your holy smell upon me so that others may come to know of you. Amen.

Today's Reflection

The young white male asked the beautiful black woman why she proclaimed God. It didn't make sense that she could possibly love a God that allowed her ancestors to be slaves. The black woman smiled. She told the young man, "You don't know like I know." Perhaps the question belies the need for the young man to be convinced of the power of God. If this black woman could love God, perhaps he, too, could. Looking at the bigger picture, the question begs for clarity on the part of the believer. It doesn't mean using fancy words or witty clichés. It means straight talk. When Paul came to the true understanding of the Christ, he wanted to do more than proclaim it. He didn't want people to follow God out a misguided notion associated with other religions. He wanted people to be drawn to and led of God through God's own fragrance of life. Give God a chance and you, too, will see.

Today's Song: "Blessed Assurance," #118

Journal Notes

February 11

A Closer Walk

"If any of you is lacking in wisdom, ask God, who gives to all generously and ungrudgingly, and it will be given to you."
JAMES 1:5

Today's Prayer

Speak through me every day, Lord. Let your words speak volumes to those in need. Give me wisdom to follow you faithfully and to use this wisdom to proclaim your word. Amen.

Today's Reflection

Getting stronger in your walk with Christ is God's plan in action. As your faith strengthens, your hope for humankind increases. God's generosity is shown when we knowingly ask of God, believing that our unselfish wants will be granted.

Over time, tests will come. Our struggle comes when our needs and wants are out of step with what God wants from us. In the book of James, we are given the tools to stay in step with God. First, we must ask. It is not that God doesn't know what we need. Sometimes we must ask of God what God would have us ask. That's all right! James shows us the source for it all. When we realize where the source is, we become lights upon the path. As we lean on him, we can manifest the attributes of those who love God. As James points out, leaning on God rids us of destructive behaviors and puts us in step with God's will for our lives. So ask. God is waiting.

Today's Song: "Just a Closer Walk with Thee," #253

Journal Notes _____

_____

_____

_____

February 12

Get Up and Go

*"Now the L*ORD *said to Abram, "Go from your country and your kindred and your father's house to the land that I will show you. So Abram went as the Lord had told him."*

GENESIS 12:1, 4

Today's Prayer

Lord, give me the peace that comes from knowledge of your love and protection. Let your holy wind stir me from apathy and light a fire that can be seen in all that I do and say. Amen.

Today's Reflection

What faith! The Lord says, "Go," and according to the account that has been handed down to us, Abram seems to take off without question or hesitation. God does not even tell Abram where he is going, only that he should leave behind everything that is familiar and familial and go to "the land that I will show you." What faith!

It was an amazing thing then as now, in the 21st-century, with all our long-range planning and strategies. It takes great faith to take off without a full understanding of what lies ahead. The first step is to get up and go, and do whatever we are called to do for the sake of the gospel—knowing that whatever happens, we go with God.

Today's Song: "Be Not Dismayed Whate'er Betide," #200

Journal Notes _____

_____

_____

_____

February 13

The Stand

"If you keep silent at such a time as this . . . you will perish."
ESTHER 4:14

Today's Prayer

Lord God, throughout history your prophets have struggled to proclaim your will and your word. We, too, are called to share our resources and care for all your creation. Loosen our tongues to speak out against evil in all its forms. Give us a glimpse of your vision of justices that we may do to be a part of that vision. Amen.

Today's Reflection

"Why was I ever born?" The lament of many a teenager, in every generation, and probably even you. These words are usually uttered when some well-meaning plan has fallen through. But questioning the why and wherefore of the circumstances of one's birth is a serious theological step. Why are you where you are right now?

All blessings come from God, but they come through human agents. People sit in churches every week and pray for those who are homeless, and those who are sick, and those who suffer from injustices. But who will be moved to speak out against those injustices? What is the face of the homeless person and what are we doing to make sure that God's will is done? God does not will that people sleep in doorways, or that children go hungry. It may be easier to retreat to our comfort zones, but the problem is that the comfort zone is always shrinking. And sooner or later we will be moved to take a stand—one way or the other. If we do not speak out against evil, then through our silence we speak up for evil.

Today's Song: "How Lovely on the Mountains," #99

Journal Notes _____

_____

_____

_____

February 14

Real Love

"Love never ends."
1 CORINTHIANS 13:8

Today's Prayer

Lord, teach us how to love each other, how to forgive one another, how to bear each other's burdens, how to share each other's joys, and even how to laugh with each other. We pray that you would bind us with cords that cannot be broken, so that in community we may continually feel your loving presences among us. Amen.

Today's Reflection

It has been said of 1 Corinthians 13 that if you substitute the word *Christ* for the word *love*, you will have a better understanding of what Paul was trying to say to the people in the church at Corinth. This kind of love is no ordinary, human love. It is the love of the one who gave up equality with God to live among us, who died because of us, but who conquered death for us and loves us still. This kind of love is a model for everyone in Christ to achieve.

Today's Song: "Precious Lord, Take My Hand," #193

Journal Notes

_____

_____

_____

_____

The Idleness of Idleness

"Go to the ant, O sluggard; consider her ways, and be wise."
PROVERBS 6:6

Today's Prayer

Lord, take me and use me for the building of your kingdom. Wake up your church, lest we die in our sleep. Make us ever vigilant for your word and your will. Make in us that apathy for the gospel, and idleness may not be our sins. Amen.

Today's Reflection

Have you ever seen an ant at rest? That is not to say that ants don't rest, just that they always seem to be working. Is this the wisdom that is being imparted? As people of God, we are commanded to sanctify the holy day, take a day of re-creation, even rest.

But let us be reminded that it is one day of rest per week and not seven. We have all received some God-given talent. It is our sacred obligation to return to God what has been given, whether it be artistic abilities or business and organization skills, or even silent time to meditate and watch the sun rise.

Some people put a lot of effort into exercising on a regular basis. But what are we doing for the kingdom of God? Are we working just one hour a week? Go to the ant, O sluggard. Consider her ways and be wise.

Today's Song: "Let Us Talents and Tongues Employ," #232

Journal Notes

_____

_____

_____

_____

February 16

Staying Salty

"You are the salt of the earth, but if salt has lost its taste, how shall its saltiness be restored? It is no longer good for anything."
MATTHEW 5:13

Today's Prayer

O Lord, my God, I pray that you keep me near you. Keep my faith in you strong, and actions toward others loving, so that I may able to serve you through the best and worst of what happens in my life. Amen.

Today's Reflection

With all the warnings about cutting back on salt in out diets, we might think this is no longer a good metaphor—but think again. We will always have salt with us. It literally is in our blood.

Christians are an integral part of the cosmos—and just like salt, some are better for the cosmos than others. The questions we must each ask of ourselves is this: "Am I the good stuff or the not-so-good stuff?" In Baptism we were made new creations in Christ, who fought the battle of sin and won.

But in response to the work of Christ, we are called to be more than just seasoning. In Jesus' time, salting food meant the difference between being able to have something to eat or going hungry, because the food was not preserved. Today, our participation in the life of the church can mean the difference between someone being spiritually fed or going hungry—and that someone may be you.

Today's Song: "All to Jesus I Surrender," #235

Journal Notes

February 17

The Transformers

*"Do not be conformed to this world, but be transformed
by the renewal of your mind."*
ROMANS 12:2

Today's Prayer

Awesome God, source of life, healing, and strength, you alone hold our times in
your hands, and you alone know the ending to the story of our lives. Calm the raging storms that plague my life, and let me surrender fully to your will. Let me feel the
joy of your salvation, and let that joy glorify you, that others may know the healing
power of your love in Jesus Christ. Amen.

Today's Reflection

Several years ago, there was a popular line of robot-like toys on the market called
"Transformers." The concept was that with some slight adjustments—a turn of an
arm, a twist of a leg, a pushing down on the head—the robot would "transform"
into an entirely different toy, such as a car or plane. The toys were a hit because the
transformation took place in just moments.

Anyone who is in Christ knows that real transformation takes a lifetime to accomplish. It is not simply a mere adjustment here and there that turns us into changed
beings. It starts with water and the Word in Holy Baptism. Then, we spend the rest
of our lives fulfilling our baptismal promises of study, prayer, praise, thanksgiving,
and being a worker of the kingdom of God. Through the repetitive actions of being
a member of the body of Christ, transformation takes place.

Today's Song: "Take Me to the Water," #117

Journal Notes _____

_____

_____

_____

February 18

Requiem

"If the foundations are destroyed, what can the righteous do?"
PSALM 11:3

Today's Prayer

Lord God, comfort with the grace of your Holy Spirit all who are surrounded by the shadow of death. Give them courage, peace, and joy—the joy that only those who live and die in you can know. Comfort those who mourn with the hope of eternal life with those they love. Amen.

Today's Reflection

In an adult Sunday-morning class, one woman recounted her story of surviving a tornado: "As I saw the spinning dust cloud in the distance, I was seized with fear. I knew that was the day I would die, and I prayed to God to let it be a quick death. No cuts or lacerations, no concussions or brain damage, just quick and painless."

"You lost your faith in God!" shouted another participant in the group.

"People die every day. Isn't that what funerals are all about?" the woman countered. It was an eye-opener for many others that day.

We all consider it a blessing to escape a close call, but what about when one does not escape? What do we call that? The psalmist tells us there is no place to run except to the Lord—especially when we seem to face a sure and certain death. We believe that the grave is only a gate, because we are in Christ. Whether we live or die, we are in Christ.

Today's Song: "All the Way My Savior Leads Me," #259

Journal Notes _____

_____

_____

_____

February 19

Trusting in the Promises of God

"Abram believed the Lord;
and the Lord reckoned it to him as righteousness."
GENESIS 15:6, NIV

Today's Prayer

To the God whose promises are true and overflowing, let me never doubt that what you have said will come true. I depend on your promises daily, for they are what carry me through. Help me to believe in you with the same fervency as Abraham. Amen.

Today's Reflection

The time for Abraham's death was drawing near. Abraham was becoming concerned that he had no heir in which to leave his estate. God told Abraham not to worry for he would have a son. Abraham came to believe in the provision and the faithfulness of God.

We, too, can develop a right relationship with God. God has a plan for our lives. It is up to us to cultivate our relationship with God to hear that plan. God's promises are true for God will protect and provide everything that we need.

Today's Song: "We've Come This Far by Faith," #197

Journal Notes _____

_____

_____

_____

Taking Courage

*"On the third day Esther put on her royal robes and stood in
the inner court of the king's palace, opposite the king's hall.
The king was sitting on his royal throne inside the palace
opposite the entrance to the palace."*

ESTHER 5:1-3

Today's Prayer

I thank you, God, for the courage to face my challenges daily. Teach me not to be afraid of what the consequence could be when I take a stand. May your love strengthen me as I leave my comfort zone and risk to do things differently. Amen.

Today's Reflection

God wants us to face our challenges with courage. God wants us to look them in the eye and take a stand. Esther knew she was risking her life to go before the king without being summoned. But she was determined to help her people; she knew that the destruction of the Jews was at stake and she had to do something.

Like Esther, when faced with difficult decisions, we too should not fear or doubt that God is able to help us meet our challenges. We are to stand firm, take courage, go before our God in prayer. Just as God saved the Jews through the courage of Esther, God will save us, if we have courage and faith.

Today's Song: "Be Not Dismayed Whate'er Betide," #200

Journal Notes

February 21

Wait with Patience

"How long must I wrestle with my thoughts and every day have sorrow in my heart? How long will my enemy triumph over me?"

PSALM 13:2, NIV

Today's Prayer

To my Savior Jesus Christ, I thank you for your presence in my life when I need you most. Lord, I know that you hear my cry and will answer when the time is right. I will wait and wait on you Lord until you have decided what is best for me. Amen.

Today's Reflection

Waiting on the Lord is not always easy. We tend to be anxious and uptight, and to put too much nervous thought into our situation. Our thoughts get cloudy and we cannot always remember what God did for us the last time we were in a difficult place. In our cloudiness, if we can remember how God has brought us through many a storm, then it would be easier to wait on God. Putting the focus on God and not the problem makes the waiting easier. When we wait patiently on God, no matter how the situation looks, God will work things out for our good pleasure.

Today's Song: "When the Storms of Life Are Raging," #198

Journal Notes _____

_____

_____

_____

Know Where You Are Going

"All at once he followed her like an ox going to the slaughter . . ."
PROVERBS 7:22a, NIV

Today's Prayer

Oh God, I pray for your wisdom for my life that comes from knowing your word. May the word give guidance to my life and assist me to walk in your path. Lord, speak now that I might follow your will for my life. Amen.

Today's Reflection

In our text, because this man did not understand God's vision for his life, he was walking down the wrong road and encountered an immoral woman. Because he did not have God's vision for his life, he could not resist the sweet and seductive works of the temptress. People who don't know God's vision for their lives spend their time wandering aimlessly down the wrong roads. A lack of direction and inquiry for guidance allows them to be vulnerable to many and diverse temptations. Knowing God's word gives us wisdom to avoid the pitfalls that lead us down the road to temptation. Knowing God's word helps us to discern God's direction for our lives.

Read and study for God's direction in your life that you may be put on the right road to a fulfilled future.

Today's Song: "I Can Hear My Savior Calling," #146

Journal Notes _____

_____

_____

_____

Does God Know You?

"Not everyone who says to me, 'Lord, Lord,' will enter the kingdom of heaven, but only he who does the will of my Father who is heaven."
MATTHEW 7:21, NIV

Today's Prayer

God, give me true mercy and compassion for hurting and needy people. May I show my love for you by visiting the sick, clothing the naked, feeding the hungry, and being with those in prison. Amen.

Today's Reflection

There are many people who perform the correct ritual and the right religious observance but for the wrong reasons and wrong motivation of heart. The right religious observance is not enough. We must be able to truly live the word in our own lives, showing our obedience to the Savior that we might receive our reward in heaven.

God says in this text that everyone who does right religious observance will not enter the kingdom of God. Everyone who quotes the word of God is not necessarily in right relationship with God. The text says, "Not everyone who says to me, 'Lord, Lord'" will enter the kingdom of God.

The Christian that acts out their biblical faith among the poor and needy is the one that can say, "Lord, Lord," and enter the kingdom.

Today's Song: "I Heard the Voice of Jesus Say," #62

Journal Notes _____

_____

_____

_____

God Accepts the Weak to Make Them Strong

"Welcome those who are weak in faith,
but not for the purpose quarreling over opinions."
ROMANS 14:1

Today's Prayer

Loving God, the one who is accepting of everyone, I thank you for how understanding you are of me when I don't always have the right answers. I know that sometimes my thinking is off the mark, but thank you for sticking with me and urging me to turn my thinking around. It is because of the love you show me that I can show that same love to others. Amen.

Today's Reflection

In the church there are different levels of Christian maturity. Each person has decided what to believe in their heart and usually there are many very different perceptions of right and wrong. Many people answer the very same question differently. Paul is saying to us in this verse that those of us who are seasoned in our faith are not to criticize those who have not experienced Christ in the way we have. Paul advises us to give people time to mature and discover God's truth in their own lives. Most of us can remember times when we adamantly believed or practiced something, and time and experience came to show us that our thinking and behavior needed adjustment. God was patient with us as we were growing. Paul admonishes us to have the same patience with others that God had for us.

Today's Song: "Shine, Jesus, Shine," #64

Journal Notes _____

_____

_____

_____

Maintain the Unity of the Spirit

*"May God who gives endurance and encouragement give you a
spirit of unity among yourselves as you follow Christ Jesus."*
ROMANS 15:5, NIV

Today's Prayer

Gracious God, peace is what we desire today. There is conflict everywhere. May we strive together to maintain the unity of the spirit in the church. May we truly become one that we would show love and forgiveness one to another. May we rely on your Spirit that gives endurance, encouragement, and unity. Amen.

Today's Reflection

This text points out that we cannot get unity out of our own efforts. We must realize that God gives unity to the church. We must strive to maintain the unity of the Spirit by living in faith and giving situations of conflict and unforgiveness to God. Acknowledging that God is able to work things out in God's own time and God's own way. Our task is to keep our eyes on God and not each other. If we keep our eyes on God and the unity of the Spirit, we will not be self-centered, but concerned for others. Our daily attitude will reflect the endurance and encouragement that will unite the people of God together in Christian love.

Today's Song: "Oh, Let the Son of God Enfold You," #105

Journal Notes _____

_____

_____

_____

Anxiety

"You are the God who sees me . . ."
GENESIS 16:13

Today's Prayer

Heavenly Father, may we always seek your guidance and wisdom for all of our decisions. May we always walk in your will and in your ways. Amen.

Today's Reflection

It's hard to imagine a wife asking another woman to conceive her husband's child. Yet this is what Sarah asked Hagar. She wanted to make sure that Abraham had an heir. Sarah didn't think of God's power, nor the question: "Is there anything too hard for the Lord?" (Genesis18:14a).

She wanted results. Hagar obeyed and conceived, but animosity set in between the two women. Hagar fled to the desert to escape Sarah's anger. In her brokenness and desperation, God came to her with a word of comfort and hope. Hagar said, "You are the God who sees me."

In our despair, we can be assured that God will also see us.

Today's Song: "Why Should I Feel Discouraged," #252

Journal Notes _____

_____

_____

_____

Empowered to Trust in God

"The midwives however feared God."
EXODUS 1:17

Today's Prayer

Kind and loving Father, bless us with the understanding that we are made strong by adversity. Teach us to accept your will for our lives, whether its in joy, sadness, or trials. Amen.

Today's Reflection

The Hebrew midwives Shiprah and Puah were given a cruel command by Pharaoh: "Kill the male babies that are born." Those words by the king put extreme pressure on those women, life if they obeyed the king and death if the didn't.

Pressures and adversities in life are in built in facets of living. They are inevitable. They will come our way sooner or later. God empowered them to disobey the order of the king. They were rewarded for their faithfulness. The same Holy Spirit that empowered the Hebrew midwives will do the same for you.

Today's Song: "I Will Trust in the Lord," #256

Journal Notes _____

_____

_____

_____

Our God Will Satisfy

"My soul will be satisfied as with the richest of foods;
with singing lips my mouth will praise you."

PSALM 63:5, NIV

Today's Prayer

Praise the Lord! Praise the Lord! Lord we are satisfied in you. You have done so many great things in our lives and we are satisfied with you. Words cannot express how grateful we are that you are in our lives. And for our satisfaction we glorify and adore thee giving thee honor and praise. Amen.

Today's Reflection

When David was in the wilderness hiding from his enemies, he felt discouraged, uncertain, and alone. David called on the Lord. In this place of wilderness and starvation, David praised God and proclaimed that God would satisfy him, and did.

There are times when we, too, are in difficult places, when emotional stress and tension are high. In those times, we are to look to God. We are to open our mouths and to praise God, proclaim the blessings of God, and bring forth praises to God. Just as God met David in the wilderness, God will comfort us.

Today's Song: "Great Is Thy Faithfulness," #283

Journal Notes

A Dwelling Place in God

"Lord, who may dwell in your sanctuary."
PSALM 15:1

Today's Prayer

O Gracious God, may the rays of your glory illumine our hearts. May we dwell in your presence in humility and gratitude. Amen.

Today's Reflection

"Lord, who may dwell in your sanctuary" is a valid question. It's not who may visit, but who may dwell and "Who may live on your holy hill?" Each of us are confronted by the same question. How do we answer? The psalmist gave the criterion for the dwelling place in God. It is a place of quiet rest and peace. It is here that we can bring all of our cares and concerns to God. We have security to keep us safe in the midst of Satan's attacks.

We find shelter and rest in the shadow of the Most High. It is in our relationship with God that we have the assurance of dwelling in his presence, his sanctuary, and his holy hill.

Today's Song: "Blessed Assurance," #118

Journal Notes _____

_____

_____

_____

March 2

Faith in Action

"Go! It will be done just as you believed it would . . ."
MATTHEW 8:13

Today's Prayer

Compassionate God, look on us with compassion. Increase our faith and grant us the ability to know how to trust and act on your word. Amen.

Today's Reflection

"Go! It will be done just as you believed it would." The humility of the centurion reminds us that we must come to Jesus in faith. Our lives are governed by faith—however, doubt can negate faith. As a man of limited power, the centurion had grasped the fact that he had encountered the One with limitless power. Out of his humility he made his request: "Lord, I do not deserve to have you come under my roof, but just say the word, and my servant will be healed."

Jesus hears and answers our prayers. He is not bound by time, space or circumstances. Our responsibility is to trust him and act on his word. Faith is not only believing, but action as well.

Today's Song: "My Hope Is Built on Nothing Less," #192

Journal Notes

Temptations Will Come

"When the Devil had finished all this tempting,
he left him until an opportune time."

LUKE 4:13

Today's Prayer

Gracious Father, empower through the Holy Spirit to withstand the temptations and not yield to them. Amen.

Today's Reflection

Jesus has shown us how to overcome temptations. They will come! Usually in our moments of vulnerability, we encounter the enemy of our soul. His ways are subtle and sneaky. Satan chooses every opportunity available to tempt us away from God. He awaits his moments in order to be effective.

There are all kinds of temptations that will come into our lives. We can be strengthened or we can succumb to them. We have the scriptures to empower us. Jesus didn't argue with this enemy, he simply said, "It is written. . . . We can do the same.

Today's Song: "Yield Not to Temptation," #195

Journal Notes _____

_____

_____

_____

March 4

Unity in Christ

"That all of you agree with one another . . ."
1 CORINTHIANS 10b

Today's Prayer

Loving Father, disagreements will come. May we be able to disagree and do it lovingly, not in hatred or strife. May we always remember that we are a royal priesthood and a holy nation. Amen.

Today's Reflection

Strife within the Body of Christ is divisive and destructive. We are called to be one, united by God's gift of salvation to all. We are not called to be clones of another, nor agree with everything. It is the abiding presence of the Holy Spirit that will prevent our disagreements from becoming acrimonious. Christ binds and empowers to us, fulfill the command, that we have been given.

Today's Song: "In My Life, Lord, Be Glorified," #248

Journal Notes _____

_____

_____

_____

All Things Possible

"Is anything too wonderful for the LORD?"
GENESIS 18:14a

Today's Prayer

Dear God, please help me in my doubt so that I can face life's obstacles with the knowledge that all things are possible with you. Amen.

Today's Reflection

Is anything too wonderful for the Lord? At the set time I will return to you, in due season, and Sarah shall have a son. Life is filled with challenge, obstacles, and tunnels that seem to have no light at the end. Yet, when we read Genesis 18:14, we can be assured that God is with us and that there is nothing too hard for the Lord. In verse 14 the Lord is removing an obstacle that seems impossible to remove by assuring Abraham and Sarah that Sarah will conceive and have a son. What the Lord is saying here to Abraham and Sarah, the Lord is also saying to us—that all things are possible with God.

Today's Song: "Lead Me, Guide Me," #70

Journal Notes _____

_____

_____

_____

Egoism is a Sin of Pride

"Who is there the king would rather honor than me?"
ESTHER 6:7b

Today's Prayer

Merciful God, forgive our selfish pride and egotistical behavior. Teach us love one another in our diversity as you love us. Amen.

Today's Reflection

Selfishness, hidden anger and resentment of others will ultimately manifest itself in hatred. Haman despised Mordecai his hatred became like smoldering embers of fire awaiting the right time to flare up. Haman methodically devised ways that would ensure the destruction of his Jewish adversary, even if it meant killing all Jews.

Oddly, he designed the method of death for himself. For Haman was hung on the gallows he built for Mordecai.

Racial, gender, and cultural bigotry are insidious. The tentacles of bigotry become suction cups of hatred, disabling all humanity. But the joys of diversity within humanity reflect the beauty of God.

Today's Song: "Lord, I Want to Be a Christian," #234.

Journal Notes

Anger, Rage, and Violence

"The king rose from the feast in wrath and went into the palace garden, but Haman stayed to beg his life from Queen Esther, for he saw that the king was determined to destroy him."
ESTHER 7:7

Today's Prayer

Lord, let your peace rule in my heart that I might be able to control my anger and rage. Amen.

Today's Reflection

The king rose from the feast in wrath. Sudden and uncontrolled anger was common for King Ahasuerus. How common is it in our lives? Our lives are so stressful that often we live only one word or comment away from the same kind of anger and rage displayed by the king. We see, on an increasing scale, the rise in violence resulting from anger and rage. Road rage is an example of this type of violence. While Ahasuerus and Esther provide us with no direct solutions, the passage points us toward the providence of God. God was present with Esther during the king's outbursts and God is present with us today in the midst of all the violence and rage in our world. We must trust that, with God's presence and help, we will someday be ruled by peace.

Today's Song: "There Is a Balm in Gilead," #185

Journal Notes _____

_____

_____

_____

Forgive the Words of My Mouth

"If you try my heart, if you visit me by night, if you test me,
you will find no wickedness in me: my mouth does not transgress."
PSALM 17:3

Today's Prayer

Dear God, I pray for forgiveness of my transgressions and for the strength to obey your will. Amen.

Today's Reflection

I have a friend who gave up complaining for Lent; more specifically, she gave up complaining about others. This is a very noble and difficult Lenten discipline, especially if viewed in light of what the psalmist says, that even if God tests the heart and visits at night, God will find no transgressions of the mouth.

It is common for us to talk and complain about each other. Our home, workplaces, communities, and churches are full of gossips and complainers. The psalmist is asking supplication for a clean heart and mouth. Realizing that we are human and subject to mistakes, the psalmist addresses a powerful and loving God, confident in God's merciful promise to forgive our transgressions and to remember them no more.

Today's Song: "Go, My Children, with My Blessing," #161

Journal Notes _____

_____

_____

_____

Hope Against Fear

"So do not be afraid; you are of more value than many sparrows."
MATTHEW 10:31

Today's Prayer

Thank you, Lord, for sending Christ to be our constant protection against the fears we face in our daily lives. Amen.

Today's Reflection

The sparrow is a small bird that often goes without notice. Yet Jesus reminds us that not even one sparrow goes without God's notice and God 's protection.

Fear has one of the most life-draining effects on our human existence. We all face fear in our lives on a daily basis. Fear can affect all aspects of our life. Jesus reminds us that we are of more value than many sparrows to our God. God's presence and protection is with us continually, providing us with the assurance that God through Christ is our hope against fear.

Today's Song: "I Want Jesus to Walk with Me," #66

Journal Notes _____

_____

_____

_____

Called to Life

After this he went out and saw a tax collector named Levi,
sitting at the tax booth; and he said to him, "Follow me."
And he got up, left everything and followed him.
LUKE 5:27-28

Today's Prayer

Lord, help me to discern your call and to become a faithful follower of Christ.
Amen.

Today's Reflection

Notice the type of people Jesus calls; they are people like you and me, people
who represent a wide variety of lifestyles. In these verses, Jesus calls a tax collector,
a wealthy person with little respect from the community. The people disliked tax
collectors because they worked for the Romans, and they cheated their own people
to gain wealth.

When asked why he associated with people like this, Jesus said he came not just
to the righteous but to everyone. Jesus calls all of us to be disciples of Christ, to
follow the Christ who came to bring us life—and not just life, but life abundant. It
is very comforting to know that you are included in this call to life.

Today's Song: "A Wonderful Savior Is Jesus," #260

Journal Notes

Being Part of the Family

"And you belong to Christ and Christ belongs to God."
1 CORINTHIANS 3:23

Today's Prayer

I give thanks to you, O Lord, for the gift of salvation through Jesus Christ. Amen.

Today's Reflection

Most psychologists would agree that having a sense of belonging is one of the most important factors in living a healthy life. My fondest memories are of growing up in a family where I felt loved and cared for, and I had a sense of belonging. That assurance gave me the things I needed to go out into a world where it's every person for themselves. But even when we have that type of family, and there are many who don't, there will be times when life throws its curves and we will feel lost, alone, forgotten, and with no sense of belonging. It is at those times that the words of Paul bring me consolation. I'm consoled by the fact that, through Christ, I belong to God. That consolation gives me hope and joy.

Today's Song: "Blessed Quietness," #110

Journal Notes _____

_____

_____

_____

God Was Gracious to Sarah

*"The LORD dealt with Sarah as he has said,
and the LORD did for Sarah as he had promised."*
GENESIS 21:1

Today's Prayer

Gracious, all-knowing God, forgive me for the times when my faith is weak and I, like Sarah, fail to believe your word. When I face difficult situations, help me to remember that nothing is too hard for you. Lord, this day, help me to trust you completely and not try to fix it myself. Amen.

Today's Reflection

At any age, God's promises are true. And God's miraculous presence is seen and felt every day. A baby is born and we celebrate. Miniature perfection, tiny nose, just enough fuzz to be called hair. Ten perfect fingers and ten perfect toes. Sarah laughed at God's promise that she would have a child. Too old? Not for God. Too hard? Not for God. At any age, God's promises are true. That which God promises, God is able to perform.

Today's Song: "I Will Trust in the Lord," #256

Journal Notes _____

_____

_____

_____

Who Am I?

But Moses said to God, "Who am I that I should go to Pharaoh, and bring the Israelites out of Egypt?"
EXODUS 3:11

Today's Prayer

O Great and Everlasting God, the God of our forebears, I come to you humble in heart and on bended knee to acknowledge your awesome power and wonder in this world and in my life. I ask that you will use me as you see fit and empower me to do your will. Amen.

Today's Reflection

"Who am I?" Moses asked God before performing this mighty task. I am sure Rosa Parks asked, "Who am I?" two months before she refused to go any farther back on the bus. "Who am I" Martin Luther King Jr. asked when, as a young minister, he was asked to lead the Montgomery Bus Boycott.

Moses raises a second question: "Who are you?" God responded, "I AM WHO I AM." When I go in God's name, it doesn't matter who I am, because "I AM WHO I AM" is going with us. God will never assign a task to us that we cannot accomplish because it is not "who I am" that matters but rather that "I AM WHO I AM" is there with us.

Today's Song: "Go Down, Moses," #87

Journal Notes _____

_____

_____

_____

If It Pleases the King

". . . and Ester rose and stood before the king."
ESTHER 8:5a

Today's Prayer

Lord, when I fail to invite you into my plans and my decision making, life seems hard and thoughts overwhelm me. When I attempt to do anything without your favor, the simplest task becomes difficult. If it pleases the King, I pray your favor upon my life as you favored Esther. "Favor, my King," is what I stand in need of. For with your favor I will be able to do all that is required of me this day. Amen.

Today's Reflection

Have you ever asked someone to do a favor for you? I have, and it usually works out fine. Especially if the end results are what I anticipated. The favor is done and you move on. Have you ever asked God for favor—it's extraordinary. The end results are always more than you anticipated, even more than you could imagine. Doors seem to open that were closed, a resounding NO turns into an accommodating YES. People seem to be nicer to you because you walk in God's favor and even your enemies know it. I am blessed and highly favored.

Today's Song: "I Want Jesus to Walk with Me," #66

Journal Notes

_____

_____

_____

_____

In My Distress I Cried to the Lord

*"The LORD is my rock, my fortress, and my deliverer, my God,
my rock in whom I take refuge, my shield, and the horn
of my salvation, my stronghold."*

PSALM 18:2

Today's Prayer

I love you, O Lord, my strength. Guide me as you guide the sunrise and direct the stars. Keep me in your holy, precious care as you care for the birds of the air and the lilies of the field. In my distress, shield my mind and guard my heart. Lord, I hurt. Hear me, help me, heal me. Lord, I've lost my way. Hear me, help me, guide me. Lord I need your guidance; hear me, help me, show me. Today, Lord, this hour, this moment, in my distress, hear me Lord, help me Lord, heal me Lord. Amen.

Today's Reflection

From the lion's den, God heard Daniel's prayer. When the Israelites cried out while in slavery, God heard and delivered. When my father died suddenly, something within me closed. When my sister died in her sleep, three years later, something within me cracked. But when my son died of suicide at age 26, my heart broke. In my distress I called to the Lord. I cried to my God for help. God heard me, God helped me, God healed me. There is no place we can be where God won't hear us. There is no situation so great that God can't help us. There is no sorrow too deep that God can't heal us. Today Lord, this hour, this moment, in my distress, hear me Lord, help me Lord, heal me Lord.

Today's Song: "When the Storms of Life Are Raging," #198

Journal Notes _____

_____

_____

_____

The Kingdom Is Like . . .

"Listen! A sower went out to sow."
MATTHEW 13:3b

Today's Prayer

Mysterious and Majestic God, thank you for the seed of your word that was planted in the soil of my heart many years ago. I pray your word will take root in me until it produces fruit that bears witness to your awesome love for me. Thank you for your kingdom, where my name has been changed from "sinner" to "saint" through the waters of my baptism. Lord, help me today to get past my issues. Help me, Lord, to remember that I am forgiven, justified, sanctified, and qualified to be in your kingdom by grace through faith, so that I may fully walk in your kingdom. Amen.

Today's Reflection

Jesus upset the apple cart. His kingdom rules seemed to be contrary to the religious laws that held the people hostage. Jesus was accused of disrespecting the Temple by healing on the Sabbath. There are times when we need to step out of the box of religiosity in order to walk more fully in the kingdom. The kingdom of God is the reign of God. The reign of God is the rule of God. Where God reigns there is peace, justice, and mercy for all. The demons of racism, classicism, ageism, and sexism are put on notice that the kingdom is near, and they tremble and flee.

Jesus said the kingdom of God is within us. When we are nourished by the Word of God, the seed of faith takes root in the soil of our hearts. Then, the desire for justice, mercy, and peace become the way we live, act and treat one another.

Today's Song: "How Lovely on the Mountains," #99

Journal Notes

_____

_____

_____

_____

March 17

Disorder in the Church

"Do you not know that the saints will judge the world?"
1 CORINTHIANS 6:2a

Today's Prayer

Loving God, help me to seek your will, your way, and your word when there appears to be irreconcilable disagreement in the church, or when I feel I have been wronged by a sister or brother. Help me to remember that your Word prescribes a way to handle disputes that differ from the world's legal system. Amen.

Today's Reflection

The church is in the world (society), but not of the world. The church is called to be an example and a witness to the world. When the church, that is Christians, forget that we move to the beat of a different drummer (Scripture), disorder and chaos result. As Christians we have the Holy Spirit, the mind of Christ, and a law book (Scripture) to help us resolve conflict. Society has the legal system where disagreements are resolved in court with attorneys, judge, and jury. What image does the church give when Christians are taking Christians to secular court?

When we use the legal system of the world to resolve church issues, lawsuits make the church look bad and cause people to focus on its problems rather than its purpose. Christians are in the world to bear witness that the God we imitate is just, merciful, long suffering, and forgiving. Let us remember when conflict arises among Christians, instead of rushing to court, let us rush to our Christian law book and read Matthew 18:15-17, and act accordingly.

Today's Song: "All to Jesus I Surrender," #235

Journal Notes

_____

_____

_____

_____

Blind from Birth

One thing I do know, I was blind but now I see.
"As he walked along, he saw a man blind from birth."
JOHN 9:1

Today's Prayer

O gracious, wonderful God, my redeemer, my salvation, my healer. Thank you for opening my eyes to see your blessings in my life. Forgive me, Lord, for complaining and whining when I relapse into moments of temporary blindness. Help me to trust you where I can't trace you. I magnify you, O awesome God. For you called me out of darkness into your marvelous light of new life, new joy, and new possibilities. Hallelujah to your name. This one thing I know—I once was blind but now I see. Hallelujah! Hallelujah! Amen.

Today's Reflection

Can you imagine the joy of an unexpected miracle? Blinded eyes opened. The man was born blind, he could see nothing. Then Jesus came by and the miraculous happened. Jesus put a mud patch on his eyes and told him to go wash in the pool of Siloam. The blind man did as Jesus said and he was healed. He could see. This incident created no small stir. We, too, were born blind. Blind to God's will, blind to God's way, blind to God's word. Blind to our need for salvation—until we accepted Christ as our Savior. In the waters of baptism, we were cleansed and given a new life. The scales of self-centeredness dropped from our eyes and we saw the glory of God in our lives, our minds, our bodies, and our affairs. We once were blind, but now we see. Praise God! Praise God! Praise God!

Today's Song: "Praise Him! Jesus, Blessed Savior," #285

Journal Notes

The Lord Will Provide

"On the mount of the LORD it shall be provided."
GENESIS 22:14

Today's Prayer

Eternal God, your ways are not our ways, and your thoughts are not our thoughts. We often forget this when we find ourselves caught between the rocks and hard places of life. We focus on our discomfort instead of our faith in you. Thank you for showing us that there are no tight spaces where your Spirit cannot enter and no sore spots that your love cannot soothe. In those times when what we face seems too difficult, assure us once again that you have a ram in the bush for every situation. Amen.

Today's Reflection

Abraham's faith is sorely tested by God's request to sacrifice his son Isaac. A request of this magnitude may not be made of us. However, there are issues and circumstances outside of the realm of the holy that put our faith, our patience, our sanity,, and even our purse strings to the test. In life we will be tested—there's no way around it—but as Christians we endure, we go through, and we triumph with trust and faith in God who will provide.

Today's Song: "Let Us Talents and Tongues Employ," #232

Journal Notes _____

_____

_____

_____

Please Send Someone Else

"Oh my LORD, please send someone else."
EXODUS 4:13

Today's Prayer

Our Creator and Sustainer, the very idea that you would call us into service is often overwhelming. It is such a privilege, and yet the responsibility is awesome. Help us not to fear those things that you would lead us to do if we keep our eyes on your divine purpose instead of our human frailties. Lord, work through our fears and insecurities so that we may faithfully serve you and be a blessing to others. Amen.

Today's Reflection

Moses was a bit reluctant to say the least. Sound familiar? Has God asked you to go where you would rather not go and do what you would rather not do? Do you feel that you just don't have what it takes to meet the challenge, lead the charge, or answer the call? God not only calls us into service, God equips. The request that we most fear from God may well be a defining moment, the turning point, the way out of no way, or the ultimate blessing. Be of good courage. This is why God reminds us that what is important is not what we can do but rather what God can and will do through us.

Today's Song: "When the Storms of Life Are Raging," #198

Journal Notes _____

_____

_____

_____

March 21

Uprooting Fear

*"All doing the king's work helped the Jews because
the fear of Mordecai fell upon them."*
ESTER 9:3

Today's Prayer

Mighty God, let us remember that there will be times when we must diligently confront unrighteousness. Keep us mindful of all of your people and those who still struggle for the ordinary freedoms we take for granted. Let us know, Lord, that we always have you with us as an ally against evil. We thank you for your power and your protection. Amen.

Today's Reflection

Mordecai may well have been the Dr. Martin Luther King Jr. of his day. This story of Esther, the Jews, and King Ahasuerus is still a profound one for us. It's about a people's right to freedom, helping those who exist under oppression, and holding the oppressors accountable. It shows that a person can become the recipient of unexpected blessings. Mordecai sought the well-being of his people and rose to prominence not by blind ambition, but by the hand of God.

Today's Song: "Would You Be Free," #76

Journal Notes _____

_____

_____

_____

God Fulfills Our Desires

"You have given him his heart's desire."
PSALM 21:2a

Today's Prayer

Oh God, how good it is to know that you are a God that hears and answers prayer. In our silence when words refuse to come, you are aware of the deep rumblings of our soul. In our anguish you comfort us, in our joy you lift us up! When we place our petitions upon your altar, you respond, you bless, you encourage. Thank you for bringing us peace and comfort in knowing that you lovingly give us the desires of our hearts. Amen.

Today's Reflection

When was the last time you had a praise report? God delivered you from a situation, blessed you with an opportunity, helped you mend a broken relationship, or just granted you a great day? Surely every time we breathe there is something to be grateful to God for. Why not take a moment out of each day, in fact right now, to identify one thing that God has done for you and then . . . PRAISE GOD!

Today's Song: "Oh, I Woke Up This Morning," #166

Journal Notes _____

_____

_____

_____

What Is in Your Heart

*"But what comes out of the mouth proceeds from the heart,
and this is what defiles."*
MATTHEW 15:18

Today's Prayer

Gracious God, patient with our human misinterpretations and values in the name of what is holy. Some have false notions but, are well-meaning, hard working servants. By your Spirit, Lord, show us that love and compassion are the keys to your heart and your kingdom. Amen.

Today's Reflection

What makes one holy? If you took a survey, everyone would have a different answer. Some of us think it's what you wear and don't wear, where you go and don't go, who you associate with or who you avoid. Others think it is certain church practices or activities. Still others will say it is consistent prayer and Bible study. Jesus, gets to the heart of the matter. If one is sincere and attempting to live the Christian life with integrity, then they will know that we are Christians by our love. Our words will reflect our purity of spirit. We will think about, care for, and treat others with respect for their humanity. It's okay to try to do all of the right things but it is better to develop true character and live in the right way. This is God's commandment, that you love one another, as God has loved you.

Today's Song: "Don't Be Worried," #212

Journal Notes _____

_____

_____

_____

Growing with God

"In whatever condition you were called, brothers
and sisters there remain with God."
1 CORINTHIANS 7:24

Today's Prayer

God, your infinite patience knows no bounds. You see us just as we are. You know our thoughts before we think them. You have even numbered the hairs on our heads. Each and everyone of us has significance and meaning in your sight. You embrace us as is, warts, scars, and all. You see in us what others cannot see and what we have yet to discern within ourselves. We ask you heavenly parent that even though you accept us as we are, please continue to work your will in us so that we may become all that you need us to be. Amen.

Today's Reflection

We seem to forget that our spirituality and our relationship with God are two commitments that are enriched and developed over time. No one accepts Christ one day and is perfected the next. If you remain faithful, there will be a process of continuous growth. The good news is that God is willing to aid us in our development by gently, patiently and lovingly fashioning us into worthy vessels.

Today's Song: "In the Morning When I Rise," #165

Journal Notes _____

_____

_____

_____

Getting Away

"Jesus went up on a mountain by himself to pray."
MATTHEW 14:23

Today's Prayer

Heavenly Spirit, there are so many different ways we try to connect with you. Like Elijah we look for you in the wind, in the fire and in the earthquake. Sometimes, the best way to show you that we care is to spend some one on one time with you. God, may we be able to do that in order to be closer to you . . . there are times when we must be with you. Amen.

Today's Reflection

Go away! That's right, go away. Just go away, I said. Go away from the phone, the television, the game, the CD player, whatever and whoever is occupying your space and energy. It really is okay . . . after all Jesus did it. Between twelve disciples, multitudes of people, powers, principalities and Pharisees, he needed time. Time to regroup, recharge, reflect, to hear and understand his instructions and his purpose from the heavenly one. Occasionally, the most meaningful way to reach, be with, hear from and to know God is, is to just go away.

Today's Song: "Lord, I Hear the Showers of Blessings," #120

Journal Notes _____

_____

_____

_____

Pray Expecting

*"Isaac prayed to the Lord for his wife, because she was barren:
and the Lord granted his prayer, and his wife Rebekah conceived."*
GENESIS 25:21

Today's Prayer

Creator God, author of life, I thank you for the special love between husbands and wives. Please be with those couples who desire to have children but are experiencing infertility difficulties. Hear their prayer and answer them in the precious name of Jesus. Amen.

Today's Reflection

Genesis 25:20 tells us that Isaac married Rebekah at age 40, and that Rebekah was having problems conceiving. In biblical times a woman's identity was tied to being someone's wife and mother. If a wife was unable to have children, she was labeled "barren," which was considered a curse. Isaac loved Rebekah he prayed on her behalf that God would grant her mercy. God heard Isaac's prayer and Rebekah conceived and gave birth to twin sons Esau and Jacob. There is power in intercessory prayer. When we are asked to pray for one another the request must be taken seriously, because someone is depending on a blessing from the Lord.

Today's Song: "Give Thanks," #292

Journal Notes _____

_____

_____

_____

March 27

Do You Care?

"Since I first came to Pharaoh to speak in your name,
he has mistreated this people, and you have done nothing
at all to deliver your people."
EXODUS 5:23

Today's Prayer

God of mercy, I thank you for being God almighty! I pray that you build up with courage and strength your messengers who advocate for the poor and powerless in our society. Amen.

Today's Reflection

Moses and Aaron dared to confront the Egyptian slave system. They faced Pharaoh directly asking on behalf of the enslaved Israelites for their release from hard labor, and the opportunity to worship God freely in the wilderness. However, their request was not only denied, but the Israelites received an additional amount of hard labor!

Moses was angry with God. He felt that God had mistreated the people because their situation grew worse instead of better. We need to remember that when our situations in life seem to get worse, we can be real with God and tell God our true feelings, too.

Today's Song: "Be Not Dismayed Whate'er Betide," #200

Journal Notes _____

_____

_____

_____

A Caring Leader

*"For Mordecai the Jew was next in rank to King Athasuerus,
and he was powerful among the Jews and popular with his many
kindred, for he sought the good of his people and interceded
for the welfare of all his descendants."*
ESTHER 10:3

Today's Prayer

God of justice and liberation, I thank you for your servant Mordecai, a man who loved his community to the point of risking his own life on their behalf. Help me, to develop this same type of passion and love for my community. Amen.

Today's Reflection

Mordecai, who was a Jew, didn't keep silent! Once he learned about the plot to massacre all the Jews in the country, he got busy to stop this evil plan. He boldly approached Queen Esther, who was also a Jew in the King's Court. He reminded her who she was, and that the plot to destroy the Jewish community included her as well. Mordecai helped Queen Esther to see that her position "was for such a time as this" to save her people from mass destruction. Mordecai's love for his community saved their lives. God calls all of us to love our community and to be an advocate for the poor and oppressed. One person can help to make a difference.

Today's Song: "Time Is Filled with Transition," #231

Journal Notes _____

_____

_____

_____

Alone?

"My God, my God, why have you forsaken me?"
PSALM 22:1

Today's Prayer

Precious Lord, I thank you for being there for me when I feel alone and discouraged. If you turn away from me what would I do? Never leave or forsake me because without you I can't make it. Amen.

Today's Reflection

"My God why have you forsaken me?" Jesus asked this question to God while he was dying on the Cross. Have you ever felt forsaken by God? Was it because of an unanswered prayer request, or because God failed to change a situation in your favor? Psalm 22 shows us clearly that we are encouraged to come to the Lord just as we are with our pain, disappointments and fears. We serve a loving God who desires to be part of our everyday lives.

Today's Song: "Blessed Assurance," #118

Journal Notes _____

_____

_____

_____

March 30

Do You Know?

He said to them, "But who do you say that I am?"
MATTHEW 16:15

Today's Prayer

Lord Jesus, thank you for making yourself available to me. Help me to be a bold witness about who you are to me. Let me not be afraid to tell somebody how you changed me and claimed me as your own. This I ask in your name. Amen.

Today's Reflection

Jesus asked his disciples, who did they say he was? They were the closest people to him on a daily basis. They were the ones who were present at all of the miracles, healings and other signs and wonders. They were the ones who witnessed how the religious establishment tried to discredit his authority because he dared to challenge their interpretation of the law.

Yes, Jesus wanted to know if the disciples knew who was in their mist. Peter identified Jesus as the Messiah, the Son of the living God. Jesus gave hope and new life to all he encountered. Who do you say Jesus is? Is he your friend, one you can depend on? Can you say that he is your Savior and redeemer? You are given the invitation to know Jesus for yourself, will you accept?

Today's Song: "He Is Lord," #95

Journal Notes _____

_____

_____

_____

Doing What It Takes

"To the weak I became weak, so that I might win the weak.
I have become all things to all people, that I might by all
means save some. I do it all for the sake of the gospel,
so that I may share in its blessings."
1 CORINTHIANS 9:22-23

Today's Prayer

Creator God, thank you for identifying with each human condition. You are always reaching out to your children who are the poor in society. Help me to walk with the orphans, people who are homeless, people living with AIDS, and others who are excluded in our society. Amen.

Today's Reflection

In Paul's letter to the Corinthians he identifies himself as an apostle of the gospel. Not only has Paul dedicated his life in spreading the good news of Jesus Christ, he also makes it relevant to the community he is serving. By relating to personal conditions or circumstance that people experience, he is able to demonstrate that Jesus cares about all of our issues. There is nothing to bad or shameful that Jesus can't fix.

Today's Song: "Give Me Jesus," #165

Journal Notes _____

_____

_____

_____

April 1

God's Love

"So we have known and believe the love that God has for us. God is love, and those who abide in love abide in God and God abides in them."
1 JOHN 4:16

Today's Prayer

God of love, thank you for your abiding presence in my life. Thank you for always dwelling with me. I know that you love me because you gave your only Son to die for me. Continue to keep your Holy Spirit in me, so all who see your love will be drawn to you. Amen.

Today's Reflection

Do you know that you are loved today? You are loved because of God's Holy Spirit that abides within you. Sometimes because of life's hardships and struggles it may be hard to believe that God is with you. However, we are reminded in 1 John 4:16 that God is love and God's love abides in us. The challenge we face is will we abide with God?

Today's Song: "I Want Jesus to Walk with Me," #66

Journal Notes _____

_____

_____

_____

April 2

Lord, Is That You?

And that very night the LORD appeared to him and said,
"I am God of your father Abraham."
GENESIS 26:23

Today's Prayer

Lord God, you are truly amazing! I thank you for loving and caring for me in spite of my faults. Help me to love others as you love me. Speak to me God speak to me. Amen.

Today's Reflection

The writer of Genesis tells us in no uncertain terms that the Lord appeared to Isaac and told him exactly what to do. How many times have we prayed for God to speak so plainly? We have a longing for dramatic communication from God, in Red Sea fashion! God speak to me.

Today's Song: "Every Time I Feel the Spirit," #241

Journal Notes _____

_____

_____

_____

April 3

God Is Yet Able

*". . . they would not listen to Moses, because of their broken spirit
and their cruel slavery."*
EXODUS 6:9

Today's Prayer

Merciful God, sustainer of all that is, help me to believe in your promises of grace
when my spirits sags, my soul aches, and the cares of life threaten to overshadow
your love for me. Be near to all who are broken-hearted this day, let us see the light
of your will for our lives. In the precious name of Jesus, I pray. Amen.

Today's Reflection

God commanded Moses to tell the Israelites that freedom was on its way. Prayers
answered! Deliverance! Freedom! This was good news! Misery had become a part of
the Israelites' daily lives for so many years they could not believe God's message of
liberation above the racket of their "broken spirits and their cruel slavery." In many
respects we are no different. God's voice becomes muffled beneath the weight of our
sagging, sore spirits and the screaming pain of our circumstances. We get so
embroiled in our situations that we can forget that God is near.

But if we dare to hope, and meet God in prayer we find, like the Israelites, that
despite our pains, betrayals and circumstances, God is yet able to save, deliver and
set us free.

Today's Song: "We Are Marching in the Light of God," #63

Journal Notes _____

_____

_____

_____

April 4

Lord, Do Something!

"Why do you make me see wrongdoing and look at trouble?"
HABAKKUK 1:3

Today's Prayer

Praise you, God, for the gift of sight, and being able to see both the beautiful and the wretched. We thank you for empowering us to mend the brokenness of our communities through Jesus Christ our savior and brother. Amen.

Today's Reflection

Daily we see all manner of destruction, wrongdoing, violence and trouble. The skeletal remains of abandon houses dot the landscapes of our urban centers. The AIDS epidemic is attacking African-Americans at an alarming rate. Our children are no longer safe in school. Lord, do something! God, "sic 'em" we scream. This is exactly what the prophet Habakkuk did: "Why do I have to see wrongdoing and trouble! Destruction and violence are before me." The prophet's desperate cry, like ours, is "Lord, do something—anything!" But God has done something. God has acted decisively in our baptisms and calls us to "do something." What God calls us to do, God equips us to handle. So get active in church, find a ministry or engage in a cause to help alleviate suffering. It is your turn—now go do something!

Today's Song: "What a Mighty God We Serve!" #295

Journal Notes _____

_____

_____

_____

April 5

For the Chronically Ill

"The LORD is my shepherd."
PSALM 23:1

Today's Prayer

Merciful Father, we lift before you those who are chronically ill. Wrap them in your embrace and assure them of your love, care, and protection. In Jesus' name, I pray. Amen.

Today's Reflection

We usually hear Psalm 23 at funerals but the "shepherd's psalm" also gives assurance of God's love and protection in the face of chronic illness.

As a pastor, I visited the homebound members in the congregation. One day I visited two women. First, I saw one who had had a severe stroke and was barely able to speak. Through tears, she cried, asking God, "Why?" Why the stroke, why did her husband have to die. After her lament, in her warbled speech, she recited Psalm 23. Despite her frustration, she was assured of God's care for her.

Later that afternoon, I saw another Mother of the Church, she was in the late stages of Alzheimer's disease. Her caregiver led her into the kitchen and planted her at the table. She had a faraway look in her eyes. As I prepared communion, a look of recognition came over her face. In a moment of absolute clarity, she said, "the Lord is my shepherd."

Two different women: one imprisoned by her body and one imprisoned by her mind and yet both find comfort in God's word.

Today's Song: "Precious Lord, Take My Hand," #193

Journal Notes

April 6

For Reconciliation in the Church

"If another member of the church sins against you."
MATTHEW 18:15

Today's Prayer

Gracious Lord, we thank you for the gift of church on earth and life together in our congregation. Teach us to live out the ministry of reconciliation with each other and the world. In Jesus' name. Amen.

Today's Reflection

There are no folks like church folks. We worship together on Sundays. Some of our richest relationships are with our sisters and brothers in church. When a church member experiences a death in the family, there is an outpouring of concern. We celebrate the critical moments in our lives in the context of the church: baptism, confirmation, and marriage. While we know how to do "church" well, we tend not to handle the simplest of misunderstandings well. Misunderstandings can churn into a full-scale "church fight" which can leave hurt feelings in its wake.

"If another member of the church sins against you, go and point it out when the two of you are alone," Jesus tells us. Don't complain to Sister "so-in-so." Go to that brother or sister under cover of prayer and in the spirit of Christ then speak from the heart, with the highest hope that reconciliation will take place. Paul tells us (2 Corinthians 5:18) that each of us has been called to the ministry of reconciliation.

Who are you holding a grudge against? Try your hand at reconciliation today, its what we're called to do!

Today's Song: "Lord, I Want to Be a Christian," #234

Journal Notes _____

_____

_____

_____

April 7

For the Spirit of Generosity

"Truly I tell you, that this poor widow has given
more than all of them."
LUKE 21:3

Today's Prayer

Lord God, giver of every gift, we thank you for blessing us with the gift of life and breath. All that we have comes from you; stir up in us the spirit of generosity to support the mission of the church at home and in the world. In Jesus' name. Amen.

Today's Reflection

During my pastoral internship in India, the story of the poor widow came alive. One Sunday, toward the middle of worship, a woman walked into church. Her sari was clean but threadbare as gauze. I watched her make her way through the pews, careful to find a seat—for it is considered improper for a single woman to sit next to a man she doesn't know. She found a seat near a few older women like herself.

During the offering of thanksgiving, she gave a generous offering of five rupees (India dollars) in the collection plate. As she gave her offering, she softly spoke. I turned toward the interpreter. "She said, she thanks God for her many blessings and life." Shortly before the benediction, she quietly slipped out. Curiosity got the best of me. As soon as worship was over, I hurried out to follow her. Down the street, she found her place on the curb and sat down. This woman was a beggar! She lived on the streets but yet she gave an offering with thanksgiving. I probably will never see this woman again, but she challenges all of us not to give to the church out of our abundance but to give of our "first fruits" for the building of the realm of God.

Today's Song: "Let Us Talents and Tongues Employ," #232

Journal Notes _____

_____

_____

_____

April 8

The Eucharist

"For as often as you eat this bread and drink the cup,
you proclaim the Lord's death until he comes."
1 CORINTHIANS 11:26

Today's Prayer

Merciful God, we praise you for every opportunity to feast at your holy table. May this gift continue to nourish us, heal us, empowers us through your Son, Jesus the Christ. Amen.

Today's Reflection

What a holy mystery we share in the Eucharist! Eucharist is true "soul food." In it we are nourished and strengthened for the Christian journey for all time and eternity. We bring our brokenness to draw from Jesus' boundless grace and mercy. Reconciliation, restoration, healing, and forgiveness are found there.

In the Eucharist, divisions of time and eternity are bridged. As we gather around the table, so does a great cloud of witnesses from every time and age. I was reluctant to take an extended trip because I was afraid that my very aged grandmother would die while I was away. I told her of my fear. She smiled and said, "I don't intend to die while you are away but in any case, if the Lord comes for me, I will just see you next Sunday at the communion table." Thank you God for your precious gift of Eucharist and for the wisdom of the older saints.

Today's Song: "Let Us Break Bread Together," #123

Journal Notes _____

_____

_____

_____

Blessed Before the Lord

*"Bring me game, and prepare for me savory food to eat,
that I may bless you before the LORD before I die."*
GENESIS 27:7

Today's Prayer

Holy One, we thank you for the young people in our lives. They are your gift to us for the future. We ask that you would bless them richly. Help them to dream big dreams and to achieve them. Keep them safe from the dangers around every corner. Grant them longevity and prosperity. Fill their lives with the richness of your presence and never leave them alone. For Christ's sake. Amen.

Today's Reflection

In this story of sibling rivalry and betrayal, Isaac prepares to bless his oldest son. Tradition emphasizes Jacob's deceit. However, we should not overlook the example set by Isaac; he prayed that the Lord would bless his child.

In recent years we have been inundated with reports describing our young people as lost and predicting that they are the first generation who will not do as well as their parents. In this era, Isaac's example resounds. We need to lift our youth up to the Lord and ask our God to bless them richly. Any success that we have had is in part because our mothers and fathers, grandmothers and grandfathers stayed on their knees before the Lord for us. Perhaps its time we went down on our knees for the next generation.

Today's Song: "Bless the Lord," #273

Journal Notes _____

_____

_____

_____

April 10

A God of Action

"The Egyptians shall know that I am the LORD."
EXODUS 7:5

Today's Prayer

Holy One, I thank you that you are a God of action. You have not left me to suffer alone or to struggle by myself. Whenever I have been in need, you have been with me, working out the details behind the scenes. Help me to rely completely on you. In Jesus' name. Amen.

Today's Reflection

The Lord is fed up! God gave Pharaoh a sign to encourage him to send the Hebrews forth, but Pharaoh would not be persuaded. It was then that the Lord set the plagues in motion that would lead to the eventual liberation of the Hebrews enslaved in Egypt. "Thus says the Lord, 'By this you shall know that I am the Lord.'" It was not enough for the Lord to tell Pharaoh; God had to show him that there were consequences for defying his will.

Isn't it good to know that God is not just a God of words, but of action? God is actively at work on our behalf, making a way for us behind the scenes, planning our way of escape. Whatever you are going through, know that the Lord will stretch out a hand to bring you out. By this you will know that he is the Lord.

Today's Song: "A Mighty Fortress Is Our God," #133

Journal Notes _____

_____

_____

_____

April 11

Silence in the Storm

"The LORD is in his holy temple;
let all the earth keep silence before him!"
HABAKKUK 2:20

Today's Prayer

Holy One, I am silent before you. Speak to me your will and embolden me to live it out in the world today. When the world's troubles threaten to overtake me, lead me back to your throne and help me find my peace in you. In Jesus' name. Amen.

Today's Reflection

It is perplexing that Habakkuk utters words of peace in this chapter. Amid the noise produced by injustice in the world, false gods vying for Israel's attention, and the cataclysmic destruction that the prophet foretells, he ends this chapter with plea for reverent silence.

But this call for reverent silence should not take us by surprise. We experience such cacophony every day in our busy lives. The storm of deafening noise in our world does not relent for our times of devotion. Yet as we seek the Lord amid the clamor, we can find the peaceful eye of the storm in the Lord's sweet presence. When the noise of this world threatens to overwhelm you, return to that quiet space found only in God.

Today's Song: "The Lord Is in His Holy Temple," #143

Journal Notes _____

_____

_____

_____

An Uplifted Soul

"To you, O LORD, lift up my soul."
PSALM 25:1

Today's Prayer

Holy One, I lift my soul to you. Holy One, I raise and hold myself before you. Holy One, I bear myself before you. Holy One, I lay bare my soul before you with all my vulnerabilities, weaknesses, and faults. I am naked before your penetrating gaze. Stripped of the masks I hide behind, my veneer removed I stand exposed. Search me Lord from my skin to my sin deep within. "For your name's sake, O Lord, pardon my guilt, for it is great." Make me whole as you are whole. To your whole, knit my soul and live anew in me. For Christ's sake I pray. Amen.

Today's Reflection

In God's presence, we find renewal and transformation. Imagine if we began each day of our life raising our souls up to God, asking the Lord to renew us, and requesting a fresh anointing of the Holy Spirit. Imagine if we began each day with a prayer reaffirming our utter trust in the Lord. How would that transform our interaction with our families and coworkers? How would that transform our daily witness? How would that transform our world? As you engage in the activities of the day, keep your soul lifted up, in constant communion with Christ, and see how it transforms you.

Today's Song: "I Was Sinking Deep in Sin," #188

Journal Notes

_____

_____

_____

_____

April 13

Blessed Anyhow

*"Am I not allowed to do what I choose with what belongs to me?
Or are you envious because I am generous?"*
MATTHEW 20:15

Today's Prayer

Holy One, I come before you confessing my enviousness. I have envied the good fortune that you have granted to others. I have taken for granted the way you have blessed me. Help me to recount today the many blessings you have given me in spite of who I am, what I have done, and what I have left undone. Thank you for being extraordinarily generous to me. In Jesus' name. Amen.

Today's Reflection

What a peculiar thing is God's grace. The blessings that flow from on high are available to everyone. In fact, the Lord makes the "sun rise on the evil and on the good, and sends rain on the righteous and on the unrighteous" (Matthew 5:25). How easy it would be to begrudge our brothers for the blessings they get and to hold our sisters' good fortune against them because we believe we are more deserving; we have worked harder, struggled longer, and been more faithful than they have. Yet, they are being blessed anyhow.

Perhaps that's when we should remember that we are also unworthy: "Our righteous deeds are like filthy cloth" (Isaiah 64:6). There is nothing we can do to earn God's grace. So let us rejoice that God blesses us anyhow.

Today's Song: "Thank You, Lord," #293

Journal Notes _____

_____

_____

_____

Using Our Gifts for the Church

*"So with yourselves; since you are eager for spiritual gifts,
strive to excel in them for building up the church."*

1 CORINTHIANS 14:12

Today's Prayer

Holy One, I thank you for the gifts that you have placed in me. I recognize that you have not given them to me for my own glorification, but for the edification of the body of Christ in this world. Use me Lord! I (re)commit myself and my gifts to you, and wait anxiously to see how you will use me to help build your Church in this world. For Christ's sake. Amen.

Today's Reflection

Did you know you have charisma? As Christians we each have charisma, gifts that God has given to us. Although we each have them, they are not all the same. These gifts often find expression in the careers we have chosen, in the talents we possess, and in the activities we enjoy. But like every blessing, these gifts come with a responsibility.

We are responsible to give these gifts back to the body of Christ and to use them to strengthen the Christian community. In this regard, we all have a ministry to which we are called. Have you discovered yours? Take some time today to entreat Christ to help you discern what your gifts are and how you can develop them. You and your gifts are important parts of God's plan of redemption. You may be surprised by what God has in store for you.

Today's Song: "Let Us Talents and Tongues Employ," #232

Journal Notes _____

_____

_____

_____

Walk in Love

"There was a man sent from God, whose name was John."
2 JOHN 1:6

Today's Prayer

Holy One, make your love real in me. Transform the way I treat others. Let your love unite where there is division, mend where there are fractures, and bring peace where there is strife. Grant me your power to love both my adversaries and my friends. Let someone see the light of your love in me and come to you. In Christ's name. Amen.

Today's Reflection

When Christ's commandments to us are described, they always come back to one issue: love. Love should move us to strive for justice for those who have been victimized, recompense for those who have been wronged, and harmony for those who are in conflict. It should circumscribe the way we treat each other; it should govern our behavior at all times.

But love is more than just a matter of behavior; love is a matter of character, defining who we are. The more we are submitted to Christ's will for our lives, the more this love expresses itself in us. Can people see Christ in you by the way you love those you interact with every day? Today, make it your goal to walk in love. Who knows, someone might find Christ because of God's love reflected through you.

Today's Song: "I Can Hear My Savior Calling," #146

Journal Notes

When Enough Is Never Enough

"Esau went to Ishmael and took Mahalath
daughter of Abraham's son Ishmael."
GENESIS 28:9

Today's Prayer

Dear God, forgive me for those times when I felt a need to win the respect of others by changing who I am. Amen.

Today's Reflection

Every society has expectations that accompany marriage. In ancient Israel, men were expected to marry their father's brother's daughter—a cousin. Ishmael married Canaanite women. To make up for marrying the wrong person and to win the favor of his parents, Esau took another wife—his father's brother's daughter (this was Mahalath, Ishmael's daughter). Yet, legally, this too was an incorrect marriage because Ishmael's mother was Hagar, a woman without status in the clan. Esau's effort to please his parents backfired. We know this because of the way the biblical story later unfolds.

Sometimes enough is never enough. We are pressured on all sides. If we do what others expect of us, we become people-pleasers, and this is a dead-end road. We should strive to understand and act on God's perspective. When we do that, it is always enough for God.

Today's Song: "Have Thine Own Way, Lord," #152

Journal Notes _____

_____

_____

_____

April 17

Courage to Confront a Hardened Heart

Then the LORD said to Moses, "Go to Pharaoh and say to him,
'Thus says the LORD: Let my people go . . ."
EXODUS 8:1

Today's Prayer

Creator God, please grant me the courage to confront a person who abuses their authority and who has a hardened heart. I also pray for the wisdom to refrain from pleading with hardened hearts, unless you send me, as you sent Moses. Amen.

Today's Reflection

In chapter 8 we find an unquestioning Moses, a Moses who returns to Pharaoh knowing that he will refuse him. And yet, Moses returns anyhow, trusting that God is with him. God is with us, too.

Today, God's Spirit is calling us to release people who are still bound by oppressive structures at home, at work, in the church, and in the world: "Let my women go!" "Let my children go!" "Let those who are homeless go!" "Let those who are ill go!" Let us trust that God will supply us with the courage and skills to confront hardened hearts, or to withhold our voices until God says speak.

Today's Song: "I Will Trust in the Lord," #256

Journal Notes _____

_____

_____

_____

April 18

Respecting God's Wrath

"I hear and tremble within; my lips quiver at the sound."
HABAKKUK 3:16

Today's Prayer

Dear God, when I am tempted the most, please help me to remember your love, as well as your wrath. Lead me in the way of righteousness. Amen.

Today's Reflection

We often emphasize God's mercy, steadfastness, lovingkindness, and blessings because God's wrath is so frightening. But today, let us take a moment to consider how enraged God becomes at unrepentant sin and injustice. The prophet Habakkuk said that he "trembles within." For a moment, let us tremble before our mighty and just God.

Today's Song: "When the Storms of Life Are Raging," #198

Journal Notes _____

_____

_____

_____

April 19

God Will Not Forsake Us

"If my father and mother forsake me, the LORD *will take me up."*
PSALM 27:10

Today's Prayer

Thank you, God, for sticking closer to me than any friend or relative. If I have unjustly forsaken someone, please reveal it to me, O Lord. Amen.

Today's Reflection

Sometimes the closest people to us turn away. Sometimes it is caused by our mistakes. Sometimes it is an error in communication. Sometimes we are dealing with an obstinate or judgmental personality. Whatever the case, it can feel extremely lonely and even devastating. It takes time to heal when loved ones forsake us. It takes time to learn to trust again. But in the meantime, the psalmist reminds us that God is always there waiting to take us up when human hands fail us. Indeed, like a loving parent takes on the needs of a child, the Lord will take you up.

Today's Song: "Precious Lord, Take My Hand," #193

Journal Notes _____

_____

_____

_____

April 20

Dealing with Critics

"Neither will I tell you by what authority I am doing these things."
MATTHEW 21:27

Today's Prayer

Dear God, I pray for the ability to deal wisely with those who criticize me, whether maliciously or from ignorance. Amen.

Today's Reflection

There are many episodes in Jesus' life that may instruct us in ours. For example, in Matthew 21, the chief priests and elders challenged Jesus' abilities and credentials. As African-Americans, our credentials are often challenged. This can be a terrible burden in the workplace, in church, or in school. Yet Jesus understands and helps us because he knows exactly what that is like.

How did Jesus respond to a question designed to trick him and get him into trouble? He responded with a question, and when the priests and elders could not answer, Jesus refused to answer them also. Is there a revelation in this for you that will help you at your job, home, or church? Jesus understands. Sometimes Jesus had such an unloving audience that he had to refuse to keep explaining himself, and sometimes we have to do the same.

Today's Song: "In the Name of Jesus," #265

Journal Notes _____

_____

_____

_____

Don't Let Anyone or Anything Turn You Around

*"Therefore my beloved, be steadfast, immovable,
always excelling in the work of the Lord . . ."*
1 CORINTHIANS 15:58

Today's Prayer

O God, help me to remember that your son Jesus gives us strength and power to overcome. Amen.

Today's Reflection

O death, where is your victory? O unemployment, where is your victory? O divorce, where is your victory? O sickness, where is your victory? O infertility, where is your victory? O racism, where is your victory? O sexism, where is your victory? O drug addiction, where is your victory? O prison, where is your victory? Although we may have problems, and might not be able to figure out what God is doing in our lives, let none of these things turn us around. God has a plan for your life and mine, and God has already worked it out.

"This battle is not for you to fight . . . see the victory of the Lord on your behalf" (2 Chronicles 20:17). Therefore, "be steadfast, immovable, excelling . . . because you know you do not labor in vain."

Today's Song: "Ride On, King Jesus," p. 182

Journal Notes _____

_____

_____

_____

April 22

Supporting Christians

*"Therefore, we ought to support such people,
so that we may become co-workers with the truth."*
3 JOHN 8

Today's Prayer

Dear God, show me how to be supportive of those in ministry who need my support. Amen.

Today's Reflection

John speaks of support that covers the basic needs someone must have do ministry without hindrance. Take a moment to reflect upon how you feel about supporting those in ministry. The average pastor or associate minister gives far more than he or she ever receives. Often, pastors and ministers give out of their personal earnings to families in need because some parishioners do not want to open church coffers. John is trying to help us overcome any tendency to withhold support. The assumption that John makes is that we are supporting ministers, missionaries and pastors who are not abusing the people or their trust in any way. Where there is abuse, it is just to end support and redirect it until change has come. John challenges us to find God's faithful servants who depend on us and to give them our support so that the hopeful, healing, and liberating power of God may go forward unhindered.

Today's Song: "What Shall I Render," #239

Journal Notes _____

_____

_____

_____

April 23

Divine Order

"The LORD watch between you and me,
when we are absent one from the other."
GENESIS 31:49

Today's Prayer

God of infinite wisdom, I trust you to always care for me and to guide me along the pathways of my life. I confess that I am often confused by the events and circumstances I encounter. I can't always explain why things happen, nor do I understand why I make the choices that I do. Grant me your gifts of good judgment, and give me confidence that all things in my life will work for good, according to your will. Amen.

Today's Reflection

Things are not always as they appear. I have learned this the hard way. People have deceived me, and I have deceived others. Why does dishonesty often seem to be the easy way out of my problems? I am so often tempted to be less than truthful, especially in my personal life. I call upon God's power today to fill me with the courage to both tell the truth and to recognize the truth in what others say to me. Watch over me, God, so that the truth will set me free.

Today's Song: "Do, Lord, Remember Me," #178

Journal Notes _____

_____

_____

_____

What God Can Do

*"This is why I have let you live: to show you my power,
and to make my name resound through all the earth."*

EXODUS 9:16

Today's Prayer

Praise the Lord, who can do all things and who does all things well. Praise the God who made heaven and earth, the God who made me and continues to keep me alive. Praise the Creator who will give life to my dreams and joy to my heart this day. Hear my prayer of praise today, God Almighty. Amen.

Today's Reflection

As I read about Moses and Pharaoh, I wonder how someone could be so stubborn. God had to do awful things to Pharaoh and his people to make them free their slaves. Am I this stubborn toward God? What does God want me to do differently? What changes do I need to make in my life? Today I will open myself up to God's messages to me. With the help of God, I will stop turning away from God's word to me. Speak now, Lord, in the way that is best for me to hear from you. Your servant is listening.

Today's Song: "I Believe I'll Testify," #225

Journal Notes _____

_____

_____

_____

A Brand New Me

"Be strong, and let your heart take courage,
all you who wait for the LORD."
PSALM 31:24

Today's Prayer

Jesus, Master, Guardian of my soul, hear my prayer. Let your strong Spirit fill me today with courage and strength, so that I may follow you and serve you. You know that I am often impatient with myself. I confess that I have also been impatient with you. Reveal to me the wisdom of your plan for my life. I trust you to show me what to do and when to do it, even if today is a day that I need do nothing but wait on you. Amen.

Today's Reflection

Martin Luther King Jr. once wrote about the strength that people need in order to truly love each other. He knew that this kind of strength was often hidden in the character of people whose lives were marked by suffering and injustice. I know people who have this kind of strength. They resist the temptation to return evil for evil. They combat violence with a spirit of peace. They are not weak, nor are they fools. Today they remind me that I have something important to accomplish with the strength that God has given me. Today I will be strong for God and of service to someone else.

Today's Song: "Let Justice Flow Like Streams," #48

Journal Notes _____

_____

_____

_____

_____

The Sankofa Invitation

*"I will restore your judges as at the first,
and your counselors as at the beginning."*
ISAIAH 1:26

Today's Prayer

Ancient and Invisible One, my prayers today celebrate your power which was made known to my ancestors. I thank you for your presence with them and your faithfulness to them. I praise you for the greatness of my people's history. May I never forget the testimony of past generations, for through their stories I learn so much more about you. You are the same yesterday, today, and forever. Hallelujah and amen.

Today's Reflection

Sankofa is a concept from West Africa that invites me to use the best wisdom and traditions of the past as my foundation for the future. Sankofa teaches me to cherish the lessons of history and remember the truth that has already been revealed. Sankofa also connects me to the ancestors who lived before me and lifts them up as evidence of my own potential. I am somebody because I come from a proud and noble people. Let me honor them today in all that I say, do, and believe.

Today's Song: "Lift Every Voice and Sing," #296

Journal Notes _____

_____

_____

_____

Have I Forgotten Something?

"Give therefore to the emperor the things that are the emperor's, and to God the things that are God's."
MATTHEW 22:21

Today's Prayer

God my provider, everything I have comes from you. You have given me the gift of life itself, and you support me with all the blessings I find in my community. Teach me to be more like you by becoming a more generous person. Show me how to share with those who are in need, and in so doing let me give honor to you. Amen.

Today's Reflection

If I were to write down everything I need to do today, would I include those things I need to do for God? The Bible is filled with wisdom reminding me that God expects something from me. God wants me to work for justice, to serve others, and to maintain a personal life that is morally and physically healthy. God also wants me to take time out for prayer. These actions can take many forms, but they must be done joyfully. Let me live today in thanksgiving to the God who is everything to me.

Today's Song: "What Shall I Render," #239

Journal Notes _____

_____

_____

_____

Continuing to Rise

*"Indeed, we felt that we had received the sentence of death so that
we would not rely on ourselves but on God who raises the dead."*
2 CORINTHIANS 1:9

Today's Prayer

God of new life, you have never known defeat. Your power is always available,
and your Spirit is always at work. Be at work in my life today, especially in the
circumstances that are so discouraging to me right now. Teach me again that even in
the midst of my personal failures, you can show me the victory of faith, hope, and
love. Amen.

Today's Reflection

No matter what obstacles are placed in my path and no matter what emotional
pain causes me to suffer, I have a confident attitude about myself and my potential.
I do not foolishly deny that I face very serious challenges. I see these challenges
every day, but my spirit sees much more. My spirit sees the power of God that was
revealed when Jesus was raised from the dead. I am God's child, too, and I, too, will
rise today.

Today's Song: "God Sent His Son," #93

Journal Notes _____

_____

_____

_____

April 29

Sad but True

*"They are waterless clouds carried along by the winds;
autumn trees without fruit, twice dead, uprooted."*
JUDE 12b

Today's Prayer

Giver of divine direction, you are able to guide me through the maze of voices and choices and influences that confuse and disturb my life. You continue to teach me to be careful in how I live and to be wise in choosing friends. Let your wisdom take control of me today, so that I will walk along a path that is pleasing to you. Keep me from evil and fill me with your goodness. Amen.

Today's Reflection

When I was a boy, my father used to say, "When the crowd goes this way, you go that way." My father was warning me about the seductive ways of careless living. The things that bring shame into our lives often appear to be popular and exciting. How easy it is for me to assume that just because everybody else is doing something it must be all right. I thank God for my father's wisdom. Sometimes, I need to remember the counsel of wise people who know that if I am to reach my God-given potential, some things and some people are better left alone.

Today's Song: "Gracious Spirit, Heed Our Pleading," #103

Journal Notes _____

_____

_____

_____

April 30

Holding On

But Jacob said, "I will not let you go, unless you bless me."
GENESIS 32:26b

Today's Prayer

God, you have promised that you would bless me and provide for me. Help me to be confident while you are moving on my behalf. Help me not to be anxious or unsettled, but instead give me the courage to wait until you bless. Amen.

Today's Reflection

Often, we find ourselves desperately seeking a blessing from God. It can be for improved health, financial gain or relationship restoration. To be sure, it is right for us to turn to God for God to meet our need; God is our provider. But there is also an attitude that can prepare us to fully access what God has for us. This posture encourages us to determine that regardless of what things look like, we will not give up faith or hope. We will continue to hold on to God until our blessing is realized.

Today's Song: "Precious Lord, Take My Hand," #193

Journal Notes _____

_____

_____

_____

May 1

The Worth of the Word

*"The tablets were the work of God, and the writing was
the writing of God, engraved upon the tablets."*
EXODUS 32:16

Today's Prayer

Thank you, God, for giving me instruction on how to serve and worship you.
Thanks for not leaving me to my own devices and personal agenda. Show me how
to honor your word with a life that gives witness to your direction. Amen.

Today's Reflection

Sometimes we forget that there are some things that we don't have to personally
ponder, figure out, or even fully understand. God has already given us direction and
revelation through the life-giving power of God's word. Indeed, the commandments
of the Bible are the very work of God, written for us so that we might continue along
the path of spiritual maturity and development. Without a doubt, the Word is priceless. It is not simply for our information; instead the Word has been given to form
and shape us.

Today's Song: "What a Mighty God We Serve!" #295

Journal Notes _____

_____

_____

_____

Free to Fail

"Happy are those whose transgression is forgiven,
whose sin is covered."
PSALM 32:1

Today's Prayer

Lord, I pray for those held hostage by a fixation with perfection. Give them strength to face their sins. Help them, and me, to receive your grace. Amen.

Today's Reflection

In a competitive society, it easy to fall prey to the widely pervasive push to be better or best, if not perfect. Moreover, recognition seems to be given to those who are either able to get through life without significant error or who have mastered the ability to cover up transgressions and shortcomings. But God suggests that happiness is not lodged in perfection, but springs forth from our willingness to acknowledge our sins. We can walk in joy when we realize that God does not refuse to love us simply because we make a mistake. Indeed, God invites us to acknowledge our sins. We are free to fail, because God's forgiveness is freely given.

Today's Song: "God Forgave My Sin in Jesus' Name," #187

Journal Notes _____

_____

_____

_____

Faceless Faith

*"What do you mean by crushing my people, by grinding the
face of the poor? says the LORD God of hosts."*
ISAIAH 3:14

Today's Prayer

God of provision, I confess that I have ignored the cries and the needs of your people. Sometimes it has been easy to walk past people who are homeless without even taking notice. Forgive me for not seeing the faces of the oppressed. Help me to resist the evil of over-consumption. And give me the strength to share the resources that you have given us. Amen.

Today's Reflection

It is easy for us to get comfortable with all the material possessions that we have. We are quick to enjoy the items that we have acquired and hesitant to disguise our satisfaction. And sometimes this becomes prideful arrogance. However, God reminds us that our indulgence and fascination with goods is grinding the face of the poor. As such, we must chose to give our faith a facelift. We are called to make life choices that give witness to our oneness with all people.

Today's Song: "Our Father, Who Art in Heaven," #100

Journal Notes _____

_____

_____

_____

Being Awake

*"Keep awake therefore for you do not know
on what day your Lord is coming."*
MATTHEW 24:42

Today's Prayer

God, help me to not be distracted by the competing concerns in my life. Cause me to be aware of what you are doing and where you are working. Help me to do what you have asked me to, without wavering. Amen.

Today's Reflection

An interesting thing about babies is that it is difficult for them to stay awake. When they feel tired or irritable, there is not much to stop them from grabbing a blanket or climbing into the lap of an awaiting parent.

However, many people have long passed infancy and adolescence and find it both difficult, if not impossible, to stay focused on God's divine plan and difficult to be acutely attentive to the movement of God. Often a lulling complacency comes upon us and we are asleep to the mandates of Christian confession and behavior. But Jesus reminds us that we must be prepared for the Lord's return.

Today's Song: "Lead Me, Guide Me," #70

Journal Notes _____

_____

_____

_____

The Smell of Victory

"But thanks be to God who always leads us in
triumphal procession, and through us spreads in every place
the fragrance that comes from knowing him."
2 CORINTHIANS 2:14

Today's Prayer

Loving God, you continue to be with me in hard times, in the midst of personal and corporate battles. In every situation, you consistently show me the paths to victory. Thanks for ordering my steps and for directing my path. Help me to be a reminder of your unfailing love, protection, and provision. Amen.

Today's Reflection

Sweat socks. Gold medals. Stuffy locker rooms. These are often the symbols of participation in and the markers of victory. The winner is often the one who played the hardest and lasted the longest. However, when we are in Christ, we have already joined in the winning side. Victory has been promised and the outcome has been secured. We needn't depend on any particular event, because God always leads along the path of triumph. Our faith and obedience, become the witness to those who don't believe. God's favor in our lives is so pervasive that it is like the sweet smell of expensive perfume.

Today's Song: "I Heard an Old, Old Story," #97

Journal Notes _____

_____

_____

_____

May 6

Choosing Life

*"You are a hiding place for me; you preserve me from trouble;
you surround me with glad cries of deliverance."*

PSALM 32:7

Today's Prayer

In the midst of chaos and confusion, Dearest Lord, have mercy on me. Even as I look upon my circumstances and surroundings, let me know that you are near. Give me comfort and help me to be a comfort to others. Amen.

Today's Reflection

David knew what side his bread was buttered on. He had flaws, and his personal choices often got him in hot water. But, he knew that the best part of him was when he relied on God. David knew that calling on God was always the right choice.

Life can be unbearable at times. Add to this our inability to lead perfect lives, and what is unbearable becomes unlivable. A friend once remarked that when she and her brothers were young, they would get into trouble with their childish pranks. Their mother, upon discovering them would admonish them with the words, "You better choose life." What she gave them was a choice sometimes between a spanking and straightening their act. "It was usually an easy choice," the friend remembers.

God brings life to us daily. Choosing life is what God requires of us.

Today's Song: "God Sent His Son," #93

Journal Notes _____

_____

_____

_____

May 7

Undeserved Forgiveness

"But Esau ran to meet him, and embraced him,
and fell on his neck and kissed him."
GENESIS 33:4

Today's Prayer

Gracious God, I thank you for my family. Please God give me the strength to put past hurts behind me. Give me the courage to love those who may have wronged me. Give me an open heart to forgive and receive them, that I may be an agent of healing. This I ask in the name of Jesus. Amen.

Today's Reflection

You know the wounds, the painful memories and the heartbreak that only those we love can inflict. We ask God to give us a forgiving heart, for in forgiving those who have wronged us, we heal ourselves. We remember what God requires of us is not judgment, blame, or ridicule, but love. "How many times must I forgive my sibling?" Jesus answers, "seventy times seven." Today, forgive a grudge. Today, give that one family member who lies outside of your grace another chance.

Today's Song: "Spirit of the Living God," #101

Journal Notes _____

_____

_____

_____

May 8

Deadly Defiance

"But the Lord hardened Pharaoh's heart,
and he would not let the people of Israel go."
EXODUS 11:10

Today's Prayer

Most Gracious God, I thank you for the hard places, the difficult situations that force me to make a move. Thank you for those moments, for often, in those moments, I get a glimpse of what you would have me do, who you would have me to be. As I go about this day, Lord, I ask that you open my spirit to see the vision of possibility you hold for me. Amen.

Today's Reflection

Sometimes God's hand is found even in the hard places. The places that are uncomfortable, those situations that are unjust. For when we are forced between a "rock and a hard place" we are forced to make a move. The Israelites had the option of being comfortable with the oppression they knew, or moving on. Even with the promise of God, it seemed an uncomfortable and frightening walk toward freedom. Sometimes we must trust God enough to let Pharaoh go!

Today's Song: "Guide My Feet," #153

Journal Notes _____

_____

_____

_____

Don't Sweat

"Do not fret because of the wicked;
do not be envious of wrongdoers."

PSALM 37:1

Today's Prayer

God, I ask for patience this day. To be firm and steadfast, walking inside your will. Lord, I affirm your love, your power, and your goodness. I pray with the assurance of one who knows you are a righteous God and justice will prevail. Amen.

Today's Reflection

By all appearances, those who don't honor God, those who lie, steal, and cheat DO prosper. How do we reconcile this fact? David assures us that righteousness will be rewarded. Our charge is to trust in the Lord and not let the appearance of inequity "worry our nerves," for as the psalmist reminds us, "I have been young, and now am old, yet I have not seen the righteous forsaken nor his descendants begging bread!"

Today's Song: "Be Not Dismayed Whate'er Betide," #200

Journal Notes _____

_____

_____

_____

May 10

Staying Ready

"Keep awake therefore, for you know neither the day nor the hour."
MATTHEW 25:13

Today's Prayer

Most Gracious God, give me a discerning heart that I may be ready to serve you, ready to praise you, ready to do your will here on earth. Save me from distractions and move me toward faithful service. This in Jesus' name I pray. Amen.

Today's Reflection

How prepared are you in your personal life? Are you always disorganized, always running late? How can you better prepare yourself to meet your daily challenges? If that perfect job, that perfect mate, or that perfect opportunity came along, would you be ready? The same thing holds true spiritually. We must be in a constant state of preparation; loving, learning, serving, witnessing, and praising God so we won't be caught unprepared and left outside of God's will for us.

Today's Song: "Soon and Very Soon," #38

Journal Notes _____

_____

_____

_____

From the Get-Go

"In the beginning was the Word."
JOHN 1:1

Today's Prayer

Dear Lord, give me courage to proclaim my faith. "Let your praise continually be in my mouth." Direct my tongue. "May the words of my mouth and the meditation of my heart be acceptable to thee, Lord, my rock and my redeemer." Amen.

Today's Reflection

Words are powerful! Once something harsh or unloving is spoken it's hard to take back the hurt it's caused. John's Gospel says the Word became flesh. If your words took form, what would they look like? How would your words manifest? Would they be beautiful and flowing, or rigid with a point? Would they be warm and inviting, reverent and peaceful, or cold and hard? Speak a good word today. Think about how your words effect others today.

Today's Song: "He Came Down," #37

Journal Notes _____

_____

_____

_____

Uncovered

"But when one turns to the Lord, the veil is removed."
2 CORINTHIANS 3:16

Today's Prayer

God, I thank you for all the beauty that surrounds me; for colors soft and colors radiant, for textures jagged and smooth. Open my eyes that I can see past the mess, past the confusion, past the injustice, past the uncaring to the brilliance of your possibility. As I move through this day, help me see the certainty of your love, evidence of your power. Amen.

Today's Reflection

There are many things that veil the radical brilliance of God. What stuff is making it difficult for you to see God? What is obscuring the power of God in your life? Is it the sameness of your routine, or perhaps the limitations of tradition? Is it the weight of living in a corrupt world where disappointment, anger, resentment, or even jealousy gets in the way of you seeing God? Today, don't let your familiarity with the world block your vision of who God is and whose you are. Today, look for the sacred around you.

Today's Song: "All Hail the Power of Jesus' Name!" #267

Journal Notes _____

_____

_____

_____

May 13

Driving or Driven

"Have you not made distinctions among yourselves . . . ?"
JAMES 2:4

Today's Prayer

God, I know you see all people as equal. Lord, keep me from seeing people only as the world sees them. Help me to see the child of God before me and not just the car someone drives, or the clothes someone wears. Help me to see the heart of those I encounter. This I can do with your help. Amen.

Today's Reflection

First impressions impact us powerfully. We so often judge the worth of our brothers and sisters, not by who they are but by the labels on their backs, the cars they drive, their income, and even where they live. The Bible cautions us against this sin. Consider today, who and what you value, and why.

Today's Song: "Yield Not to Temptation," #195

Journal Notes _____

_____

_____

_____

Dreamers

They said to one another, "Here comes this dreamer."
GENESIS 37:19

Today's Prayer

Gracious God, creator of all things, please supply me with a vision for my life and the strength to hold on as I go through the challenges that life will present. Amen.

Today's Reflection

This particular narrative begins by telling of an already strained relationship that Joseph had with his brothers. As the narrative unfolds, God gives Joseph the gift of prophecy or vision. When Joseph begins to disclose his visions, the level of hostility within the family escalates. It peaks when Joseph discloses a vision wherein the symbols project him as being in a position of power while his family is in a position of subjugation. There are several lessons that one can learn about discretion in disclosing the revelations of God, especially when it threatens the comfort level of others. However, we learn that God's divine agenda can not be altered!

Today's Song: "God Has Smiled on Me," #190

Journal Notes _____

_____

_____

_____

Passing Over

*"The blood shall be a sign for you in the houses where you live:
when I see the blood, I will pass over you, and no plague
shall destroy you when I strike the land of Egypt."*

EXODUS 12:13

Today's Prayer

Holy God, who provides a means of salvation in troubled times, I thank you for passing over my sins through the blood of Jesus. Amen.

Today's Reflection

This particular account in Exodus is a story of a people who are held in bondage. God is about to deliver them from servitude. For the Christian community, the unblemished lamb, the blood of the lamb, and the Passover are signs that communicate the Christ event. They symbolize God's plan for deliverance to all humanity. The blood of the Lamb still provides salvation.

Today's Song: "I Know It Was the Blood," #75

Journal Notes _____

_____

_____

_____

Just a Visit

"For I am your passing guest, an alien, like all my forebears."
PSALM 39:12b

Today's Prayer

Oh Lord, help me to be as mindful of my own words as I am as mindful of the words of others. Amen.

Today's Reflection

This particular psalm mirrors the movement and emotional anxiety that we all experience from time to time. Sometimes the words of others can push us to the edge. Hurtful words can cause us to doubt. The realization that life on earth is temporary and filled with pain can compel us to examine the permanence of God and the hope and expectation of better days in God's presence. Know that God's words of promise are sure and that suffering cannot endure forever. Like the psalmist, in the midst of suffering, hope and faith in God are what we have to cling to.

Today's Song: "Time Is Filled with Transition," #231

Journal Notes _____

_____

_____

_____

This Is a Really Good Day

*"On that day the branch of the LORD shall be
beautiful and glorious."*
ISAIAH 4:2a

Today's Prayer

Lord, help me to be cleansed of the things that are not like you. Strengthen me that I might endure a positive change. Amen.

Today's Reflection

Often times we want to move to the next stage of growth in our lives because we believe that it will bring peace and security as well as other good things. Much like children in elementary school, we can't wait until promotion to the next level. But in matters of the spirit, maturity is a process that requires the individual to address their personal shortcomings before they can move on. The old folks would use the term "going through the fire" to symbolize the process. It was figurative speech to indicate the refining of gold: a process that requires the burning off of all impurities. The process is usually painful but the result is "beautiful and glorious."

Today's Song: "Give Me a Clean Heart," #216

Journal Notes

Jesus' Blood

*"For this is my blood of the covenant that is poured out
for many for the forgiveness of sins."*
MATTHEW 26:28

Today's Prayer

Lord of life, creator of all things, grant me knowledge and understanding of the ongoing covenant of love that you have with your people. Amen.

Today's Reflection

The words *covenant* and *blood* highlight two of the prevailing themes that are connected by threads of family relationships within the Bible. The Passover was celebrated in remembrance of the covenant that God had with God's people. The Passover was a time to remember this relationship and the blood that was shed to save the covenant community. Jesus' words in this chapter symbolize a new covenant with a new Passover lamb. The sacrifice that is about to take place in this account will atone for all the sins of those who believe (see Leviticus 17:11). There will be no need to sacrifice any more animals. In infinite wisdom, God has chosen the unblemished Lamb to die so that we who believe might be passed over during the day of judgment. It's not what we have done, but what God has done. Thanks be to God.

Today's Song: "Lamb of God," #35

Journal Notes _____

_____

_____

_____

Vision Correction

"In their case the god of this world has blinded the minds of unbelievers, to keep them from seeing the light of the gospel of the glory of Christ, who is the image of God."

2 CORINTHIANS 4:4

Today's Prayer

Father in heaven, open our hearts and spirits so that we might comprehend the eternal things of life. Amen.

Today's Reflection

The faith community within the Bible had to live in tension with those who saw the world differently. The world has changed little in that respect. Materialism, immediacy in results and effective outcome models have taken a root and grown in our world. What people cling to and rely upon in times of trouble is rightfully their god. Paul draws upon that contrast in this chapter as evidenced in the last line. "Because we look at not what can be seen but at what cannot be seen; for what can be seen is temporary, but what cannot be seen is eternal." These contrasts in world-views are ever present in our Christian reality. Where is your focus.

Today's Song: "Some Folk Would Rather Have Houses," #236

Journal Notes _____

_____

_____

_____

Lying Tamer

"But no one can tame the tongue—
a restless evil, full of deadly poison."
JAMES 3:8

Today's Prayer

Gracious and Holy God, help me to think carefully before I speak. Amen.

Today's Reflection

Today's meditation gives one reason to be very careful in the words that one utters. The author ends this chapter by drawing a contrast between wisdom from above and earthly wisdom. Now what were you getting ready to say?

Today's Song: "If I Have Wounded Any Soul Today," #170

Journal Notes _____

_____

_____

_____

Distressed but Determined

"She is more righteous than I."
GENESIS 38:26

Today's Prayer

Lord God, I give you thanks and praise for being a God of justice and love. I give you thanks for being mindful of me even when I'm not mindful of you, and for protecting me when I feel vulnerable. When all else fails and everyone has turned their backs on me, I can depend on and trust in you, O Lord. You know everything, and nothing is hidden from you. Amen.

Today's Reflection

Like Tamar, we often have done what we thought was the right thing. followed the rules, and yet found ourselves distressed and in the midst of a mess. Like Tamar, we have often trusted and believed promises, yet found ourselves betrayed.

Tamar's father-in-law knew her humiliating plight if she remained childless. He attempted to carry out the tradition in giving her his next oldest son. When that son died, he said he would give her his youngest son, but he didn't. God knows our situation and will use what was intended to be a stumbling block and turn into into a stepping stone.

Today's Song: "Like a Ship That's Tossed and Driven," #251

Journal Notes _____

_____

_____

_____

May 22

Getting Home, the Long Way

"So God led the people by the roundabout way of the wilderness."
EXODUS 13:18

Today's Prayer

Eternal God, show me the way that I must go to fulfill your will in my life. Help me to stay on the path you've set before me. Keep me in your loving care. I thank you for loving me and for saving me. Amen.

Today's Reflection

The children of Israel learned a lot about themselves and God. Finding the fastest way to the promised land was not the most important thing—but rather it was what they learned on the journey that was important.

The children of Israel learned that God could supply all of their needs. They worried about food, and God provided manna from heaven. Wilderness experiences are neither pleasant nor convenient. Wilderness experiences can be time-consuming and uncertain, yet priceless. We can learn so much about ourselves and our creator in the wilderness. We can see our weakness and our strength. We can see our loyalty, but most of all we can see that God is with us and that we are not by ourselves.

Today's Song: "Lead Me, Guide Me," #70

Journal Notes _____

_____

_____

_____

May 23

Change of Heart

"I have told the glad news of deliverance."
PSALM 40:9

Today's Prayer

I give thanks to you, O Lord, for hearing my distress and comforting me. For hearing my joy and taking delight in it. Lord, I thank you for your unconditional love and your endless mercy that meets me at my point of need. Amen.

Today's Reflection

For many of us, a tragedy or a crisis can put us in a position of having to rely and depend on someone else. When disaster strikes and we don't know what to do, when we are overwhelmed with a sense of hopelessness or where to go, and when it seems that no one can help—at those times we turn to God as our last resort. God doesn't always change the situation but sometimes changes us in the situation. The situation that seemed impossible or hopeless before now has possibilities and options. We thank God for the strength to go forward and not give up. We want to repay God, but God only desires from us our love and obedience.

Today's Song: "Be Not Dismayed Whate'er Betide," #200

Journal Notes _____

_____

_____

_____

May 24

Learning to Love

"He expected justice, but saw bloodshed."
ISAIAH 5:7

Today's Prayer

Merciful God, creator of every good and perfect gift, help me to be a follower of Christ. Help me to love my neighbors as you have loved me, and to treat them as I want to be treated. Keep your hedge of protection all around me. Help me to do what is required, O Lord, to walk with you. Amen.

Today's Reflection

With care we were created, and showered with unconditional love. God has supplied our every need: air, water, and food in abundance. God provides warm weather, a place to live, companionship, and surrounds us with the beauty of creation God gives us these things freely, not because we earned them or even because we deserved them, but simply because he wants us to have them.

In response, humanity is destroying the land. We hurt one another, and charge one another ridiculously high prices for things God has freely given us. We disrespect and dishonor one another because of the color of our skin, gender, religious choices, economic status, and illnesses. If we are to walk with God, we must learn to love.

Today's Song: "In Christ There Is No East or West," #214

Journal Notes _____

_____

_____

_____

Seeing Jesus

"I know who you are, the Holy One of God."
MARK 1:24b

Today's Prayer

Gracious God, for your unconditional love found in Jesus, I thank you for opening my heart to understand who the Holy One of God is in my life. For it was Jesus, the healer, who touched me and made me whole. I thank you for the privilege of knowing him for myself. Bless all who call on Jesus with health and strength. Amen.

Today's Reflection

As Jesus began his public ministry, many things happened with him in the presence of others. It was very clear to all who heard and saw Jesus that there was something very special about him. When Jesus astounded and amazed people, they never once considered who he really was. Like those people, many of us are in the presence of Jesus yet do not know him. The Holy One of God is the one who loves and blesses us. He can bring joy into our lives. No matter what the problem is, Jesus can fix it. He can free us from the bondage of racism, sexism, poverty, and drugs. When Jesus touches our hearts, our lives are forever changed. He is a friend like no other. We can do all things through Christ, who strengthens us. He was the sacrifice for us and is available to us if we would only ask, believing.

Today's Song: "What a Fellowship, What a Joy Divine," #220

Journal Notes _____

_____

_____

_____

_____

May 26

The Miracle of Grace

"He gave us the ministry of reconciliation."
2 CORINTHIANS 5:19

Today's Prayer

Loving God, the one who heals from the inside out. Fill me with your Holy Spirit so that I may know your love for me. Fill me with your wisdom that I might worship you in spirit and in truth. Amen.

Today's Reflection

There are many forms of human suffering. One of the most common forms of suffering is guilt. Guilt that we cannot forgive long after the event itself has passed. This guilt takes on many forms, including self-indulgence, self-pity, low self-esteem, and an overwhelming sense of unworthiness.

In the ministry of reconciliation, where God reconciles the world through Jesus Christ, we can overcome guilt. Jesus' way of dealing with this sense of guilt is not to excuse the wrongs. Rather, through his love for us to forgive the person and to blot out those wrongs. The guilt is no longer a barrier in our lives. This is the miracle of grace, found on the cross at Calvary.

Today's Song: "We Praise Thee, O God," #100

Journal Notes _____

_____

_____

_____

Drawing Near

"Draw near to God, and He will draw near to you."
JAMES 4:8

Today's Prayer

Merciful Creator, give me a clean heart so that I might serve thee. Help me to be a light that shines in the darkness, the peacemaker in the midst of conflict, and the loving one in the midst of hatred. I thank you for molding and making me into a vessel that can be used by you. Amen.

Today's Reflection

The bottom line of the goodness is transformation, a change of mind and heart. No matter how selfish or rebellious we have been, if we repent and confess our sins before God, God will certainly answer. God will answer because God loves and cares for us.

If only we would just humble ourselves, realizing that everything we have comes from God. If we submit ourselves to God, God will welcome us with open arms, embracing us with unconditional love. In good times and in bad, in sickness and in health, God loves us and blesses us.

Today's Song: "I'd Rather Have Jesus," #233.

Journal Notes

God Was There

"The LORD was with him."
GENESIS 39:23b

Today's Prayer

Gracious God, creator of all things, it is through difficult times that we need your blessed assurances. I pray that you would be with all who find themselves in difficult times. Use me to help others, as others have helped me. Amen.

Today's Reflection

Genesis 39 tells the reader that Joseph was "bought," from the Ishmaelites. The second and the last verse within Genesis 39 give emphasis to God's presence in the midst of situations that appear to go from bad to worse. Others influenced Joseph's condition of forced servitude to incarceration. However, Joseph controlled his attitude and the text reveals that Joseph tried to make the best of a bad situation. It also reveals that through harsh circumstances the Lord is with us.

Today's Song: "Why Should I Feel Discouraged," #252

Journal Notes _____

_____

_____

_____

May 29

In Plain View

"Israel saw the great work that the LORD did."
EXODUS 14:31

Today's Prayer

Lord God, as we go through life's transitions we pray that your saving power would be discernible to us as well as to others. Guide us in times of darkness and distress. Amen.

Today's Reflection

Exodus 14 is an account of a community in transition. The past was lived in captivity. There are several voices within the text. There are the voices of the Lord, Moses, the Egyptians and the community. The Lord's voice reveals intention, directions, and purpose. The voice of Moses reveals encouragement. The voice of the Egyptians reveals wavering and indecision and the voice of the people reveal protest. Often captivity can be comfortable. The people were uncomfortable with leaving captivity. Sometimes, in our spiritual lives, we too are easily seduced into captivity, but the Lord is revealing new intentions, directions, and purpose. Be encouraged. Listen and watch for the great work that God is doing, for you, while you are in transition.

Today's Song: "Do, Lord, Remember Me," #178

Journal Notes _____

_____

_____

_____

My Hope Is in God

"Hope in God; for I shall again praise him, my help and my God."
PSALM 42

Today's Prayer

My Lord and my God, it is your presence that sustains life. Please sustain me in the parched places of my journey. Allow me to drink from the well that sustains my spirit. Amen.

Today's Reflection

The voice of the psalmist is focused on memories of better times, hope for the future and questions of when, where and why. We all go through periods in our lives when our faith is challenged. The psalm is clear evidence of our not being the only ones to have experienced this dilemma. The words express the deepest dread of the faithful, to be abandoned by God. But in the final verse of the psalm the desperation has moved to hope. "Hope in God; for I shall again praise him." Our faith is our hope. A hope that assures us that God will not abandon us.

Today's Song: "I Will Trust in the Lord," #256

Journal Notes _____

_____

_____

_____

A Holy Volunteer

"Here am I; send me!"
ISAIAH 6:8

Today's Prayer

My Lord and my God, I realize that I live around and work with many who do not know of your ability to take away sin. I pray that you would use me as a vessel to deliver a message of good news. Amen.

Today's Reflection

The prophet Isaiah had a life altering experience in the temple. His encounter with God and the heavenly host made him realize that his life, being interwoven with those around him, was not respectful of the holiness of God. "Yet my eyes have seen the King, the Lord of hosts!" was proclaimed with amazement. Isaiah was astonished in the realization that God was merciful and had provided a way for his guilt and sin to be taken away. Not only was his guilt and sin taken away, but also the Lord had sought out a messenger. Isaiah, being moved by this redeeming experience, offered himself as a vessel to deliver the word of God. We are much like Isaiah in many ways. And God will always be God. Ready to redeem us and use us as vessels for noble use. The only requirement for Isaiah was to face the truth about himself and to be willing to be used by God. The Lord still seeks out vessels. "Here am I; send me!"

Today's Song: "I, the Lord of Sea and Sky," #230

Journal Notes _____

_____

_____

_____

6/1/04 *Start*

Restored

~~Daughter~~
Daughter *"Son, your sins are forgiven."*
MARK 2:5

Today's Prayer

Gracious God, thank you for sending Jesus to bring healing to this world. I pray thee; make me whole again through the healing power of your love that comes in Jesus Christ. Help me to know Jesus as my Lord and Savior. Amen.

Today's Reflection

Jesus came into the world to restore it to wholeness. The paralytic was one among those needing to be made whole again. He knew what it was like to live as an outsider because of his physical disability. Those who witnessed the healing realized it could only come from God. Jesus restored to wholeness, one who was an outsider. Jesus had compassion on the man and made him whole again. In our world, there are many who live as outsiders. But like the paralytic, we too can be restored to wholeness in Jesus. Through a relationship with Jesus Christ, we receive access to God's healing power in our lives. It is in Jesus that we are accepted and received as children of God.

Today's Song: "I Was Sinking Deep in Sin," #188

Journal Notes My understaning of this short to Restored is: understanding that I must Build a Relationship and with Jes Then I may recieve Access to God. But keeping in mind that God is the head of my Life, Then ~~accept~~ Jesus! Christ Amen

June 2

Sacred Space

"For we are the temple of the living God."
2 CORINTHIANS 6:16

Today's Prayer

Lord God, I pray that the work that you are doing on me, in me and through me might be manifest in all situations. Let me be a living temple of the living God. Amen.

Today's Reflection

This portion of Paul's second letter to the Corinthians addresses the extreme ends of the conditions of life in which the servants of God find themselves. These extremes are not unique to the community of the faithful; they are a part of life's challenges to all people. However, it is our belief in God that makes us respond differently under such trying circumstances. A young man approached his minister and asked, "Why does God test me with such difficult circumstances and conditions? I thought God knew everything." The minister replied, "God does know everything. And if God is testing you, it's not to find out about you, it might be to show you things that you need to know about yourself."

Today's Song: "In the Morning When I Rise," #165

Journal Notes _____

_____

_____

_____

June 3

Weight Lifting

"The prayer of the righteous is powerful and effective."
JAMES 5:16b

Today's Prayer

Lord, in a broken and ailing world, I pray for those who are sick, shut in, and less fortunate. I pray that you would heal my infirmity and shortcomings and help me so that I might not be judgmental toward others. Amen.

Today's Reflection

In our profit-oriented world, we often become blinded by what has become a common term in our daily jargon: the bottom line. This portion of James's letter begins by addressing the issue of ill-gotten gains through unjust methods and moves to ways of the prophets and the power of their prayers and ends in restoration of those who have wandered from the truth. The letter is intended for a community of believers. It is this community that is called to respond, in love, to those who have wandered away from the truth. Not only is prayer powerful and effective but so is our desire and love to save those within our community. God's desire and love for us can be shared in how we respond to others.

Today's Song: "Sweet Hour of Prayer," #242

Journal Notes _____

_____

_____

_____

June 4

The Big Payback

*"But remember me when it is well with you; please do me
the kindness to make mention of me to Pharaoh,
and so get me out of this house."*

GENESIS 40:14

Today's Prayer

Heavenly Father, thank you for the communities that nurtured and supported us as we grew to adulthood. Help us to replenish our communities with all that we've received. Amen.

Today's Reflection

John-John was his pet name, but he's now called John. John is a stockbroker, and only the twinkle in his eyes gives him away. There are others, too—look at them now. Brian Earl is a lawyer. Little Effie owns a big service station down the street.

Like Joseph, our parents, grandparents, and members of our communities did us a huge favor. They nurtured us. They instilled us with values. They taught us lessons and encouraged us to be the best in our fields. And like Joseph, they don't want much in return. Remember them in ways such as mowing the grass or taking out the garbage. Telephone and visit with them often. The best way to repay them is to remember them in words and deeds.

Today's Song: "Somebody Prayed for Me," #246

Journal Notes _____

_____

_____

_____

Praise God in Everything You Do

"The LORD is my strength and my might, and he has become
my salvation; this is my God, and I will praise him,
my father's God, and I will exalt him."

EXODUS 15:2

Today's Prayer

Hear me, O Lord, as I petition you to talk with me like you talked with my parents, grandparents, and ancestors. I will sing gladly their songs of strength and renewal. Amen.

Today's Reflection

The book of Exodus invites us to hear the freedom song. As the children of Israel marched out of Egypt toward freedom, they knew that their strength came from God. When we look back on our history, we see the strength of the Lord in our parents and ancestors. We know they survived through song, praise, and worship. We saw how God brought them through.

God lives today. When we praise and exalt God above all else, we are renewed and strengthened for the tasks of each day. We, too, stand on the Exodus trail of hope, for God has brought us a mighty long way.

Today's Song: "We've Come This Far by Faith," #197

Journal Notes _____

_____

_____

_____

June 6

Message in a Sunrise

*"Be still, and know that I am God. I am exalted among
the nations, I am exalted in the earth!"*
PSALM 46:10

Today's Prayer

I am so thankful to be called yours, Lord. In the stillness, I feel your presence.
In the quiet I hear your voice. Amen.

Today's Reflection

Busy, busy, busy, yet each day I found myself getting further behind. Not good.
So when the call came to do a workshop in Belize, I jumped at the chance for a
little relaxation. I wasn't even thinking about God.

In Belize, the nights were black and the waves were the only sound I heard. Late
one evening, I walked out on the steps. I didn't know the time. I turned to the sound
of the waves, and then it was there. First, an azure line. Slowly, it turned colors and
for the first time I saw a sunrise like no other. In that instant, I knew the power of
the Lord.

I learned that nothing is ever so important that we can't take a few moments to
enjoy God's power—even in a sunrise.

Today's Song: "Jesus, the Light of the World," #59

Journal Notes _____

_____

_____

_____

I Love to Tell the Stories

"But you shall receive power when the Holy Spirit has come upon you; and you shall be my witnesses in Jerusalem and in all Judea and Samaria and to the end of the earth."

ACTS 1:8

Today's Prayer

As your wonder working power flows through me, Lord, use me to share this message with others. Amen.

Today's Reflection

The great writers of our time have borne witness to God's power. From their pens we have the stories of Harriet Tubman's mission and Martin Luther King Jr.'s dream. We witness through these writings not only the heartache of African-Americans, but its triumphs! And it is through these triumphs that we witness the power of the Holy Spirit that Jesus promised upon his ascension.

When we seek this power, we will be empowered by it. Embrace it. Then we can be the witnesses for the next generations to come. It is through God's authority alone that we are able to stand and bear witness at all.

Today's Song: "I Love to Tell the Story," #228

Journal Notes _____

_____

_____

_____

Some Rules Are Made to Be Broken

*And he said to them, "Is it lawful on the Sabbath to do good or
to do harm, to save life or to kill?" But they were silent.*

MARK 3:4

Today's Prayer

If not now, Lord, when? Don't let me be swayed by unjust rules. Help me help others now. Amen.

Today's Reflection

There were rules growing up. We always said, "Yes, ma'am and sir," to our elders. We didn't interrupt grown folks talking, and we certainly didn't talk back to them. Those were rules that aided in our maturity.

There were other rules. We couldn't sit at certain counters or drink from certain fountains. We rode at the back of the bus. Someone said enough. Our humanity said that we were entitled to the same privileges. It was the message Jesus gave that day to the Pharisees. He told them that each person is entitled to health and wholeness seven days a week, 24 hours a day. Who are we to argue?

Today's Song: "When Israel Was in Egypt's Land," #87

Journal Notes _____

_____

_____

_____

A Parent Who Understands

"For even if I made you sorry with my letter, I do not regret it
(though I did regret it), for I see that that letter
grieved you, though only for a while."

2 CORINTHIANS 7:8

Today's Prayer

Help me to be a good parent, Lord. It is not important that I be perfect, for perfection lies in my faith and trust in you. Just lead me so that I may lead my children in your ways and in your light. Amen.

Today's Reflection

Unlike the rap song written years ago by actor Will Smith, I wanted to be a parent who understood. Instead I found myself at odds—first with the toddlers I bore and then with the adolescents they became, who made me cringe at the way they dressed, talked, and acted.

We are not in a popularity contest as parents. We will say and do things that our children will find exception to. And it will hurt our hearts to have to say and do what it takes to guide our children in the ways of God. Don't fret. It may hurt, but the hurt will be far worse if you don't. In the end, facilitating our children's growth in God pays off in volumes.

Today's Song: "He Leadeth Me," #151

Journal Notes _____

_____

_____

_____

Time to Get It Right

*"But in these last days he has spoken to us by a Son,
whom he appointed the heir of all things, through
whom he created the world."*
HEBREWS 1:2

Today's Prayer

Help me to live this day as if it were my last, but don't let me waste one day of these end times. Amen.

Today's Reflection

Staring at the results of her medical test, the young woman saw the word she had dreaded for weeks. It was cancer. At that moment she felt such despair. What should she do now? Write her will? Tell everyone? Tell no one? Then she remembered.

"I am your child." She spoke these words aloud, and they gave her comfort. Every cell in her body belonged to God, and God would not abandon or forsake her. She was going to live, and live she has. From the creator of the world, God asks us to live this life and not waste a moment of it. No matter the hour, we still have time to get it right.

Today's Song: "Pass Me Not, O Gentle Savior," #150

Journal Notes

_____

_____

_____

_____

June 11

What Is It?

When the Israelites saw it, they said to one another, "What is it?"
For they did not know what it was. Moses said to them,
"It is the bread that the LORD has given you to eat."
EXODUS 16:15

Today's Prayer

God of heaven and earth, you continue to hear the concerns of my mouth and the hushed cries of my heart. Thank you for attending to the details of my life, even those desires that others might overlook or misunderstand. Help me to recognize and appreciate your provision. Amen.

Today's Reflection

It is often easy to recognize God's provision when the divine action plan results in clearly identifiable miracles. Most Christians would agree that unexplained healing and indescribable safe passage from major accidents testify of intervention from the Deity. However, there are times when God interrupts our daily existence in ways that are suspiciously familiar, un-excitedly regular. We can desire the extraordinary and abundance and, instead, God gives daily bread and sufficiency. What we truly need may not look like anything we've ever seen before. Therefore, we need people in our lives to help us to see the miracle of the manna.

Today's Song: "Like a Ship That's Tossed and Driven," #251

Journal Notes _____

_____

_____

_____

June 12

Gaining Wisdom

"Give me now wisdom and knowledge."
CHRONICLES 1:10a

Today's Prayer

Gracious God, thank you for meeting every one of my needs and many of my wants. When I ask of you, you always answer me. When I need you, I find you close. When I don't know what to do, I hear you telling me which way to go and what to do. Please continue to direct, guide, and shape me. Amen.

Today's Reflection

When we were children, we were often amazed and mesmerized by the infinite power and influence of cartoon characters and fairy-tale protagonists. But as we matured, it became easier for us to believe that knowledge was found solely in books, research, and careful intellectual pursuit. That is, there was little room for information from non-scientific sources. However, King Solomon realized that it was more than common sense and scholarly study that ensured success. He rightly discerned that we must first seek God's wisdom on how to serve God's people.

Today's Song: "Seek Ye First," #149

Journal Notes _____

_____

_____

_____

June 13

Internal Truth

*"You desire truth in the inward being,
therefore teach me wisdom in my secret heart."*
PSALM 51:6

Today's Prayer

I confess that my self-destructive behaviors, unkind words, false witness, and irresponsible use of the world's finite resources are not only transgressions against my fellow humans, but also a sin against you. When I make choices that compromise the truth, have mercy on me. Please forgive my frailties and failures. Amen.

Today's Reflection

One expects that the proponents of education and holders of knowledge possess a level of understanding that is founded on truth. Scholars, professors, teachers, pastors, and activists should speak beyond conjecture and speculation. However, it is possible to memorize facts, but not allow truth to impact our behavior and influence our choices. We can know truth and not live it. God invites us to experience truth on the inside, to be impacted and guided by a profound and deep personal encounter with the truth, who is Jesus. Such a relationship encourages a life of faith rooted in truth.

Today's Song: "Give Me a Clean Heart," #216

Journal Notes _____

_____

_____

_____

A Round-Trip Religion

*"Assyria will not save us; we will not ride upon horses;
we will say no more, 'Our God' to the work of our hands.
In You the orphan finds mercy."*

HOSEA 14:3

Today's Prayer

God of glory, you are so faithful in your love toward me. When I chose to stray from you, you wait for me to return. When my sins, transgressions, and iniquities seem to multiply and increase, your love and mercy abide. Thanks for always receiving me back. Amen.

Today's Reflection

Experienced airline travelers often testify to the financial benefits of purchasing a round-trip ticket. Vacations and business trips alike are less stressful when the traveler is assured that they can get back home. Likewise, our hope in God provides us with the comfort of knowing that our ultimate destiny is not limited to a non-refundable, one-way salvation that can be canceled out if we miscalculate or make a mistake. God, in Christ, has confirmed a way back to our divine destiny. Yes. Repentance is our return ticket from our side excursions on the isle of iniquity. God's unfailing mercy allows us to come home.

Today's Song: "He Is Lord," #95

Journal Notes

June 15

More or Less

And he said to them, "Pay attention to what you hear: the measure
you give will be the measure you get, and still more will be given
you. For to those who have, more will be given; and for those who
have nothing, even what they have will be taken away."

MARK 4:24-25

Today's Prayer

Lord, forgive me when I hoard the gifts and talents that you have given me.
Forgive me when I refuse to share my time and resources with others. Help me to see
the ways and opportunities that you give me to give of myself. In Jesus' name. Amen.

Today's Reflection

Many of us find ourselves somewhere between a preoccupation with accumulating more things and a focus on saving our money and time. However, the paradox of our faith is that we gain when we give, and we lose when we save. Hence, the challenge for many Christians is not necessarily fiscal responsibility, but a sound management and accounting of how we demonstrate our faith. We must practice free giving and deep living.

Today's Song: "Let Us Talents and Tongues Employ," #232

Journal Notes

_____

_____

_____

_____

June 16

A Time to Finish

*"And in this matter I am giving my advice: it is appropriate
for you who began last year not only to do something but, but even
to desire—to do something—now finish doing it, so that your eager-
ness may be matched by completing it according to your means."*

2 CORINTHIANS 8:10

Today's Prayer

God, I thank you for allowing me to be a part of your plan for the transformation of my community. I praise you for inviting me to be a laborer in the building of the kingdom. Help me to finish what I have started for you. Amen.

Today's Reflection

It is no secret that most people in our ever-expanding society are often inundated with long to-do lists coupled with multiple assignments. We must do more in increasingly shorter periods of time. Yet, in the midst of our countless objectives, it is not unusual for us not to find enough time to complete all that we began. And not only are our reports or home repairs incomplete, but so are our commitments to God and the church. The challenge is to remember what God said to us, reflect on what we promised to God, and to begin to complete them.

Today's Song: "Lead Me, Guide Me," #70

Journal Notes _____

_____

_____

_____

June 17

Pre-Test Preparation

"Because He Himself was tested by what he suffered,
he is able to help those who are being tested."
HEBREWS 2:18

Today's Prayer

God of glory, when I am overwhelmed by the situations and circumstances that surround me, help me to know that you are there with me. Remind me that while human help can fail, divine assistance is never far off. In Jesus' name. Amen.

Today's Reflection

When students take a test, they seem to score higher when the questions have been clear and the answers found in the previous class materials. Tests can be endured when the teacher has not only prepared the students through lectures, but when she or he has been diligent enough to take the exam first, to make sure that the test is doable. Likewise, Jesus endured suffering so that we might be convinced that we can, and will, be victorious in the midst of our distress.

His work on Calvary reminds us that the trials in our lives are not insurmountable examinations.

Today's Song: "God Sent His Son," #93

Journal Notes _____

_____

_____

_____

God Provides

*The LORD said to Moses, "Go on ahead of the people, and take some
of the Elders of Israel with you, take in your hand the staff with
which you struck the Nile, and go."*
EXODUS 17:5

Today's Prayer

Most gracious and eternal God, the Exodus is the historic frame of reference for
so many of us. Our freedom is rooted in your goodness and care for us. May our
gratitude be as eternal as your love and our memory as sure as your promises. In the
name of Jesus we pray. Amen.

Today's Reflection

A thirsty people questioned their leader, Moses, in the hardship of the wilderness.
In desperation, Moses seeks the help of the Lord. God's grace is always as specific as
our need. God reminds Moses that he already has what he needs: God is still with
them, and the rod that struck the Nile River is still in Moses' hand. When he uses
it to strike the rock water flows readily and sufficiently. May we, in our own lives
witness to the sovereignty of God.

Today's Song: "When Israel Was in Egypt's Land," #87

Journal Notes _____

_____

_____

_____

God's House Is Greater

"The house that I am about to build will be greater,
for our God is greater than other gods."
2 CHRONICLES 2:6

Today's Prayer

O Eternal God, I read the biblical history of a people whose kings are measured by their faith in you. I am amazed at their progress. I am aware that whatever wisdom or knowledge is mine in this day in which we live is needed in building community—your kingdom. This is what Jesus taught his followers. Enable each one of us, by your Holy Spirit to love enough to be your temples of strength and love in this needy world. Amen.

Today's Reflection

2 Chronicles continues the history of David's royal line. His son, King Solomon, is inspired to lead the people in building *the* great temple in Jerusalem. I reflect on his leadership and know that I am required to do more than build physical structures to the glory of God. The message of Christianity is to be used by a Great God to build relationships with people throughout the world; to contribute to a community of love that accepts all people as children of God; and to build economic systems that eradicate poverty and ensure peace.

Today's Song: "God Has Smiled on Me," #190

Journal Notes

_____

_____

_____

_____

June 20

Don't Be a Fool!

"Fools say in their hearts, 'There is no God.' They are corrupt,
they commit abominable acts; there is no one who does good."

PSALM 53:1

Today's Prayer

Have mercy upon us, O Lord. Have mercy upon me! I seek to do good in a world where goodness is measured materialistically. I am blessed and I am grateful. Help me to understand that there are many people seeking to close the gap between those who have more than they need and those who have nothing. Let me never denounce your presence either in my heart or that of others. I know that I cannot make it, we cannot make it without you. Forgive us our godlessness and restore us to your powerful presence. Amen.

Today's Reflection

The grace note in this psalm is the expectation of God. God constantly seeks those who struggle to be faithful. "God looks down from heaven on humankind to see if there are any who are wise, who seek after God." God always expects someone to choose God's side. This is the message of the cross and the pentecostal power of the Holy Spirit. No matter how dire circumstances may be, God awaits the opening of the doors of our hearts so that God may dwell within us. I must want to be used by God to make a difference. I want you to use me, O Lord!

Today's Song: "All to Jesus I Surrender," #235

Journal Notes _____

_____

_____

_____

True Repentance

*"Rend your hearts and not your clothing. Return to the LORD,
Your God, for God is gracious and merciful, slow to anger, and
abounding in steadfast love, and relents from punishing."*

JOEL 2:13

Today's Prayer

Gracious, loving God, where would I be without your love? How could I survive without your mercy? I place myself within your open arms. Equip me with the power of your Spirit so that I may be your true servant. Let your will be done in and through my life. In the name of Jesus, the Christ, I pray. Amen.

Today's Reflection

The preaching of Peter at Pentecost is so rightly set in the prophecy of Joel. The time of which the prophet speaks is being experienced. God's Spirit is being poured out on all flesh, "and your sons and your daughters shall prophesy, and young men shall see visions and old men dream dreams." The inexplicable has been explained centuries before. God is a creative God, always re-creating, constantly restoring. Praise God! Praise is the only proper response. God remains faithful.

Today's Song: "Have Thine Own Way, Lord," #152

Journal Notes _____

_____

_____

_____

June 22

Getting Clean

"When he saw Jesus from a distance he ran and
bowed down before him and he shouted at the top of his voice,
what have you to do with me Jesus, Son of the Most High God?
I adjure you by God, do not torment me."

MARK 5:6-7

Today's Prayer

O Gracious Master, help me to share faith in you. I know what you have done for me, and I stand amazed in your presence. Give your church proclamation power in these needy days. In your name we pray. Amen.

Today's Reflection

The healing story of the man with an unclean spirit is marked with authenticity by the one who knows who Jesus is. He knows that Jesus can do anything because of who he is. He does not realize that the love of Jesus will heal him, relieve him, give him new life. No wonder he wanted to join those who followed Jesus, but Jesus refused to take him and said to him, "Go home to your friends and tell them how much the Lord has done for you, and what mercy the Lord Lord has shown you . . . he went away, proclaiming the healing of the Lord, and everyone was amazed!"

Today's Song: "There Is a Balm in Gilead," #185

Journal Notes _____

_____

_____

_____

Investing by Giving

*"You will be enriched in every way for your great generosity
which will produce thanksgiving to God through us."*
2 CORINTHIANS 9:11

Today's Prayer

Gracious God, your word holds the answers to our attitudes in this market conscious society. Wealth is not the answer for our happiness. No amount of security can deny the violence of our society. Open our hearts and our lives so that our knowledge may effect the abundant life for all. In the name of Jesus, I pray. Amen.

Today's Reflection

Paul writes to the Christian community at Corinth, encouraging them to contribute to the poorer Christian community in Jerusalem. Those who have enough of everything are urged to freely share, expressing their own gratitude to God who has so blessed them. Paul's teachings and writings help us to understand that belief in Jesus Christ is best expressed in sharing with others. In God's bounty there is enough on God's earth for all. Inequities are caused by our assumption of power! Poverty is a problem we can solve in God's world.

As medical science is advanced, treatment is needed for illnesses by everyone. Making our technological and scientific advantage available to all, committing them to peaceful purposes demands self-limitation on profit motives. Education is not personal choice—it is public responsibility.

Today's Song: "Here I Am, Lord," #230

Journal Notes

Listening for Jesus

Therefore as the Holy Spirit says,
"Today if you hear his voice, do not harden your hearts as in
the rebellion, as on the day of testing in the wilderness."
HEBREWS 3:7-8

Today's Prayer

Dear Savior, you lived in this world as a human being, subject to all the inequities of life. You chose to do the will of God, faithful unto death. Your presence with us, through the power of the Holy Spirit, still directs and guides, enables and strengthens. Forgive our weakness. Give us the will to do your will, until the day shall come when we shall see you face to face and tell the story of your amazing grace. Amen.

Today's Reflection

The life, death, and resurrection of Jesus Christ forces a shift in the paradigm of what life is all about. For believers in him, those first century Christians, it was undergoing much persecution. Many of these Jewish Christians were tempted to return to Judaism. The author of Hebrews urges them in such a way that they will hold fast to their confessed belief in Jesus Christ. For them he is both sacrificial lamb and priest. The stories of the faithful ones may comfort them, but the substance of faith itself must grow weary for them as they wait for the return of Jesus. The building up of the spirits of this community of faith rests solely on their own shoulders. They, like us, became partners with Jesus Christ. The Holy Spirit bears witness that the faithful journey is not in vain. Can you hear Jesus calling you?

Today's Song: "Lift Every Voice and Sing," #296

Journal Notes _____

_____

_____

_____

You Cannot Do It Alone

"You will surely wear yourself out, both you and these people with you. For the task is too heavy for you; you cannot do it alone."

EXODUS 18:18

Today's Prayer

Great God of liberation, you have given us much ministry to do. Grant us wisdom to work together, to ask for help, to create community. In Jesus' name. Amen.

Today's Reflection

Fresh out of seminary, I worked with two other pastors sharing ministry in New Jersey. Patti and John were wise counselors and wonderful teachers. The most important lesson I learned from them and the churches we served was the importance of teamwork.

We took turns preaching; we divided other tasks based on our gifts. Moses' first elders came to be because a wise counselor, his father-in-law, Jethro, recognized that Moses was on the road to burnout. To lead God's people on his own would wear him out, and the people, too. There is so much to do in God's kingdom. We're called to do our part. We cannot do it alone. Teams are God's gift to keep us fresh for the journey.

Today's Song: "Let Us Talents and Tongues Employ," #232

Journal Notes _____

_____

_____

_____

The Church's One Foundation

*"He set up the pillars in front of the temple, one on the right,
the other on the left; the one on the right he called Jachin,
and the one on the left, Boaz."*
2 CHRONICLES 3:17

Today's Prayer

Great God, help us to build our foundation on your word, your strength, your peace. Through Jesus Christ. Amen.

Today's Reflection

At the annual New Church Development conferences I used to attend, seminars and conversations sometimes focused on the building needed for the congregation. Land had to be purchased, specifications drawn up and funding secured. It was exciting to come the next year and hear about groundbreakings, fresh new sanctuaries where God's praises were sung, and multiple-use spaces for ministry to the whole person.

Solomon must have been excited building the temple of the Lord. The account of its construction in 2 Chronicles is rich with detail about its foundation and specifications: length and height; wood and gold adornments; cherubim and curtains—all described so that we can almost see it for ourselves. Solomon put two pillars in front of the temple; their names say perhaps more about its foundation and specifications than anything else. Jachin means "God establishes." Boaz means "In God is strength." May God establish our foundation; In God may we find strength.

Today's Song: "A Mighty Fortress Is Our God," #133

Journal Notes

Blessings Are Assured

"But surely God is my helper, the Lord is the upholder of my life."
PSALM 54:4

Today's Prayer

Holy, holy, most holy God, you are our help, our refuge and our strength. Continue to hear and answer us, we pray. In your time. Amen.

Today's Reflection

Early childhood is such an important time in our personal and spiritual development. When we cry out of hunger or distress, the response of those who care for us shapes our outlook. When they come, we learn to trust them and our environment. With this assurance, seeds of faith are planted. We come to believe our parents are good, we are good and the world we know is a safer place. Our faith in the goodness of God grows in this rich soil.

As we grow we learn the world is not so safe. We suffer, others suffer. We make mistakes and hurt others, and they hurt us. We cry out to God, hungering for peace and relief from our distress.

God responds. God comes, like no other. In God's way and in God's time. Surely, God is our helper. God upholds our lives and calms our fears. God feeds us with the bread of life. God protects us and keeps us—rest assured.

Today's Song: "Blessed Assurance," #118

Journal Notes _____

_____

_____

_____

June 28

Like Shelter in a Storm

*"The LORD roars from Zion, and utters his voice from Jerusalem,
and the heavens shake. But the LORD is a refuge for his people,
a stronghold for the people of Israel."*

JOEL 3:16

Today's Prayer

Keep us safe, O Lord, our strength. Hide us in the cleft of the rock; give us shelter from the storms of life. In Jesus' name. Amen.

Today's Reflection

Summer showers invite us to get wet. We may shed umbrellas and turn our faces up to the rain. We feel refreshed and rejuvenated. Summer storms are different. The wind whips and roars like an angry lion. Lightening flashes. The earth and the heavens shake. Then the sky splits open and water pours forth. Summer storms make us run for shelter.

Same rain, different experience. God is like that. God is a formidable enemy to the foes of God's people. Desolation and famine are arrows in God's quiver, used to defeat wickedness. On the other hand, God's people are nourished with sweet wine and flowing milk.

God is like a summer storm to the wicked; God is refuge and refreshment for his people. Let us turn our faces toward God.

Today's Song: "We Are Often Tossed and Driven," #206.

Journal Notes _____

_____

_____

_____

Time Out

"And they went away in the boat to a deserted place by themselves."
MARK 6:32

Today's Prayer

Eternal God, our peace, meet us in a quiet place today. There, may we find in you solace, and in ourselves a quiet joy. In Jesus' name. Amen.

Today's Reflection

Most of us are so busy these days: we live by our calendars or palm pilots. Without them, we are lost sheep—off track and disorganized. Juggling priorities is a challenge, and often times we collapse at the end of the day, dissatisfied that we have not accomplished all of our objectives.

How do we balance the demands of work and family? When do we find time to exercise and play? How do we act as good stewards of God's creation, our own time and our talents?

These are questions that Christians answer each day. If we are clever, we search the scriptures for clues. If we are faithful, we may hear Jesus' voice giving clear guidance. Surely we will hear Jesus telling us to go in to the world together, with very little, to teach, heal and forgive. We will also hear Jesus inviting us, compelling us to take a time out. "Come away to a deserted place all by yourselves and rest a while," he says in verse 31. The disciples respond and do as Jesus commands.

Jesus, a good rabbi, understood the value of Sabbath time. If it was good enough for him, perhaps we might find it of some value.

Today's Song: "Joys Are Flowing like a River," #110

Journal Notes _____

_____

_____

_____

June 30

Bragging Rights

"Let the one who boasts boast in the Lord."
2 CORINTHIANS 10:17

Today's Prayer

Humbly we approach your throne of grace, Holy God, knowing that we stand only on you. In you, we have peace; in you we have life. Thank you for this free gift. Amen.

Today's Reflection

My brothers were all so cute when they were children. That certainly was something to brag about. Gifted, strong, charismatic, brilliant. Passionate, courageous, brave, beautiful. Patient, kind, joyful, prayerful. God has certainly bestowed gifts and blessings on us all.

We can all find something to be proud of, to celebrate. When we cannot see it for ourselves, others may see it is us. But we give God the glory. For it is only in the Lord that we boast.

Today's Song: "My Hope Is Built on Nothing Less," #192

Journal Notes _____

_____

_____

_____

Come Boldly

*"Let us therefore approach the throne of Grace with boldness,
so that we may receive mercy and find grace to help in time of need."*
HEBREWS 4:16

Today's Prayer

Lord, we want to come boldly to the throne of grace. There at your feet may we find healing and forgiveness, through Jesus Christ. Amen.

Today's Reflection

I enjoy a nice party, I must confess. Occasionally my life is so full that I will need some encouragement to get there. I know that I am invited, but I need some coaching to get me moving.

"Come on, everyone will be there. I am going," a friend might say. We have all been invited to sit at the table with our Lord, to be in communion with the saints, to live lives free of sin. God has invited us. And sometimes we are reluctant to get moving.

There is one who urges us to come. He is the one called Jesus. He is our high priest, one who understands our weaknesses.

How? Well, Jesus was fully human. Fully. He understands our trials. He understands our fears and failures. Jesus is saying, "Come, boldly to that which lies before you!" Come boldly to the throne of grace. There is peace, there is joy, there is rest.

Today's Song: "Come, Thou Fount of Every Blessing," #108

Journal Notes

_____

_____

_____

_____

Climbing up the Mountain

*"When the LORD descended upon Mount Sinai, to the top
of the mountain. The LORD summoned Moses to the
top of the mountain, and Moses went up."*
EXODUS 19:20

Today's Prayer

God of truth and inspiration, I believe in your power to speak to me and to show me signs of your presence in my life. I hear your voice in the sounds of nature. I see your face among the people who call out to you for strength and protection. I feel your Spirit in the worship and praise that honors your name. continue to reach out to me, I pray, so that I may know your will for me in all things. Amen.

Today's Reflection

Today I, too, will climb the mountain. I will go up like Moses did and have a little talk with God. I will go up like Jesus did and have a meeting with my ancestors. I will go up like Dr. Martin Luther King Jr. did and look over and see the promised land. I will go up like Dr. Maya Angelou did and learn why the caged bird sings. Even if I have to climb up the rough side of the mountain, I m going up. Where is my mountain today, O God, the place where I must go to hear your voice and see your face? I m ready to go up.

Today's Song: "Every Time I Feel the Spirit," #241

Journal Notes _____

_____

_____

_____

The Glory of God

"The glory of the LORD filled the house of God."
2 CHRONICLES 5:14

Today's Prayer

God of wonder, you are the creator of all things, the source of all life. Your majesty is known throughout heaven and earth. Your greatness is beyond measure, yet you have reached out to me in love. I thank you for coming into my life and calling me your own. Fill me today with the blessing of your presence. Come into my heart, I pray. Amen.

Today's Reflection

How wonderful it is to know that God regards me as a temple where God's Spirit can abide. I am just a human being, yet God calls me the crown of creation. I have faults and I have fears, but God says I am a royal priest because I am a part of the body of Jesus Christ. Even now, God is ready to enter into the deep places of my being and fill my darkness with sacred light. My faith has prepared me for this gift. Today let the glory of. the Lord fill this house!

Today's Song: "The Lord Is in His Holy Temple," #143

Journal Notes _____

_____

_____

_____

True Friendship

*"My companion laid hands on a friend and
violated a covenant with me."*

PSALM 55:20

Today's Prayer

O God, in whom I trust, your own Son, Jesus, knew so well what I feel sometimes. It is painful for me to admit that—friends have disappointed me, deserted me, even betrayed me. I ask today that you allow me to remember and trust again the promise that even though friends may forsake me, you will never abandon me nor leave me alone.

Strengthen me to follow Christ today. In the name of Jesus, I release my anger and disappointment to you, and I receive your power to forgive completely. Amen.

Today's Reflection

Why are some people in my life so dishonest, cruel, and indifferent? Why do they say one thing to my face and something else behind my back? Why do they disrespect me? Why do I disrespect them? I hate to admit that I, too, have sometimes failed to be the best friend I could be. What goes around really does come around. The power of God in Jesus Christ can break this cycle. I trust you, God, to bring cleansing and healing for my spirit so that true friendship can begin with me.

Today's Song: "Would You Be Free," #76

Journal Notes _____

_____

_____

_____

The Gift of Courage

"Do not preach"—thus they preached — "one should not preach of such things; disgrace will not overtake us."

MICAH 2:6

Today's Prayer

God of power and might, I call on you today to surround me with your divine protection, for I see trouble all around. So much bad news fills the air, and so many people try to escape the harsh realities of suffering and injustice. Strengthen me, and strengthen the leaders of our community so that we will respond to these urgent needs. Give us all courage to speak the truth according to your will. We are trusting that your power will support our efforts to heal and restore troubled lives. Amen.

Today's Reflection

I have a gift that was first given by God to my ancestors. This is the gift of courage. They used this gift as they faced the tragic horrors of slavery and racism. They treasured this gift and offered it as an inheritance to their children. I am their child, and the same courage lies deep inside me. Today, I will open this gift and use it to lift up someone else. My thoughts, words, and deeds will show that God has awakened new courage in me. Today, I will speak God's truth and not be afraid.

Today's Song: "You Are the Seed," #226

Journal Notes _____

_____

_____

_____

July 6

The Beauty Inside

*"There is nothing outside a person that by going in can defile,
but the things that come out are what defile."*
MARK 7:15

Today's Prayer

Holy and ancient God, only your Spirit can cleanse my heart. Be at work in my life so that I may learn from you the way of holiness and peace. Guard my words, guide my thoughts, and direct my deeds, I pray. Make me more and more like you, so that I can serve you this day. Amen.

Today's Reflection

Some days you may feel that the world around you is full of thoughtless, selfish, and dangerous people who live by values that are completely different from your own. You may even feel stuck in such a place, wanting to live elsewhere but finding no way out. God reaches out to you today and reminds you that no matter how ugly things may get, God will always see and honor the beauty of your spirit. The power of faith working on the inside is much greater than any disturbing presence working on the outside. Wherever you find yourself today, join God in recognizing the divine beauty of who you really are.

Today's Song: "God Is So Good," #275

Journal Notes

_____

_____

_____

_____

Return to the Future

"If I must boast, let me boast of the things that show my weakness."
2 CORINTHIANS 11:30

Today's Prayer

O God, my help and my strength, I rejoice today in the power of the love you continue to show me. You have never abandoned me. You have never turned away from me. When I stumble and fall, you pick me up. When I act foolishly and with evil intention, you correct me and return me to the path of my true destiny. I praise you for these things. Hallelujah. Amen.

Today's Reflection

I sometimes wonder what would happen if I could go back in time and undo all the wrong I have ever done. What if I could take back all the unkind words? What if I could return to past relationships and make better choices than the ones I chose when I just didn't know any better? What if I could do it all over again? These thoughts help me to remember how much I have needed God in my life. I cannot go back into the past, but I can embrace my future and trust God to show me a better way to live.

Today's Song: "Lead Me, Guide Me," #70

Journal Notes _____

_____

_____

_____

July 8

Each One, Teach One

"For though by this time you ought to be teachers, you need someone to teach you again the basic elements of the oracles of God. You need milk, not solid food."

HEBREWS 5:12

Today's Prayer

Gracious God, I thank you today for your loving patience with me. You know me completely, for you have made me and called me your own. Encourage me today to keep reaching for the truth and wisdom that you have set before me.

Awaken in me a new hunger and thirst for your presence. Teach me your way so that I may teach others. Amen.

Today's Reflection

Today I see the urgency of the situation. God needs people who are ready to be messengers of the truth. No one is too young or too old, too rich or too poor. God needs people who can absorb the lessons of life and the teachings of God's word and become leaders within the community of faith.

God has already invested greatly in me, preparing me for greater service. Today, I take the next step toward this goal, because I know that God wants me to be a messenger of the truth.

Today's Song: "We've Come This Far by Faith," #197

Journal Notes _____

_____

_____

_____

Getting Help

"Wherever I cause my name to be honored,
I will come to you and bless you."

EXODUS 20:24b, NIV

Today's Prayer

Heavenly Father, hallowed be thy holy name. As you are holy, I ask that you come enter and abide in my life—that I may stand worthy to be called your child. Amen.

Today's Reflection

Sometimes we need someone else to help us interpret the things we cannot comprehend at first reading. I remember struggling to understand the writings of one of my professors in college. I was close to withdrawing from the class when I attended a lecture given by another professor on campus. I understood all the comments he made and approached him. He took time from his schedule to sit with me and translated the notes and material in language and terminology that I could easily understand.

Sometimes it's like that with God's word. Some stories and events recorded in the Bible can be hard to understand at first. When that happens we need to seek out someone who can unravel the love and power of the gospel. The Ten Commandments are sometimes seen as the "thou shall not" rules. When interpreted through the gospel we can come to know them as ten words of God's grace—good news. God spoke all of these words—and said I will honor those who honor me. Do you want to be blessed by God? Keep God's word and God will honor you.

Today's Song: "I Want Jesus to Walk with Me," #66

Journal Notes _____

_____

_____

_____

A Common Burden

"For there is no one who does not sin."
2 CHRONICLES:6:36, NIV

Today's Prayer

My Lord and my God, make your ears to be attentive to the prayers that I offer up to you in this place, this tabernacle to which you have said you would dwell within, my heart. Amen.

Today's Reflection

Those of us who follow the word of God have heard it said that Solomon was the wisest man who ever lived. In all Solomon's wisdom he was wise enough to know that there was no one who did not sin. Let the wisdom of Solomon's guide you through this day. Reflect on those words and pray for forgiveness and direction.

Today's Song: "O Lord, Open My Eyes," #134

Journal Notes _____

_____

_____

_____

July 11

Knowing Who to Trust

"When I am afraid I will trust in you."
PSALM 56:3, NIV

Today's Prayer

Dear God, when I am afraid, I will trust in you. I will not be afraid. For I know that you are with me, and that nothing is more powerful than you. Amen.

Today's Reflection

David's plight as he fled for his life from the wrath and vengeance of King Saul reminds me of a saying I once read on a poster hanging on the walls of an office-mate's cubical regarding paranoia: Yes, sometimes people are out to do you harm. When you are afraid—remember to put your trust in God. And after God provides remember to be thankful for God's deliverance . . . that God may keep your feet from stumbling, that you may walk before God in the light of life.

Today's Song: "We Are Marching in the Light of God," #63

Journal Notes _____

_____

_____

_____

July 12

Even on Bad Days

"Is not the LORD among us?"
MICAH 3:11b, NIV

Today's Prayer

God, help me to hear your word today. Help me, God, to live out your will in my life this day better than I have ever lived it before. Help me God to do my very best. Amen.

Today's Reflection

It has been said that the word of God is like a two-edged sword because it cuts two ways. The word of God can afflict and it can heal, it can convict and it can exonerate. Today I hope you have come to see how God wants us to take stock of our own lives. God wants us to search our own hearts, open our eyes to our own sins and shortcomings. God invites us to first take the log out of our eyes that we may better see how to serve and live for God showing the world the way of righteousness.

Today's Song: "Have Thine Own Way, Lord," #152

Journal Notes _____

_____

_____

_____

July 13

What Will It Take?

Jesus said to the disciples, "Do you still not understand?"
MARK 8:21, NIV

Today's Prayer

God, help me to understand your will in my life and what it is that you require of me this and every day of my life. Amen.

Today's Reflection

Okay, so you have followed the devotions. You have taken inventory of your life, made a list of your good and not so good points. Now the tasks that must be completed before you can claim perfection in your life seem greater than you can accomplish. Guess what? You are right. You will never be able to do it on your own.

Do you still not understand? It's not you—not us—but the Christ that lives within us that makes it possible.

Today's Song: "Time Is Filled with Swift Transition," #231

Journal Notes _____

_____

_____

_____

A Tale I Must Tell

"I must go on boasting."
2 CORINTHIANS 12:1, NIV

Today's Prayer

Dear God of all grace and all mercy, we thank you for your grace that is all sufficient and for your power that perfects our weakness. To you we will forever give the praise, the honor and the glory, for your greatness and your goodness, your mercy and your overwhelming love continue to keep us in awe. Amen.

Today's Reflection

Have you been thinking all along that we have been defeated? The task of being godly and Christ-like, of being a faithful disciple is impossible. Correct, if it were not for these words: "My grace is sufficient for you, for my power is made perfect in weakness" (verse 12:9a).

Take delight in the testimony of the apostle Paul, who knew what it was live in God's love regardless of the situation. "Therefore I will boast all the more gladly about my weaknesses, so that Christ's power may rest on me. That is why, for Christ's sake, I delight in weaknesses, in insults, in hardships, in persecutions, in difficulties. "For when I am weak, then I am strong" (verses 12:9b-10).

So, knowing this truth, we can live in the midst of all that we encounter and still have joy. Now boast in that today.

Today's Song: "Joys Are Flowing like a River," #110

Journal Notes _____

_____

_____

_____

Finding Confidence

*"And we are his house, if we hold on to our courage
and the hope of which we boast."*
HEBREWS 3:6b, NIV

Today's Prayer

Beautiful Savior, God of creation, Son of God, Mary's child, and my redeemer! Truly I love thee; truly I will serve thee for you are the light of my soul, my joy, and my crown. Teach me ever to adore thee. Let me live my life so the world may see and know of your glory. Let me live my life so that others needing your joy, your affirming words of commendations and affirmations, your unwavering approval and love may find their way to you and in finding you will find all that they need. Amen.

Today's Reflection

It means so much to me to hear someone say they have confidence in me. To hear it from the word of God means so much more. How about you? How does it make you feel to hear, and to know that God has confidence in you? And then in light of all your past mistakes and failures to hear someone say, "I am confident of better things in your case!"

Wow! What an evaluation, what affirmations. God has placed God's confidence in you. God has confidence in your abilities, in your faith, in your love for God. How does that make you feel? You know, no matter who doesn't believe in me, I know God does. That's what matters the most.

Today's Song: "He Understands; He'll Say, 'Well Done,'" #172

Journal Notes _____

_____

_____

_____

July 16

Rest for the Stressed

"Six days you shall do your work,
but on the seventh day you shall rest."
EXODUS 23:12a

Today's Prayer

Creator God, you have shown us the way to a balanced life—a life of work, play and rest. Yet we have made our own path of activity and busy-ness. Slow us down so that we can rest and appreciate the mystery and majesty of your creation. Place within us a deep appreciation for all that you provide. Give us the wisdom to respect and keep the Sabbath. Amen.

Today's Reflection

We spend a lot of time being busy. We rush from one task to another, often without giving our fullest attention to any one of them. Inventions designed to simplify our lives seem to do the opposite. We are working harder and longer, and we are suffering because of it. African-Americans suffer from high blood pressure, diabetes, heart disease, and cancer at rates higher than the national average. All of these illnesses are worsened by the stress we carry. We invest in all kinds of strategies to ease stress. Simple changes in diet and adding exercise can make a difference.

God instituted a safeguard against stress at the very beginning of creation. On the seventh day, God rested—and so should we! Do you remember the time when stores and businesses were closed on Sundays? Wouldn't it be nice if we could reclaim the Sabbath as a day of rest? Our very lives may depend on it.

Today's Song: "Oh, I Woke Up This Morning," #166

Journal Notes

_____

_____

_____

_____

Attitude of Gratitude

When all the people of Israel saw the fire come down and the glory of the
LORD on the temple, they bowed down on the pavement with their faces to
the ground, and worshiped and gave thanks to the LORD, saying,
"For [God] is good, for [God's] steadfast love endures forever."
2 CHRONICLES 7:3

Today's Prayer

Eternal God, you just keep on blessing me. Thank you for loving me and keeping me in your circle of care. Strengthen me for the work you have for me to do. Although I forget to say it, please know that I am so very grateful for your grace, mercy, power, love, and presence. All I have, I owe to you. Hallelujah and amen!

Today's Reflection

A common refrain in African-American churches is "God is good—all the time!" In trying times and peaceful ones, God is good. Solomon lived an attitude of gratitude. When the temple had been completed, he dedicated it to God and offered prayers of thanksgiving. Solomon knew that the accomplishment was not his but the gracious work of God. And Solomon was grateful.

We often take our blessings for granted. We think we should get what we work for and that we deserve life's advantages. Our toil is futile unless we dedicate our work and ourselves to God. All good things come from God. God simply asks that we appreciate and share our blessings. Whether big or small, we need to give thanks to God for all our blessings. Do you have an attitude of gratitude?

Today's Song: "Count Your Blessings," #173

Journal Notes

_____

_____

_____

_____

The Power of a Simple Prayer

*"Be merciful to me, O God, be merciful to me, for in you my soul
takes refuge; in the shadow of your wings I will take refuge,
until the destroying storms pass by."*

PSALM 57:1

Today's Prayer

Merciful God, I am grateful for your lovingkindness that finds me even when I am
in the depths of despair and pain. You search me out. You touch with your grace
those broken places I keep hidden from the world. Your love is too wonderful for me
to understand. I can only receive it and be thankful. Amen.

Today's Reflection

In January 1978, my maternal grandmother and my younger brother both died
within 24 hours of each other. It was the first time that my faith had ever been tested. I was so overwhelmed by grief and sorrow that I could not speak an intelligent
prayer. I repeated over and over the simple words, "Lord, have mercy." I don't
remember how long I uttered these words; but at some point I was flooded with a
peace and calmness I did not know was possible. My weeping eased, my pulse
slowed, my soul rested in the presence of my Savior. My faith was strengthened
because I felt the presence of God with me in my despair.

In our darkest moments, God hears our cries and pleas for help. God sends
angels of mercy and peace to soothe our hearts and quiet our minds. It is good to
express our deepest emotions. God will be there. On this, we can depend.

Today's Song: "His Eye Is on the Sparrow," #252

Journal Notes _____

_____

_____

_____

July 19

Plenty Good Room

"For all the peoples walk, each in the name of its god, but we will walk in the name of the LORD our God forever and ever."
MICAH 4:5

Today's Prayer

O Wise God, you have a delightful sense of humor and beauty. You have created great diversity throughout creation. Help us to see and to value the differences that make us unique. Help us to see and to value the common bond we share which makes us one. In the name of the Christ, amen.

Today's Reflection

God respects diversity and welcomes all into the divine household. God provides a space for all and embraces all. In God's realm, we are safe, secure, and satisfied. There is no superior or inferior because God does not show partiality. We are each God's child and sisters and brothers to each other. Despite outward appearances, we are created in the image and likeness of God and God makes no mistakes!

Because God has gifted and blessed us, we are to walk in the name of our God. The Bible does not deny the existence of other gods. But we know whom we serve and adore. We know our God through the life, ministry and resurrection of Jesus Christ and the ongoing presence of the Holy Spirit. It is a privilege and a blessing to claim the One who has claimed us from the beginning of time.

Today's Song: "Our God Reigns," #99

Journal Notes _____

_____

_____

_____

Nothing Is Impossible

*Jesus said to him, "If you are able!—All things can be done
for the one who believes." Immediately the father of the
child cried out, "I believe; help my unbelief!"*

MARK 9:23-24

Today's Prayer

Help me, O Sovereign One, to place my trust in you—help my unbelief! I pray with great expectations in you and I live in this hope. Through Jesus Christ, amen.

Today's Reflection

The father in this text is a mirror of us. We live in an unbelieving society, and we are not quite sure whether anything is possible. We are cynical when others declare they believe that nothing is too hard for God. Instead, we resist believing this, and we do not trust in God's power to answer the prayers we voice. Most of the time, we pray for God to undo something already in motion or we pray with a particular outcome in mind.

To the parent in this text, Jesus replies that all things can be done—for those who believe. What if we could give ourselves over completely and deeply to the belief that the One who created the heavens and the earth and all that there is can do all things? Jesus challenges us to place all hope and trust in God. We can trust God to do the impossible.

Today's Song: "Lead Me, Guide Me," #70

Journal Notes _____

_____

_____

_____

Partnership in Ministry

"I am confident of this, that the one who began a good work among you will bring it to completion by the day of Jesus Christ."

PHILIPPIANS 1:6

Today's Prayer

Ever-present God, I have heard your voice calling me to greater and deeper service and faithfulness. Instill your Holy Spirit in me that I might be energized, motivated, and sustained for this work. I present my whole self and all of my gifts to the building of your realm, which has no end. In the blessed name of our Redeemer, I pray. Amen.

Today's Reflection

God created a new thing when God raised Jesus from the tomb. The church was born and it lived with the expectation that Jesus would return to claim his own. One preacher has made it plain: "The Bible tells us that Jesus is coming back for his church, the church without a spot or wrinkle. Well, we have a lot of washing and pressing to do to get ready!"

Some of us live as though we do not believe that Jesus will come back. We do not know when or how Jesus will return to claim us, but we need to be ready. Whatever ministry or mission God has laid on your heart, now is the time to be about that business. Our work may not be as dangerous or as dramatic or as far-reaching as was the apostle Paul's. Yet any work God has for us is just as important. God has called each of us to render some service for the sake of creation.

Today's Song: "Have Thine Own Way, Lord," #152

Journal Notes _____

_____

_____

July 22

The Only One

*"For it was fitting that we should have such a high priest,
holy, blameless, undefiled, separated from sinners,
and exalted above the heavens."*

HEBREWS 7:26

Today's Prayer

Holy and forgiving God, you alone can pardon our sins and cast them into the sea of forgetfulness. Help me to repent—to turn from my sinful ways to you. Thank you for grace and mercy that surround me and keep me alert. I love you, O God! Thank you for loving me enough to sacrifice your own beloved Son, so that I might have eternal life. In the name of the Blessed Redeemer, Jesus. Amen.

Today's Reflection

In days of old, people believed they needed priests to speak for them before God. Albeit, the priests were human and needed to confess and account for their own sins as well as for the sins of the people. But Jesus changed that relationship. Because of his selfless sacrifice, Jesus has shown once and for all that all we need is him to speak to God.

It has been said, "There are only two kinds of people: sinners and sinners saved by grace!" Through the work of Jesus and the ongoing power of the Holy Spirit, we have the power to be what God intends. God extends grace and mercy even to sinners like us.

Today's Song: "Come to Jesus," #156

Journal Notes _____

_____

_____

_____

July 23

Obeying God

Then he took the Book of the Covenant and read it to
the people. They responded, "We will do everything
the LORD has said; we will obey."
EXODUS 24:7, NIV

Today's Prayer

God of our past, who knows are sorrows, we know that we have come this far because of you. Had you not been on our side and walking with us, we would have perished—if not physically, then emotionally—a long time ago. Help us to be as faithful to you as you have been to us. Help us to say, "We will obey," and then do it. In Jesus' name, amen.

Today's Reflection

Half of our woes and worries are not with us because God hasn't answered our prayers—they are with us because we have not answered or obeyed God's commands. Too often, when God gives us something to do, it's not what we had in mind, so we either delay being obedient or ignore the directive altogether. Then, when the floor falls from beneath us, we cry and weep. Pray for the strength and the spiritual integrity to do what God is telling you to do right now!

Today's Song: "We Praise Thee, O God," #100

Journal Notes _____

_____

_____

_____

Following God

*"They did not deviate from the king's commands to the priests
or to the Levites in any matter, including that of the treasuries."*
2 CHRONICLES 8:15, NIV

Today's Prayer

Most loving God, guide my feet, my hands, my mouth, my spirit, and my thoughts today. I need your direction, your words, and your guidance. Take this situation, Jesus. It is yours, not mine. I give it to you. Amen.

Today's Reflection

Too often in church there are too many chiefs. And too many times, there is one small group of people who "decide" what's best for the church and cause havoc by urging disobedience and discord. Churches fall apart when that happens—all because some people wanted to have control.

Guess what? God is the one in control, and God is perfectly able to weed out the "bad seeds" in leadership, if we would but let him. When we "decide" and plan and plot to disobey our church leaders, we are out of covenant with God. Let God be God. If the leadership is not right, take that concern to God and not to other members.

Today's Song: "Come by Here," #43

Journal Notes _____

Criminal Justice

"Do you rulers indeed speak justly? Do you judge uprightly among men? No, in your heart you devise injustice and your hands mete out violence on the earth."

PSALM 58:1-2, NIV

Today's Prayer

Loving God, you have ordained me to keep watch over part of your flock. Purify my mind, my heart, my spirit, and my intentions. I need to be cleansed by you so that I am not filled with human desire and ambition. This place of leadership is an honor that you can take away. Lord, help me to be worthy of this call. Amen.

Today's Reflection

One of the most profound statements I've ever heard is that our children are not ours—that they belong to God and that we as parents are merely caretakers. I rebelled in spirit as I thought about changing diapers, trips to the doctor, and future costs to come. And yet, it was true. Children are God's. The reality set in that as parents we must answer to God for not taking good care of them.

So must leaders answer to God for not taking good care of the flock. Manipulating people, taking advantage of them, and using them are all despicable actions in the sight of God. The flock belongs to God. Caretakers, in the form of leaders, must never forget that.

Today's Song: "Lord, I Want to Be a Christian," #234

Journal Notes

_____

_____

_____

_____

Surrounded by Enemies

*"Your hand will be lifted up in triumph over your enemies
and all your foes will be destroyed."*
MICAH 5:9, NIV

Today's Prayer

Loving God, today I feel the pull of being surrounded by enemies. I come to give my complaints and fears to you, to thank you for receiving me, and then to ask you to be a fence around me. I know that no enemy is stronger than you, but sometimes I doubt that you hear me or that you are as near as I need you to be. So today, take my spirit and calm it, and let me see your glory in the midst of the storm. Amen.

Today's Reflection

Everyone says to trust in the Lord, yet when enemies seem to come at you from every direction, it's hard to lean on arms or depend on arms you cannot see or feel. And yet, the only way to get through enemy territory in one piece is to depend on those very arms. It is maddening. Sometimes the onslaught is relentless and beats us down to a place where we think we cannot survive. But the greatest thing about God's arms is that they specialize in lifting the downtrodden from rough places to smooth terrain in the nick of time. Ask for—and expect—God's arms to give you a testimony of how you got over!

Today's Song: "What a Fellowship, What a Joy Divine," #220

Journal Notes _____

_____

_____

_____

July 27

The First and the Last

"Sitting down, Jesus called the Twelve and said,
"If anyone wants to be first, he must be the very last,
and the servant of all."
MARK 9:35, NIV

Today's Prayer

Dear Jesus, help me today to want to be a servant and to understand what it really means. I am filled with my ego and my desires, but I know this is not pleasing to you. Wipe from me my human inclinations, and make me more like you. Help me to understand the cost you paid to be a servant, and then to be willing to pay that cost myself. Amen.

Today's Reflection

The most aggravating thing in the world is to get on a plane first because you have a seat in the back but have to wait until the entire plane is served before you get your food. Oh the joy we have when we can get onto the plane first, but that joy quickly dissipates when we are hungry and are the last to be fed.

We have to remember that there are advantages to being "last." In fact, being last sets you up to be first. In other words, if we can sublimate our human desires for power and nurture the work of servanthood, there are blessings that await us that we cannot begin to imagine. Perhaps the greatest blessing, however, is the feeding we'll get from the living Christ. Our spirits will never hunger or thirst.

Today's Song: "Give Me a Clean Heart," #216

Journal Notes _____

_____

_____

_____

July 28

Centered in Jesus

"Your attitude should be the same as that of Christ Jesus."
PHILIPPIANS 2:5, NIV

Today's Prayer

Dear God, help me to be more Christ-centered. Help me to ask, in everything I do or say if this will please you. Then, give me the strength to try to emulate you. When I think of how you emptied yourself and became a human being who wasn't respected or honored by so many people, and yet you did your father's work anyway, I shudder, but I want to be like you. So cleanse me and make me a worthy servant, Jesus. Amen.

Today's Reflection

We don't get it. Just like the Jews thought that being "the chosen ones" gave them more privileges, we as Christians too often think the same way. We don't understand that being a sibling of the living Christ gives us have more responsibility. Part of that responsibility is to imitate the Christ in all situations. That means forgiving, loving unconditionally, serving selflessly, showing mercy to enemies, and seeking God in all things. We don't get it. Being a Christian is hard work, and if we try to really imitate the Christ, we realize that fact. If we don't imitate him, we're really not his at all.

Today's Song: "King of My Life," #86

Journal Notes _____

_____

_____

_____

The Covenant

*"This is the covenant I will make with the house of Israel
after that time, declares the Lord. I will put my laws in their
minds and write them on their hearts. I will be their
God and they will be my people."*

HEBREWS 8:10, NIV

Today's Prayer

O God, clean me and uncoil my spirit so that you can find residence in me. Help me to understand that unless you are in me, I am not connected to you. Help me to understand that it's not about church membership or being a church officer that's pleasing to you. Rather, it is whether or not I am in covenant with you. Direct me and remove from my life, Lord, anything that keeps that covenant from being formed and sustained. Amen.

Today's Reflection

Jesus wants us to have a new attitude, one that is far from the attitudes of negativity, depression, judging others, non-forgiving, criticism, and anger that we too often harbor. God wants his spirit in us, God wants his words in our hearts. It's a new way of being for all of us, but it is so powerful! God wants that for all of us. In letting God in, we show that we are God's people and that he is truly our God. Have you let him in?

Today's Song: "All to Jesus I Surrender," #235

Journal Notes _____

_____

_____

_____

July 30

For Another Time as This

"For it is the LORD your God who brought us and our ancestors up from the land of Egypt, out of the house of slavery, and who did those great signs in our sight."

JOSHUA 24:17

Today's Prayer

Almighty God, today we remember that we are the hope of our ancestors manifest. Their struggles, their faith and fortitude made a way for us that should not take it for granted. Amen.

Today's Reflection

The hope of the civil rights movement was one in which we sought to share in the American dream. We saw ourselves as human beings entitled to fair, equitable, and just treatment in a system that once questioned our humanity. In that dream of equality, hope did not disappoint. With one drop of God's love, our people moved through that mountain of hate. Alleluia!

The movement is alive, but the focus has changed. For what God wrought during those turbulent years we must now acknowledge with our commitment to excellence, education and growth. Removing the shackles of oppression enables us to receive what comes with calm fortitude that must be passed down from generation to generation. Let us sing the songs of freedom and live the life of the free in God.

Today's Song: "Lift Every Voice and Sing," #296

Journal Notes _____

_____

_____

_____

Tell It Like It Is

*"Moreover, that whole generation was gathered to their ancestors,
and another generation grew up after them, who did not know
the LORD or the work that he had done for Israel."*

JUDGES 2:10

Today's Prayer

Don't let the history of our people die, Lord. With clarity, let us tell the stories of our ancestors and what you have done for us through them. Help us to remember that it is on their shoulders we stand to your glory. Amen.

Today's Reflection

Every family has one. He or she is known as the family historian and can be relied upon to know who was married to whom, who died, who was born, and the other sundry events that happen in our extended family lives. For our family it was Aunt Olive. She knew everything, some of it not so pretty. Dear Aunt Olive was always telling it like it is.

Aunt Olive said the only way to really know that God has brought us from a mighty long way is to know the real history of the family. She reminded us that for every tear shed there was light and laughter at the end of those tunnels. She was fond of telling us that for all of our mistakes and foolish missteps, we were a family that always managed to keep God forever at the ready! Her mantra, "Child, Praise God for the trouble," gave us hope. What a wonderful legacy she left us— a powerful reminder that as a family, we are truly God's own.

Today's Song: "We've Come This Far by Faith," #197

Journal Notes

_____

_____

_____

_____

Only a Prayer Away

*"For this child I prayed; and the LORD has granted me
the petition that I made to him."*
1 SAMUEL 1:27

Today's Prayer

Like Hannah, we must pray for the children here and the children to come. Lord we ask your blessings upon them. Place your mark on their foreheads and claim them as your own. Protect their hearts and minds, while guiding them to the knowledge of you. Amen.

Today's Reflection

As women, we are unique in our ability to have children. We know the joys that motherhood brings because birth is such a celebrated occasion. No one prepares us for the sorrows. It is because of the times to come that we should be ever prayerful. Hannah prayed for a child, but it wasn't to fulfill her loneliness. With the joy that came from giving birth, Hannah was also willing to make the ultimate sacrifice. She knew that the child was not just hers, but God's.

We are only the vessels by which our children arrive. We must not let class, race or social status stop us from praying for all of our children. Don't just pray for your child or the members of your family, but make sure that all of God's children got prayer on their side. Only then will our communities prosper and grow.

Today's Song: "Sweet Hour of Prayer," #242

Journal Notes _____

_____

_____

_____

Clear Like Glass

*"Let them know that you alone, whose name is the LORD,
are the Most High over all the earth."*
PSALM 83:18

Today's Prayer

Use me, Lord, as an instrument of your wonderful power. Help me to be transparent so that you may be seen more clearly. Then others may know that you alone are God. Amen.

Today's Reflection

The little girl stood terrified on the side of the house. For more times than she cared to acknowledge, her father had become violent. Who could she turn to? Who would help them? She was only six and not big enough to do anything. But something clicked. With a little girl's resolve, she opened the door just as her father drew back his hand.

"Stop!" she screamed. "Daddy, God doesn't like you hitting Mommie."

In that instant the father realized that it wasn't the little girl talking to him, but God alone. Emanating from his daughter was a presence he had not felt in a long time. He fell to the floor and wept. Years later he remembered how God used his child as an instrument of peace.

If God can use a little child, he can certainly use you. Believe it!

Today's Song: "Have Thine Own Way, Lord," #152

Journal Notes _____

_____

_____

_____

August 3

More Than Getting By

*"We must work the works of him who sent me while it is day;
night is coming when no one can work."*
JOHN 9:4

Today's Prayer

Help me to do today what I usually put off until tomorrow, Gracious Father. Teach me how to create goals, to build a work ethic, and to grow in wisdom each day. Amen.

Today's Reflection

Statistics can be a plague to the African-American community when used to oppress the spirit, but God challenges us to forget what they say and concentrate on what God does best. It means doing more than just getting by.

God is the great motivator and sustainer, but you must be answer the call. Not to worry, however. Through Christ, who paid it all, we are empowered to do the work before us. It doesn't matter the academic, political, or social constructs, we must work to build our communities today or suffer for it tomorrow.

What will your legacy be? Will it be work unfinished or a job well done? It's up to you.

Today's Song: "This Little Light of Mine," #65

Journal Notes _____

_____

_____

_____

August 4

The Price of True Freedom

But Peter said to him, "May your silver perish with you, because
you thought you could obtain God's gift with money!"
ACTS 8:20

Today's Prayer

I want your gifts, O Lord. Through your grace, help me to aspire to the greater
good without selling out my community or you. Amen.

Today's Reflection

"What does it cost to be a Christian?" asked the teacher. The answers were varied.
The giving of tithes was one answer. Another answer was that one must give of their
time in order to be a Christian. Yet another said, "You must give to the poor."

The real answer is all of the above and none of the above. The truth is that the
price of our salvation is already paid. It doesn't mean that it should be taken for
granted. With the ultimate sacrifice for the precious gift of salvation, we should be
inclined to tithe, give of our time and give to others, but not to fool God into thinking we're better than we are. When you accept the gift, you want to give. The price?
It's free!

Today's Song: "God Forgave My Sin in Jesus' Name," #187

Journal Notes _____

_____

_____

_____

Do the Right Thing

*"For God didn't give us a spirit of cowardice,
but rather a spirit of power and of love and of self-discipline."*
2 TIMOTHY 1:7

Today's Prayer

I'm not brave, Lord. In fact, I'm often afraid. Dispel my fears. Give me a sense of your power so that I may always do the right thing. Amen.

Today's Reflection

In this era of political correctness, it seems that the issues of racism and prejudice have been watered down. We stay divided because no one wants to be seen as politically incorrect, plus we are too afraid to tackle the real issues. We smile at each other while seething on the inside when injustice rears its ugly head. In truth, it's not that I forget that I am a child of God, but that you are.

But if we see each individual as one of God's own; if we look upon our brothers and sisters of other races and cultures with love, we can tackle the problems without fear. As God's children, the hope is that we cannot hurt another of God's children. Yes, the issues still loom large, but they can only be conquered when we view the broader picture—that we are all children of God.

Today's Song: "We Are All One in Christ," #221

Journal Notes _____

_____

_____

_____

What Prayer Can Do

"And the LORD *repented of the evil
which he thought to do to his people."*
EXODUS 32:14

Today's Prayer

Let our prayers rise to you like incense. Give us hearts to feel for our neighbors
and that we may come to you in prayer in all boldness and confidence. Amen.

Today's Reflection

What difference can I, just one person, make in the world? The world is so big, so
complex that anything I do seems like one drop in an oversized latte mug. But one
by one the drops add up, until the cup overflows. Our intercessory prayers and
interventions on behalf of others do matter. This example of Moses' encounter with
God shows us the power of an authentic relationship with God—the kind of relationship that allows one to have a candid conversation with God, which is what
prayer is.

Today's Song: "Blessed Assurance," #118

Journal Notes _____

_____

_____

_____

August 7

No Fear or Dread

"Have no fear or dread of them."
DEUTERONOMY 1:29

Today's Prayer

O God, creator of everything that is, teach us the way to love all that you have made. Give us courage and understanding to reach out to those most different from us and the wisdom to ascertain how to do it in such a way that is in accordance with your will. Amen.

Today's Reflection

Now let's get one thing straight. Fear is not always a negative thing. Fear of sure and certain danger can instill caution in a perilous situation. Imagine where we would all be if only Adam and Eve had been just a little more cautious. The people of Israel were given a command to go into the land that the Lord had shown them. However, they refused to step outside their comfort zone and defied God.

God's will for our lives does not always give us a warm and fuzzy feeling about where we are and with whom we share our time. Remember, our times are in God's hands and the Holy Spirit, which blows where it wills, also blows us where it wills. The people we encounter, whether similar or different, are all a part of God's design. Yes, there is evil in the world and we should be careful, but we should not be fearful. Fear produces hate. The challenge is to understand, to find common ground even with those whom we believe are our enemies. Walls of separation can fall and enemies can become friends if we overcome our fear of others.

Today's Song: "Guide My Feet," #153

Journal Notes

August 8

The Sound of Silence

"For God alone my soul waits in silence;
from God comes my salvation."
PSALM 62:5

Today's Prayer

Lord, speak to me that my soul might be stilled. Lord, let me hear your voice above all others. Quiet the noise in my head and in my heart that I may be in tune with your will for my life. Amen.

Today's Reflection

In our fast and busy world, finding silence may be a difficult thing to do. But when we seek it out, even in the loudest city it is possible to hear the voice of God in the din of traffic or construction, in the crashing of waves rushing in and out on a deserted beach, and in the hum of farm machinery. It is not at midnight, but rather in those hours when it is no longer night but not quite day that are the hardest for those who suffer from adversity. But it is also in those same hours that many find they are most able to talk to, hear and understand God.

So do not fear the still of night, rather approach it with a holy curiosity. The voice of God is not found exclusively in silence, maybe it is just the only frequency most humans are tuned in to.

Today's Song: "Some Folk Would Rather Have Houses," #236

Journal Notes _____

_____

_____

_____

Restored

"Rejoice not over me, O my enemy; when I fall, I shall rise;
when I sit in darkness, the LORD will be a light to me."
MICAH 7:8

Today's Prayer

God of mercy, I call on you in the name of Christ, asking forgiveness of all the wrongs I have done, sins known and unknown. Give me a clean heart and a clear conscience that I may know that peace that passes all human understanding. Amen.

Today's Reflection

This is the confession of one who has seen trouble and anguish, has been rescued and restored, and now holds that restoration in memory to get through the next valley in life. The difference between this writer and many people of God today is that he has not only awareness of the situation but a confidence that even in the darkness God is there just as God has been there in the past and he will rise again.

Call to remembrance the last time your own sin brought trouble and anguish your way. In honesty, did you go to the Lord and confess, repent, and feel the power of forgiveness and the peace that comes from reconciliation? People who serve in prison ministries say inmates have testified that even in a prison cell there is a freedom that comes from having admitted one's guilt and knowing that they are forgiven by God, who is the highest authority in the universe. There is a hope in God's mercy. That light pierces the darkness prison in life, whether of bars or of the minds.

Today's Song: "My Hope Is Built on Nothing Less," #192

Journal Notes _____

_____

_____

_____

Jesus Triumphs

"Hosanna! Blessed is he who comes in the name of the Lord!"
MARK 11:9

Today's Prayer

Lord, give me the picture of your perfect kingdom and let me never lose sight. Give me strength to be a willing participant in the building of Christ's church that at the name of Jesus all might say, "Hosanna!" Blessed is the one who comes in the name of the Lord. Amen.

Today's Reflection

Many of us say it every Sunday, having no understanding of what we are saying. Literally it means "save (us)." And political salvation is what the people were looking for from Jesus. That is why "Hosanna" was shouted as Jesus entered Jerusalem, yet less than a week later "Crucify him" became the cry.

Those who come in the name of the Lord often don't live up to our expectations. Even the Holy Spirit, though it is "always right on time." as we say, does not always work when we want, where we want and in the manner most effective for our way of thinking. And though our piety style may not allow us to say it aloud, we silently wonder, "What in the world is God doing? I thought God knew just how much we could bear! Will we go down to the pit before God realizes what is happening and send some relief?"

Jesus came to do a new thing in a way most people were not accustomed. They tried to stop him, but there is no stopping God's will.

Today's Song: "Ride On, King Jesus," #182

Journal Notes _____

_____

_____

_____

Keep on Keeping on!

*"What you have learned and received and heard and seen in me,
keep on doing and the God of peace will be with you."*

MARK 11:9

Today's Prayer

Loving God, give me the strength that I need to resist evil and to do your holy will. Amen.

Today's Reflection

Phillipians has often been called the epistle of joy. Not only because the exhortation to "rejoice" is repeated several times, but also because the entire mood of the letter is one of joy, even though it was written from prison. The joy of being a new being in Christ helped Paul endure even while being imprisoned! Paul's testimony of joy from prison is more than mere encouragement or witness it serves to give us strength.

Today's Song: "Shine, Jesus, Shine," #64

Journal Notes _____

_____

_____

_____

August 12

My Soul Delights in the Law

"Since the law has only a shadow of the good things to come . . ."
HEBREWS 10:1

Today's Prayer

I give you thanks, dear Lord, for the gift of your word to me in scripture, in proclamation, and in Jesus, your Word made flesh. May that word be a lamp that lights my life, and may I reflect that light to bring others out of darkness. In Jesus' name I pray. Amen.

Today's Reflection

Lutherans talk a lot about Law and Gospel, but depending on which branch of the Lutheran tree one is on, one side tends to have more foliage than the other. For those who tend to cultivate the Gospel side and allow the Law side to wither a little, the first verse of this letter reminds us that the Law does indeed hold good things for us. For those who prefer to cultivate the Law side because "that Gospel side is just too free-wheeling and loose," we are reminded that the law is only a "shadow" of the good things. We need both—the Law shows us who we are, imperfect beings, sinners in need of a savior; while the Gospel tells us that Christ came for sinners and that through our faith in him we are saved.

With that in our array of tools of the Spirit, tending the garden of our souls should be a little more delightful. Although we know that the trials and temptations are sure to come we need not fear God's wrath. In God there is delight that we can go on with our lives in confidence of a right relationship with God.

Today's Song: "Give Me Jesus," #165

Journal Notes _____

_____

_____

_____

You Have a Friend in Jesus

"The LORD would speak to Moses face to face,
as a man speaks with his friend."
EXODUS 33:11a, NIV

Today's Prayer

Jesus, you are my friend. You have stood by me when I had no one else to stand with me. You have never shown any doubt that you loved me. God, I thank you for your friendship. Amen.

Today's Reflection

In Exodus, Moses often went to the Tent of Meeting to talk with God about his many concerns. Moses was able to pour out his heart to God and God was able to receive what Moses had to say. Their relationship developed to a point where truth and honesty were revealed. God was able to give clarity and encouragement to Moses so that he would not give up on the people of Israel. This relationship with God was the greatest privilege Moses could have ever had.

We, too, can have this same kind of relationship with God as we build our own tent of meeting and spend precious time with God being truthful and honest. God will listen to us and hear our deepest cries. God will take counsel with us, bring clarity to that which we are going through and will give us strength and encouragement.

Today's Song: "What a Fellowship, What a Joy Divine," #220

Journal Notes

August 14

The Judgement and Mercy of God

*Now when the last of these fighting men
among the people had died, the LORD said to me,
"Today you are to pass by the region of Moab at Ar."*
DEUTERONOMY 2:16-18, NIV

Today's Prayer

God, I thank you for your patience with me. Thank you for allowing me to serve you in faith and not exacting the level of punishment I deserve for my sins. Thank you for your mercy and grace. Amen.

Today's Reflection

The story begins with the sending out of twelve spies by Moses to check out the promised land. Ten came back saying that they were fearful because the land was filled with giants. But two, Joshua and Caleb, said that God was strong enough to give victory over the giants. The people believed the ten and decided that God was not strong enough. We must be mindful of what a lack of faith and trust in God will do. We serve a kind and merciful God. Our unbelief can be costly in our lives. Our lack of faith can cost us dearly in terms of pain and suffering. God loves us, but can punish us at times for our disobedience. But thank God, after the punishment God provides for us a way to enter the promised land.

Today's Song: "My Soul Does Magnify the Lord," #168

Journal Notes _____

_____

_____

_____

August 15

Our God Will Satisfy

*"My soul will be satisfied as with the richest of foods;
with singing lips my mouth will praise you."*
PSALM 63:5, NIV

Today's Prayer

Praise the Lord! Praise the Lord! Lord we are satisfied in you. You have done so many great things in our lives and we are satisfied with you. Words cannot express how grateful we are that you are in our lives. And for our satisfaction we glorify and adore thee giving thee honor and praise. Amen.

Today's Reflection

When David was in the wilderness hiding from his enemies, he felt discouraged, uncertain, and alone. David called on the Lord to hear his cry. In this place of wilderness and starvation, David praised God and proclaimed that God would satisfy him, and did.

There are times when we, too, are in difficult places, where emotional stress and tension are high. In those times, we are to look to God. Open our mouth and to praise God, proclaim the blessings of God, and bring forth praises to God. Just as God met David in the wilderness, God will comfort us.

Today's Song: "Great Is Thy Faithfulness," #283

Journal Notes _____

_____

_____

_____

Fearing God

"The LORD Almighty is the one you are to regard as holy,
he is the one you are to dread."
ISAIAH 8:11, NIV

Today's Prayer

Sovereign Lord, the one who has created all things. There is no one like you. No one has the power but you. Lord we humble ourselves before you, for only you can accomplish the things that you do. Amen.

Today's Reflection

God was about to bring destruction upon the king of Assyria because they had rejected the Lord God and substituted false gods. Assyria was rich with great wealth, prosperity, royalty, and a very great army able to inflict harm upon anyone who dared to challenge them. God tells the prophet Isaiah not to fear what the people of Assyria fear. The prophet is not to follow the way of the Assyrian people and not to respect what they respect or love what they love.

Like Isaiah, our trust should be in God. Reliance on anything other than God is fruitless. Do not fear and respect the things that the world fears and respects. Fear the Lord today and trust your life to God.

Today's Song: "Have You Thanked the Lord?" #270

Journal Notes _____

_____

_____

_____

God Owns Everything

"Give to Caesar what is Caesar's and to God what is God's."
MARK 12:17

Today's Prayer

God, help me to realize that everything belongs to you and to daily give you everything in my life that you deserve. Amen.

Today's Reflection

The Pharisees and Herodians came to Jesus and asked him a trick question about paying taxes. Either answer Jesus gave they would have declared him disloyal either to God or to the government. But Jesus knew the deception that was in their heart. Jesus took a coin and asked them whose image was inscribed on the coin. When they replied, "Caesar's," he said, "Give to Caesar what is Caesar's and to God what is God's." And they were amazed at his wisdom because they could not trick or trap him. Everything belongs to God. Not only does Caesar belong to God, but you belong to God as well. Give unto Caesar the things that are Caesar's and to God what is God's.

Today's Song: "He Is Lord," #95

Journal Notes _____

_____

_____

_____

August 18

The Divine Glory of Christ

"He is before all things, and in him all things hold together."
COLOSSIANS 1:17, NIV

Today's Prayer

Lord God, I thank you for coming in Christ Jesus to show your glory to the world. I thank you for the fact that nothing can obscure his glory—even heresies and speculations. Despite all human efforts, nothing can hide his glory. Jesus is Lord and supreme head of the church. Amen.

Today's Reflection

Paul wrote to the Colossians a message that stressed that Jesus was the supreme head of the church to counter heresies and philosophic speculation that tended to obscure the divine glory of Christ. Paul warned against false doctrine and urged steadfast faith in Christ. For Paul, Jesus was the center of everything.

It is good news that we serve a Lord that was the creator of all things, before all things, and the reconciler of all things. The glory of Christ shines because he is before all things and in him all things began. Praise God that Christ is the supreme head of the church.

Today's Song: "Glory, Glory, Hallelujah!" # 148

Journal Notes _____

_____

_____

_____

Faith as the Road to a Fulfilled Life

"And without faith it is impossible to please God, because anyone who comes to him must believe that he exists and that he rewards those who earnestly seek him."

HEBREWS 11:6, NIV

Today's Prayer

Lord God, I stand before you to receive the plan for my life today. I believe what you have for my life is perfect and I have faith that you will bring that plan to completion in due time. I love you Lord and I sincerely seek thy holy face to guide me on my spiritual journey. Amen.

Today's Reflection

As we read and learn about God's word, we must search for the deepest meaning of the truth of the Word in our lives. When we get that understanding, we are able to line our lives up with the Word. Lining our lives up with the Word is called faith. Without which it is impossible to please God. And when we please God there are untold blessings in store for our lives. Instead of reaching for worldly forms of happiness and love, why don't you try pleasing God first?

Today's Song: "We've Come This Far by Faith," #197

Journal Notes _____

_____

_____

_____

August 20

God's Love Never Ceases

*"The LORD, the compassionate and gracious God,
slow to anger, abounding in love and faithfulness."*
EXODUS 34:6

Today's Prayer

Kind and loving God, thank you for enveloping us in your love. May we always be mindful of the fact that we are loved. Amen.

Today's Reflection

God's words to Moses continues to remind us that the love of God is all encompassing. God's love cuts across all barriers. God's love is not limited, hampered, nor bound by human ideals and idiosyncrasies. God's love is always present. We cannot escape God's compassion and forgiveness.

Today's Song: "O, How He Loves You and Me," #82

Journal Notes _____

_____

_____

_____

Egoism Is a Sin of Pride

"Who is there the king would rather honor than me?"
ESTHER 6:7b

Today's Prayer

Merciful God, forgive our selfish pride and egotistical behavior. Teach us to love one another in our diversity as you love us. Amen.

Today's Reflection

Selfishness, hidden anger, and resentment of others will ultimately manifest itself in hatred. Haman despised Mordecai his hatred became like smoldering embers of fire awaiting the right time to flare up. Hamam methodically devised ways to ensure the destruction of his Jewish adversary, even if it meant killing all Jews. Sadly, he designed the method of death for himself, his family, and his servants. They were all hanged.

Racial, gender, and cultural bigotry are insidious. The tentacles of bigotry become suction cups of hatred, disabling all humanity. The joys of diversity within humanity are lost. Our diversity reflects the beauty of God.

Today's Song: "Lord, I Want to Be a Christian," #234

Journal Notes _____

_____

_____

_____

Deliverance Comes through Prayer

"He will turn their own tongues against them
and bring them to ruin . . ."
PSALM 64:8

Today's Prayer

Merciful God, too often we forget that you see and hear everything we say and do. Teach us to bring our complaints to you, for you are the one who answers our prayers. Amen.

Today's Reflection

Harsh words and judgements are very commonplace in our world today. There is a word of judgement against anyone who choose to slander, defame, or hurt the righteous. "He will turn their tongues against and bring them to ruin."

This particular psalm addresses itself to the unfairness of gossip and slander. Sadly to say, there are those who delight in this behavior. As members of the body of Christ, we must weigh our words carefully before voicing them. Words can destroy as well as defend.

Today's Song: "I Can Hear My Savior Calling," #192

Journal Notes _____

_____

_____

_____

Wisdom Comes from God

"For whoever finds me finds life and receives favor from the LORD.*"*
PROVERBS 8:35

Today's Prayer

Loving Father, give us the wisdom to love, desire, seek, and serve you with our whole heart. Amen.

Today's Reflection

Wisdom is based on the knowledge of God and not our intellect. It is a gift to us. All humanity has been given the freedom to choose to follow the instructions of the Lord. We have not been left alone to try to find our way to God. The remedy for our salvation was already planned before the world began. Our hope and trust comes from God, for God is wisdom. Our intellect comes out of life's experiences, that which we know and have seen. Wisdom comes from knowing and following God the Father, God the Son, and God the Holy Spirit.

Today's Song: "Where He Leads Me," #146

Journal Notes _____

_____

_____

_____

Do Not Be Afraid

"Do not fear him, for I have handed him over to you."

DEUTERONOMY 3:2

Today's Prayer

O Sovereign Lord, you have shown us your greatness in heaven and on earth. Help us always to trust in your power to defend us. Amen.

Today's Reflection

Fear and faith do not go hand in hand. Fear negates faith. Too often we allow fear to control us instead of trusting God's word. The command that was given to Israel applies to us as well: "Do not be afraid of them, the Lord your God . . . will fight for you." How many times we try to fight our own battles. We are no match for the weapons and wiles of Satan—they are too strong. But God's word comes to us in victory: "The Lord will fight for you, you need only to be still" (Exodus 14:14).

Faith in God combats fear. As a child I was taught that fear can torment us and consume us. The love of God drives out fear and perfects our faith. When we are overwhelmed by the vicissitudes of life, we need not be afraid but trust in God's word. The Lord knows how to fight our battles. We have an arsenal that is based on faith and can defeat every foe.

Today's Song: "When the Storms of Life Are Raging," #198

Journal Notes _____

_____

_____

_____

Discipline Comes from Love

"No discipline seems pleasant at the time but painful."
HEBREWS 12:11a

Today's Prayer

Merciful Father, may we always remember that you discipline us out of your love. May others see your image in us. Amen.

Today's Reflection

There have been many times when the tumult of life has caused me to cry, "Lord, why? Why am I going through this kind of pain?" No discipline seems pleasant at the time, but painful.

It was my Sunday school teacher who taught discipline comes to make sure that God can see his reflection in us. God disciplines us out of his love for us and "later on . . . it produces a harvest of righteousness and peace for those who have been trained by it."

Today's Song: "We Are Often Tossed and Driven," #206

Journal Notes _____

_____

_____

_____

Alive with Christ

*"See that no one takes you captive through
hollow and deceptive philosophy."*
COLOSSIANS 2:8

Today's Prayer

Gracious Father, thank you for the freedom of life we have through your Son,
Jesus Christ. Amen.

Today's Reflection

Over the last few decades, we have been inundated with deceptive philosophies
and pseudo-religious ideals. We have the words of Saint Paul to encouraged us to be
faithful. "See to it that no one takes you captive through hollow and deceptive philosophy, which depends on human tradition and the basic principles of this world
rather than on Christ."

Cults and psychics are not new. As religious ideologies they are empty and enslav-
ing. As Christians, we have freedom through Christ to live our lives free of that type
of bondage. It is the work of the Holy Spirit that protects us from becoming captives.

Today's Song: "I Will Call Upon the Lord," #277

Journal Notes _____

_____

_____

_____

Rest for the Journey

*"Six days shall work be done, but on the seventh day
you shall have a holy Sabbath of solemn rest to the LORD;
whoever does any work on it shall be put to death."*

EXODUS 35:2

Today's Prayer

God, thank you for giving us the Sabbath. We pray for the wisdom and strength to take it. Amen.

Today's Reflection

We work all the time. Advanced technology has made it possible to carry our work with us and access it from anywhere in the world. As a result, we don't have to take breaks.

We work on the Sabbath, while on vacation, and during what should be family time. We work all day and go home and work until late on our computers, sleep a few hours, and then go back to work. In a world like ours, God's commandment is very relevant.

It is clear from scripture that God took rest very seriously. In Genesis, even God took the seventh day off for rest while creating the world. The understanding of this commandment in Exodus 35 is take rest or die. While I don't think we need to put any one to death, the idea of Sabbath rest is very valuable to our health, well-being, and productivity. A Sabbath time of rest is good for the body and soul.

Today's Song: "Come by Here," #43

Journal Notes

_____

_____

_____

_____

August 28

Lord of Heaven and Earth

"So acknowledge today and take to heart that the Lord *is God in heaven above and on the earth beneath; there is no other."*
DEUTERONOMY 4:39

Today's Prayer

Lord, help me to remember that you rule in heaven, and on earth, and in my heart. Amen.

Today's Reflection

Growing up Christian, most of us were taught that God is in heaven and that in heaven there is joy, peace, love, and abundance because of God's rule.

In the Deuteronomy 4, Moses reminds the people of God's goodness and mercy, and that God is creator of both heaven and earth. It brings us great comfort to know that, even during times of civil unrest, natural disaster, wars, racial divisions, hate crimes, and violent rage, the Lord is God. God rules both heaven and earth. God does not leave us during troubled times, but seeks to bring us joy, peace, love, and abundance.

Today's Song: "I, the Lord of Sea and Sky," #230

Journal Notes _____

_____

_____

_____

Faithful Help

"But as for me my prayer is to you, O LORD.
All on acceptable time, O God, in the abundance of your
steadfast love, answer me with your faithful help."

PSALM 69:13

Today's Prayer

Dear Lord, thanks for the blessed assurance that you are there for me at all times and through all things. Amen.

Today's Reflection

Psalm 22 is the only psalm quoted more than Psalm 69 in the New Testament. The psalmist in Psalm 69 is clearly suffering but, with a certain hope that God will answer prayer, prays for God's faithful help. The psalms provide a great sense of help and assurance during times of suffering and pain. The psalmist does not hesitate to call upon the Lord for help and to call with a sense that the pleas for help will certainly be answered.

The psalms provide us with great examples of how we can live our lives. They remind us that we can live in the certain hope that God will and does answer prayer. They provide us with the assurance that during the lowest times in our lives that God is there supporting, guiding, and sometimes even carrying us through these periods.

Today's Song: "Blessed Assurance," #118

Journal Notes _____

_____

_____

_____

God Will Deliver Us

*"Therefore thus says the LORD God of hosts: O my people, who live
in Zion, do not be afraid of the Assyrians when they beat you with a
rod and lift up their staff against you as the Egyptians did."*
ISAIAH. 10:24

Today's Prayer

O God, you are powerful and just. We pray for your powerful and just rule in our
hearts. Amen.

Today's Reflection

God has sent Isaiah to tell the people who were afraid, who were being punished
and treated unjustly, not to worry and not to fear, because their God is powerful
and just.

It is obvious from the daily newspapers and nightly newscasts that the message of
Isaiah spoken to the people then, is very much needed today. Living in these times
of injustice, hate, violence, and abuse, we need to hear and believe the message
of Isaiah. We need to know that our God is a God of power and justice, and that
God will do for us today what Isaiah says: protect and deliver us.

Today's Song: "I'm So Glad Jesus Lifted Me," #191

Journal Notes _____

_____

_____

Living in the Light

*"The true light, which enlightens everyone,
was coming into the world."*
JOHN 1:9

Today's Prayer

Lord, thank you for the good news of Jesus and the gift of eternal life. Amen.

Today's Reflection

Can you remember as a child how frightening it gets when the lights go off and you are in the dark? Your imagination could run wild. You could imagine monsters in the corners, snakes on the walls, and bats flying around. But when your mom turned the lights on, everything was revealed and you could see what was really there. That is exactly what Jesus did for us when he came into the world. Jesus brought true light into the world and that light revealed the true story of God. That revelation gave us a clear understanding of the gift of eternal life for those who follow Christ.

Today's Song: "The Lord Is My Light," #61

Journal Notes _____

_____

_____

_____

A Spirit of Thankfulness

"And let the peace of Christ rule in your hearts; to which indeed you were called in the one body. And be thankful."
COLOSSIANS 3:15

Today's Prayer

Dear Lord, help me to remember that I am a part of the body of Christ and that I am not alone. Because of this I can live with a spirit of thankfulness. Amen.

Today's Reflection

We live in a world where we may have to make hundreds of civil decisions on a daily basis: How can I decide justly? How can I not let my prejudice or bias get in the way? How can I correct without sounding judgmental?

Paul knew these were the kinds of inner struggles that we deal with when he wrote this letter to the Colossians. Therefore, Paul gives us a helpful reminder that we should live with a spirit of thankfulness and let the peace of Christ rule in our heart. Paul was aware that, in most decisions, the heart rules the head. When we are making those hard inner decisions we should remember we are not alone, that we are a part of the body of Christ. And then, with a spirit of thankfulness, we should allow the peace of Christ to rule in our heart.

Today's Song: "Spirit of the Living God," #101

Journal Notes _____

_____

_____

_____

Holy Hospitality

"Do not neglect to show hospitality to strangers, for by so doing
that some have entertained angels without knowing it."
HEBREWS 13:2

Today's Prayer

Lord, show me how to love and accept strangers as you did. Amen.

Today's Reflection

I was fortunate enough to be a part of the bishop's delegation to visit our companion churches in Tanzania, Africa. It was a life-changing experience to witness people whose hospitality was overwhelming. The Tanzanians are very, very poor. Meat is not on the regular diet since they cannot afford it. Yet, they would prepare meals for us with meats and other foods that they could not afford to eat themselves.

Sometimes we suspected they would use all their resources to welcome us, and go without themselves. When asked about their generosity to strangers they said that visitors and strangers honor them by their visit and that you always welcome the stranger. I believe that is what Hebrews 13 is saying to us. We should practice living a more hospitable life.

Today's Song: "Jesu, Jesu, Fill Us with Your Love," #83

Journal Notes _____

_____

_____

_____

Moses Did Everything the Lord Commanded

"The Lord spoke to Moses."
EXODUS 40:1

Today's Prayer

Lord, as you dwelt in the tabernacle of old and filled it with your glory, fill me with your presence. Lord God, make me a worthy tabernacle. As Moses anointed the objects for worship, Lord, anoint my mind so my thoughts are pleasing to you. Anoint my lips so that you are honored by the words of my mouth. Abide at the altar of my heart so that you may be glorified in my life. Enable me Lord, as you did Moses, to do just as you command. Amen.

Today's Reflection

The tabernacle was God's dwelling on earth. And Moses built it according to God's specifications. There were no shortcuts. There was no substitution of materials. There was no coming up with a better idea or a better way. Moses did everything just as the Lord commanded him. Under the new covenant, Jesus did just as God commanded. He paid the wages for sin. He fulfilled the Law. There are no shortcuts to salvation. Jesus is the only way. No one comes to the Father, but by him. He did everything just as the Lord commanded him.

Today's Song: "I Will Call Upon the Lord," #277

Journal Notes _____

_____

_____

_____

Move in the Way of the Lord

"You shall have no other gods before me."
DEUTERONOMY 5:7

Today's Prayer

O Lord, my God, in whom I live, move and have my being, I am grateful that you loved me so much you gave me rules to live by. When the rules condemned me, you gave me grace and mercy through your Son, Jesus Christ. O glorious God, give me an obedient heart so that I might serve you with joy and thanksgiving. Today, Lord, help me to walk in all the way you have commanded. Amen.

Today's Reflection

The law, The Ten Commandments were rules for holy living, given to Moses by God. Each Commandment contains a small lesson on how to be in right relationship with God and with one another. Obedience to the law brought God's promises of long life, health, and prosperity. Disobedience brought condemnation and consequences.

Because the Law condemned us, our merciful and gracious God sent Jesus, not to destroy the law but to fulfill it. When we do as Jesus commands, love the Lord our God and our neighbor, we too fulfill the law.

Today's Song: "I Will Enter His Gates," #101

Journal Notes _____

_____

_____

_____

As I Was with Moses, So I Will Be with You

*"No one shall be able to stand against you
all the days of your life."*
JOSHUA 1:5

Today's Prayer

Thank you, Lord, for the word that reminds me I am never alone and I am not forsaken. It is almost too wonderful for me to grasp. When children leave home you are with me. When loved ones die, you are with me. Even when it is hard for me to be with myself, you are still there. Never alone! Thank you, God, for your constant presence. Thank you for your grace and mercy. Be with me this day Lord as you were with Moses and Joshua. Amen.

Today's Reflection

Just as God was with Joshua, he is with us no matter what challenges, circumstances, and situations we may have to face. We may not be called upon to conquer nations like Joshua, but every day we must conquer tough situations, difficult decisions, and various temptations. God promises that he will never abandon us or fail to help us. Today's reading reminds us that we, too, are never alone. By asking God to help and guide us, we, like Joshua, are empowered to conquer the every day challenges of life.

Today's Song: "Lead Me, Guide Me," #70

Journal Notes _____

_____

_____

_____

September 6

O Lord, Come Quickly to Help Me

"Be pleased, O God, to deliver me.
O LORD, make haste to help me!"
PSALM 70:1

Today's Prayer

Lord, my God, my defense and my deliverer, today I need your help and I need it quickly. Grant unto me clarity where there is confusion. Give me strength where I am weak. Turn my fear into faith. Hear me Lord. Come speedily to my aid. For I need your help, without you I can do nothing. I praise you Lord, my God and my deliverer for being a God who is always on time. Amen.

Today's Reflection

When the storms in our lives are out of control and our world is rocked as if struck by an unexpected tornado, there is little time to pray. When all we hold dear is threaten to be taken away or destroyed by the howling winds of sudden illness, divorce, death, unemployment, or out-of-control children, there is no time for bending knees. When we find ourselves long on need and short on time, "Help, God!" or "Lord, have mercy!" is more than sufficient to get God's attention.

Today's Song: "When the Storms of Life Are Raging," #198

Journal Notes _____

_____

_____

_____

September 7

God's Spirit

"The Spirit of the LORD will rest on him."
ISAIAH 11:2a

Today's Prayer

O God, how excellent is your name. How I long for the time of redemption for your whole creation. Help me to remain faithful to your word and your way, O God, when I have been wounded by racism, sexism, and gender bias. Until that day, my Lord, when peace, justice, and fairness will reign, let your Spirit of truth and wisdom rest on me so that I am quick to praise and slow to take offense. Give me the ability to deal fairly with all peoples. Help me Lord to yield to the guidance of the Holy Spirit so that peace is my intent and justice is my motive. Until you come again. Amen.

Today's Reflection

I knew a pastor who said never argue about politics and religion. Whenever someone tried to engage him in a debate about the reality of heaven and hell, his reply was always the same: "I'd rather live like there's a heaven and a hell and die and find out there is none than to live like there is none and die and find out there is."

Isaiah gives us a prophetic glimpse of what is to come. Down the long corridor of time he is able to see when God will redeem God's whole creation and justice and righteousness will be the norm. No more drive by shootings. No more teen violence or road rage. No more war on drugs. No jails, no hospitals. Peace will flow like a river and we will study war no more. I'd rather live like that's true and die and find out it isn't, than to live like it isn't and die and find out it is.

Today's Song: "When Peace Like a River," #194

Journal Notes _____

_____

_____

_____

September 8

Sending the Best, Last

Jesus said to them, "Fill the jars with water."
And they filled them up to the brim.
JOHN 2:7

Today's Prayer

Lord, forgive me for the times when I let everything run out before I turn to you. When I run out of strength, you renew me. When I run out of solutions, you show me the way. When I am impatient with myself, your patience soothes my anxieties. Help me, Gracious God, to seek you first so that my cup doesn't run out but overflows. Amen.

Today's Reflection

Do you ever wonder why we try everything before we try God? We are encouraged to ask and receive, seek and find, knock and it will be opened to us—but more often then not, God is last on our agenda instead of first.

It seems God has a way of saving the best for last. He may not come when you want him, but he's always on time. God sent judges, kings, and prophets and last of all God sent his Son. God sent the best, last!

Today's Song: "What a Mighty God We Serve!" #295

Journal Notes _____

_____

_____

_____

Encourage Each Other

"For God did not call us to impurity but in holiness."
1 THESSALONIANS 4:7

Today's Prayer

Lord, I thank you for hope that reaches beyond the grave. How grateful I am for the assurance and comfort of your word. I praise you for Jesus the Christ, my hope of glory. Thank you, God. Amen, amen, amen!

Today's Reflection

When my father died suddenly, something in me shut down. When my sister died unexpectedly in her sleep, something in me cracked. When my son died of suicide ,something in me broke. Death is a life-changing event. It seems so final when the minister says into your hands O Lord I commend their spirit.

But through the pain, grief, and sorrow, we hear the voice of Jesus, our hope of glory. "Father, into your hands I commend my spirit." "It is finished." Our Lord died for our sins and rose from the dead for our justification. Death may seem like the end, but for Christians, death does not have the final word.

Christ will break through the clouds when he comes again with those who died believing in him. The graves and the seas will give up their saintly treasures and they will accompany the Lord. Those who remain will be caught up to be with the Lord forever. If we live for him now, we shall live with him when he returns. Thank God!

Today's Song: "Thank You, Jesus," #280

Journal Notes _____

_____

_____

_____

September 10

Giving God Your Love

*"You shall love the L*ORD* your God."*
DEUTERONOMY 6:5a

Today's Prayer

Forgiving God, how can we ever totally love you the way that you deserve. We give up on you, get frustrated with you, neglect and take you for granted. You, O Lord, have been faithful beyond measure. The next time we pause to reflect on all those things that we require in a loving relationship, let us hold ourselves accountable that these same things we offer in our relationship with you. Amen.

Today's Reflection

How can you not love someone who will love you no matter what? Yet we end up giving our all to romantic relationships that aren't good for us, friendships that have long soured, partnerships personal and professional that are no longer fruitful. Hanging on when we should be moving on. It seems unfathomable that we would put our all, our everything, into these relationships. It has been proven time and time again that God's love for us is unconditional, and unwavering. God continues to love us even when we are at our most unlovable. Frankly, isn't that what true love is about?

Today's Song: "He Has Made Glad," #291

Journal Notes _____

_____

_____

_____

Scouting Out the Promise

"Give me a sign of good faith."
JOSHUA 2:12b

Today's Prayer

Ever-guiding Creator, it seems as though you ask us to do the impossible. Perhaps it appears that way because we foolishly imagine that we can accomplish those things that only you can make happen. By our obedience, faith, and commitment to you, assure us once again that no task is so daunting, no challenge so immense, no tribulation so unbearable that you will not sustain, strengthen or deliver your servants. Support will come from unexpected sources, doors will open, miracles will occur, somehow help will come when we need it the most. Thank you Lord for doing more than we can imagine and more than we have the right to expect. Amen.

Today's Reflection

Joshua was the successor of Moses, commissioned by God to distribute the Holy Land. He was confronted with a host of enemies and a surprising assortment of allies. When God sends us forth on a mission, we are never sure of who or what we may encounter. Who is it that God will send to help us? Who in the process of helping themselves may in reality be aiding God's plan? Who will we help today?

Today's Song: "A Wonderful Savior Is Jesus," #260

Journal Notes _____

_____

_____

_____

God Will See You Through

"In you, O LORD, I take refuge; let me never be put to shame."
PSALM 71:1

Today's Prayer

God, there are times when we feel so broken, so utterly diminished, that we wonder if we can be whole again. In some miraculous way, you always seem to be the glue that holds us together. You make shattered pieces fit, you put the fragmented shards of our lives back in place. Pain does not go away immediately but, the soothing balm of your steadfast care helps us to heal over time and we are grateful. Amen.

Today's Reflection

Let's face it. Life is a gift from God, but it isn't always easy. There are seasons that are particularly challenging. There are times of anguish and struggle. Yet, we almost always encounter someone else who is having a rougher time than we are, or someone whose testimony encourages us to hang in and hold onto God's unchanging hand. There was probably some dark time in life that you've already been through. But you survived, and you are here to tell the story. You have learned from your experience, and you did not do it alone. God carried you, cared for you, and continues to be constant with you in the hills and valleys of life.

Today's Song: "God Is So Good," #275

Journal Notes _____

_____

_____

_____

Well-Fed

"With joy you will draw water from the wells of salvation."
ISAIAH 12:3

Today's Prayer

Precious Lord, how can we say thanks for how constant you have been in every aspect of our lives. So often we share our sorrows, but how frequently do we share our joy? Just knowing that you are there is a comforting reality, a wonderful feeling, a profound experience that we should not take for granted. Let us promise, Lord, to consciously share the best part of us with you. In Jesus, name we pray. Amen.

Today's Reflection

Just as there are low times, there are those immeasurable times of joy unspeakable. Times of true awareness of the goodness of God, the love of Christ, and the power of the Holy Spirit. Times that make one's soul burst in happiness. These are the good times, the blessed times, the times that remind us that we do not have to do this thing by ourselves. As stubbornly independent and self-reliant we may be, there is one who is stronger, wiser, more compassionate, and more able to keep us from falling.

Today's Song: "Joys Are Flowing like a River," #110

Journal Notes _____

_____

_____

_____

I Will Be Content Where God Needs Me

"My joy has been fulfilled."
JOHN 3:30

Today's Prayer

In the grand scheme of things, O God, we are not always certain where we belong. We aim too high, or our intentions lack imagination and ambition. Help us to seek your will for our lives. Help us to discern our purpose here on earth. Then, O God, help us to pursue it with all diligence, and find our peace and contentment in whatever it is you have called us to do—no matter how great or how small. Amen.

Today's Reflection

How many of us have such a strong sense of self like John the Baptist? He knew that he was not the Messiah, although a very effective minister in his own right. He was excitedly preparing for Jesus to come on the scene. He wasn't threatened or questioning God about his role. He knew where he fit and what he was supposed to do—and he was content with it. He grew where he was planted.

Today's Song: "He Leadeth Me," #151

Journal Notes

September 15

Empowered by the Holy Spirit

"When the day of Pentecost had come, they were
all together in one place."
ACTS 2:1

Today's Prayer

Prevailing Spirit, one who is everything to us. One who can do anything through us, you are true to your word. You promised us a helper and let us allow its entry into the recesses of our hearts. Let our spirit become as one with your spirit, let your will become our will, your way our way, and the work that you would deem worthy our work. Lord, let our lives reflect the presence and the power of Jesus, now and forever more. Amen.

Today's Reflection

The gift of the Holy Spirit is for everyone. We want to regulate it to preachers, priests, or anyone that we may perceive to be holy. The Spirit, however, is not something that we can assign, nor can we accurately determine its effectiveness in someone else. What we can do is to be open to receive it, filled with it, and guided by it as we serve and share our witness with the world.

Today's Song: "Come, Thou Fount of Every Blessing," #108

Journal Notes _____

_____

_____

_____

September 16

The God of Second Chances

". . . and the grace of our Lord overflowed for me with the faith
and love that are in Jesus Christ."
1 TIMOTHY 1:14

Today's Prayer

Compassionate and caring God, you continue to look past our faults and our transgressions. Your mercies are new every morning. You have loved us when we were unlovable. You have been understanding when we have been misunderstood. You see the best in us when others would deem us unworthy. Thank you for seeing in us what others cannot see, for not giving up on us when others would think that we are hopeless. Thank you for giving us another chance. Amen.

Today's Reflection

Have you ever known someone whose life took a dramatic turn for the better? They kicked the habit, got out of jail, removed themselves from an abusive relationship, or stopped being abusive. They conquered depression, cancer, or just decided to become a better human being? Have your ever noticed how some people will tend to remind them of what is in their past instead of dealing with them as they are presently? Isn't it good to know that God wipes the slate clean. Our mistakes are a thing of the past. God looks at the heart not judging us solely on our acts. We as Christians should treat others accordingly with the same mercy, understanding and compassion.

Today's Song: "If I Have Wounded Any Soul Today," #170

Journal Notes _____

_____

_____

_____

Chosen by God

*"For you are a people holy to the LORD your God; the Lord
your God has chosen you out of all the peoples on
earth to be his people, his treasured possession."*
DEUTERONOMY 7:6

Today's Prayer

God, I thank you for making me your treasured child. You didn't have to choose me, but you did. Help me each and every day to walk in obedience to your will, so all that I say and do is pleasing to you. Amen.

Today's Reflection

What do you treasure the most in this world? Is it your life, your family, or the things that you own? For God, it was the Israelite community. God made a promise to their ancestors that one day their descendants would possess a land they could call home.

The Israelite community was God's treasured people. In response to God's love for them they were to be a holy people. They promised to live a life different and separate from the lifestyles of those who lived in the promised land before them. God has made us treasured people, too. When we were baptized God claimed us as God's treasured possession. Remember that you are God's precious child.

Today's Song: "Great Is Thy Faithfulness," #283

Journal Notes

_____

_____

_____

_____

September 18

Preparing for God's Visit

Then Joshua said to the people, "Sanctify yourselves;
for tomorrow the LORD will do wonders among you."
JOSHUA 3:5

Today's Prayer

God of wonder and might, I'm so glad you are the head of my life. Thank you for revealing yourself to me through your continued signs of love. Amen.

Today's Reflection

Joshua was preparing the people of Israel for a miracle. They were about to enter the promise land, but they needed to cross the Jordan River. God was going to divide the river so they could walk through it, but first they needed to spiritually prepare themselves to receive this miraculous act of God. Are you spiritually ready to receive a blessing from the Lord? God can still do the impossible. By placing our trust and faith in God, we spiritually prepare ourselves to receive God's blessings in our life.

Today's Song: "I Will Trust in the Lord," #256

Journal Notes _____

_____

_____

_____

All I Need

"My flesh and my heart may fail, but God is the strength of my heart and my portion forever."
PSALM 73:26

Today's Prayer

Lord, I know that I can always depend on you. When my body, friends and family fail me, I know that you will be there to see me through. Thank you, Lord, for supplying me with your unending love and devotion. Amen.

Today's Reflection

How do you over come a bad day? When everything that could go wrong does. What do you do? In Psalm 73 the psalmist had a very bad day.

Those people, who made life difficult for the psalmist, seemed to be living a life of prosperity. Sometimes it seems the more good we try to do the harder life becomes. Despite the struggles and burdens we may encounter we are called to trust and depend on God. The one who is always faithful to the righteous.

Today's Song: "Why Should I Feel Discouraged," #252

Journal Notes _____

_____

_____

_____

September 20

God Is with Us

*Then Haggai the messenger of the L*ORD *spoke to the people with the Lord's message, saying, "I am with you says the L*ORD*."*
HAGGAI 1:13

Today's Prayer

God of love and care, thank you for words of your everlasting presence. Help me to spread the message that you desire to be present with all of your children. Amen.

Today's Reflection

Everyone listened and was on one accord when the prophet Haggai told the community why they were experiencing so much hardship. It was because they had placed their needs ahead of God. By neglecting to care for God's temple first, and tending to their needs second, God wasn't pleased with their priorities. However, the people were obedient to the prophet's warning and changed their ways. God desires to have top priority in our lives. If the Lord isn't first in your life, the time is now to make God the top priority.

Today's Song: "Seek Ye First," #149

Journal Notes _____

_____

_____

_____

September 21

Going in Belief

Jesus said to him, "Go, your son will live." The man believed
the word that Jesus spoke to him and started on his way.
JOHN 4:50

Today's Prayer

Lord Jesus, there is Holy Spirit power in your word. Help me to always remain faithful in your word. Amen.

Today's Reflection

Jesus loved people and wanted them to experience the love God had for them. For the Samarian women at the well, this meant receiving forgiveness and the knowledge that she was valued. For the royal official, Jesus gave proof, that faith can change a situation. Jesus continues to love us and his words of power can change our situations. May the Spirit-filled words of Jesus Christ make a change in your life today.

Today's Song: "Jesus Loves Me!" #249

Journal Notes _____

_____

_____

_____

September 22

More Precious

But Peter said, "I have no silver or gold, but what I have I give you
in the name of Jesus Christ of Nazareth, stand up and walk."
ACTS 3:6

Today's Prayer

Lord Jesus, there is Holy Spirit power in your name! Help me to always keep my heart, mind and eyes on you. Amen.

Today's Reflection

The lame man at the temple will never be the same. After Peter and John brought physical healing to the man, they were also able to heal him from the social burden of being a beggar. In Jesus' name, Peter and John were able to give the lame man new life. What a difference from a life of despair and poverty to one of victory and possibility. The power of Jesus can do the same for you.

Today's Song: "I'd Rather Have Jesus," #233

Journal Notes _____

_____

_____

_____

Pray for Others

*"First of all then, I urge that supplication, prayers, intercession
and thanksgiving be made for everyone."*
1 TIMOTHY 2:1

Today's Prayer

God of goodness and love, continue to bless all my sisters and brothers. You know that somebody needs to hear from you. Thank you for keeping the world in your tender hands, I love you Lord. Amen.

Today's Reflection

As a community of faith we are dependent on each other. We are to pray for one another. Scripture tells us that the prayer of the righteous is powerful and effective. When we pray change happens, healing and deliverance happens. The Holy Spirit will be present in sincere prayers. There is power in prayer! Never under estimate the power of prayer that God has given to us.

Today's Song: "Sweet Hour of Prayer," #242

Journal Notes _____

_____

_____

_____

Fatal Forgetfulness

"Take care that you do not forget the Lord your God."
DEUTERONOMY 8:11a

Today's Prayer

Loving God, help my memory this day. Keep me Lord from forgetting how great and awesome you are. Today I will count my blessings and know that what I have I have because of you. Amen.

Today's Reflection

God is clear don't out grow whose you are by thinking and acting like you can do it by yourself. The Lord is clear that whatever you have is because of what God has done for you. The most simple or basic of your needs were met by God at a time when you could do nothing on your behalf.

As you prosper in this life, remember it is not your church, or some cloth, or some pastor that gives you the abundant life—it is God! God is the one who put things in your path to help and guide you. It is God who truly provides and blesses you daily. Don't make God angry by forgetting how it is God who makes a difference in your life.

Today's Song: "Blessed Assurance," #118

Journal Notes _____

_____

_____

_____

September 25

Standing on God's Promise

"Israel crossed over the Jordan here on dry ground."
JOSHUA 4:22b

Today's Prayer

Ever Faithful God, thank you for giving me solid ground to stand on. Thank you for firming up the loose dirt in my life and turning it into a solid foundation for my life. Amen.

Today's Reflection

My cousin Prince recently retired after 42 years as founder and pastor of a church in Markham, Illinois. He told me that he had other options back then but he felt "called" to this place by God. Prince crossed over the Jordan of doubt to stand on God's promise of I'll be with you. Exalted by God, 42 years later, besides several housing developments that he was instrumental in developing and scores of other honors, the expanded church still stands now on a street corner that has been renamed in his honor.

Be assured that no matter how impossible it may seem, God will keep the promises made to you. And that is something you can stand on and believe.

Today's Song: "Great Is Thy Faithfulness," #283

Journal Notes _____

_____

_____

_____

Don't Boast

I say to the boastful, "Do not boast," and to the wicked,
"Do not lift up your horn."
PSALM 75:4

Today's Prayer

Loving God, ruler of the universe, thank you for blessing me with life and the opportunity to serve you this day. I don't know all of the ways that you bless me, but I know you will. Help me to share your love with someone today. Amen.

Today's Reflection

Get a grip. To most people you are not irreplaceable. I get a kick out of listening to people who think that every achievement they have made is because of how great they are. They believe they are self-made and that no one helped them get to where they are. How foolish! There is no one who has not relied on someone else's help, whether seen or unseen to achieve. Whether it is a captain of industry or an elite athlete, somebody gave them a boost at some point.

Instead of boasting, be thankful that God provided for you when you needed someone the most. Even if you found yourself sleeping on a park bench or in a railroad station, God was working behind the scenes to help you. But you do have to reach out and inquire of God's will for your life. Once you get on the path to understanding, you will begin to see how God has always been there waiting for you to obey. Don't boast unless it is about how great God has been in your life.

Today's Song: "My Soul Does Magnify the Lord," #168

Journal Notes

_____

_____

_____

_____

September 27

Do Not Fear

"My spirit abides among you; do not fear."
HAGGAI 2:5b

Today's Prayer

Loving God, as I look out and see what appears to be ever increasing odds against my peace, I ask that your Holy Spirit will abide with me and encourage me to do your will. Amen.

Today's Reflection

We live in times that are full of dangers and hate. Yet God calls us to faithful and to struggle against racism. It would be easier to give in and not fight for justice, but God tells us not to fear because God's Spirit is with us. Like our forebears who opposed slavery and Jim Crow racism, we too must stand up against injustice.

The Lord states that all the silver and gold are ours. In other words, God holds our reward for faithful service. Even when it seems we are fighting against overwhelming odds, never give up, because God is with us and seeks to provide us with an abundance.

Today's Song: "Pass Me Not, O Gentle Savior," #150

Journal Notes _____

_____

_____

_____

September 28

Excuses

"Do you want to be made well?" The sick man answered him,
"Sir, I have no one to put me into the pool."
JOHN 5:6b-7a

Today's Prayer

Gracious God, help me to hear and know the voice of Jesus when he comes into my life. Help me to answer the question and not give Jesus an excuse for my poor behavior. Come today and help me to be restored in your sight. Amen.

Today's Reflection

Gee, isn't that like someone we know? You ask them a question and they respond with an excuse for why they didn't do something. Jesus already knew the answer to the question that he asked the man. Jesus already knows the deep desires of our hearts. But just like that friend of ours who offers up excuses, when Jesus calls us to wholeness we throw up reason after reason why we can't repent and live a better life.

Jesus already knows our situation and Jesus knows that he can make a difference in your life. What are you waiting for? You know that there is something that you need to turn over to Jesus. Stop making excuses, stand up and walk in the new life that Jesus has waiting for you.

Today's Song: "Jesus, the Light of the World," #59

Journal Notes _____

_____

_____

_____

September 29

Useless Opposition

*"When they saw the man who had been cured standing
beside them, they had nothing to say in opposition."*
ACTS 4:14

Today's Prayer

Loving God, I ask that you will help me to be your agent of goodwill in this world. Grant the assistance of your Holy Spirit to guide me as I battle against evil in this world. Amen.

Today's Reflection

If only evil would roll up and go away, but it never does. Satan is always on the go, creating strife, confusion, and hate. However, God grants us assistance. In other words, we are not alone in this battle. We have Jesus who has already won the victory on our side.

Today's Song: "I Heard and Old, Old Story," #97

Journal Notes _____

_____

_____

_____

No Doubt

"Without any doubt, the mystery of our religion in great."
1 TIMOTHY 4:16a

Today's Prayer

All-knowing and powerful God, thank you for the beauty of this day and allow-ing me to be part of it. I thank you for caring for me and helping me to serve you. Be with me this day as I grow in knowledge of you. Amen.

Today's Reflection

What is clear to some people is a mystery to others. Take a good detective story: clues are laid about for discerning readers to gather, to help them solve the mystery. God leaves us clues as well to help us solve the mystery of life in Christ. Part b of Timothy 4:16 tells us that Jesus "was revealed in flesh." In other words, he was made plain in our sight. Today, two thousand years later, Jesus is still being revealed in our sight. Think about what saved you, think about what saved others that you know from a life of sin and destruction. Don't you believe that it was Jesus who offered you salvation when you thought that salvation was only in having a good time? Well, let me share a clue with you: It was Jesus.

Today's Song: "Seek Ye First," #149

Journal Notes _____

_____

_____

_____

God's Own Possession

"For they are the people of your very own possession."
DEUTERONOMY 9:29

Today's Prayer

Holy One, I thank you for great faithfulness to me. It is in spite of my infidelities and imperfections that you love me. Deliver me from pride in my personal piety and help me to see where I am in need of repair. Help me to be faithful, as you are faithful. In Jesus' name, amen.

Today's Reflection

Moses recalls the sins of the children of Israel to remind them of one thing: they were not redeemed because of their righteousness, but because of God's faithfulness. The Lord made a promise to their ancestors to make a great nation of them in spite of their infidelity and in spite of their imperfections. They had become the Lord's own possession, brought out by God's great power. What a word of reassurance this was for wayward Israel.

We, too, have become God's possession, purchased with the high price of Christ's blood. We can be assured that in spite of the fact that our faith will occasionally wane and in spite of our numerous persistent imperfections, God will bring us out with a powerful outstretched arm. Thanks be to God that our deliverance does not rest on our righteousness, but on God's faithfulness.

Today's Song: "Great Is Thy Faithfulness," #283

Journal Notes _____

_____

_____

_____

October 2

Manna from Heaven

*"The manna ceased on the day they ate the produce of the land,
and the Israelites no longer had manna."*

JOSHUA 5:12

Today's Prayer

Holy One, I thank you for manna from on high. Day by day you provide that which I need, yet rarely do I appreciate how much you do for me. Today I want to thank you for the many things I take for granted. I thank you for . . . (*consider what God has done for you*). In Christ's name, amen.

Today's Reflection

The children of Israel subsisted for years on manna, the heavenly morsels God fed them when there was no other food to be found. But on the day that they were able to live on food of the promised land, the care packages from on high ceased just as suddenly as they came.

It is remarkable how God's grace sustains us. At the beginning of our final year of doctoral studies, my wife and I realized that our source of income was ending and that we had no other source for the upcoming school year. I remember praying about our situation, then feeling a sense of peace as if I knew that the Lord would work out the details. On a single day my wife was notified that she had received a new scholarship for which she did not even apply. A few minutes later we received a call offering us an appointment for a position that we did not know was vacant. The Lord had provided manna for which we did not know to ask, just in the nick of time.

Today's Song: "I Believe I'll Testify," #225

Journal Notes Need to define Manna and Subsisted. Also Continuing to know that God will work thing out for my-self and LC and our love ones In Jesus Christ

Name and my God Amen

October 3

God's Got Your Back

*"When God rose up to establish judgment,
to save all the oppressed of the earth."*

PSALM 76:9

Today's Prayer

Holy One, I am thankful that you care about what life is like in my skin. You know what it means to be dehumanized, despised, and denied opportunity. I thank you that you have not left me to endure my burden alone. You are with me and will deliver me from those who seek to abuse me. You will rise to ensure justice in my life. In Jesus' name, amen.

Today's Reflection

For all of us, who have been abused, forced to suffer in silence, know that God is watching. For all of us, who endure injustice daily, know that God is watching. For all of us, who have been exploited by those that have more wealth or power than we do, know that God is watching. For all of us, who have had limits placed on our potential because of our skin color or complexion, because of our gender or native tongue, know that God is watching. Not only is God watching, but our Lord will rise up to establish justice, to save all the oppressed of the earth. The awesome God of heaven has got your back.

Today's Song: "I Must Tell Jesus," #183.

Journal Notes *It's Wonderful to know that I have my Father, my God, my Angel and Christ Jesus, w/ The Holly spirit is Watching over me. I do need help in letting my temptation get the Best of my Life.*

In Gods Na and In Christ Jesu nome and the Holly spirit

October 4

Read Already

God's Justice

"I will punish the world for its evil,
and the wicked for their iniquity."

ISAIAH 13:11a

Today's Prayer

Holy One, I thank you that you care for how I am treated. You will not tolerate the abuse, disrespect, or disenfranchisement of your servants. I recommit myself to uplifting and not down-pressing my brothers and sisters, for the sake of your kingdom. Through your power, I will seek to make righteousness more than a matter of personal piety, but a matter of justice for all of humanity. In Jesus' name, amen.

Today's Reflection

Every now and then it is important to remember that the Lord will not tolerate injustice. Isaiah spoke the Lord's angry words not only against Babylon, but also against "the world for its evil, and the wicked for their iniquity." If we look carefully, we will see that the evil that provoked the Lord's wrath was the abuse of the poor by the powerful (verses 2, 11).

This is an important reminder because today Christianity often is portrayed as either a matter of morality or of personal piety. Yet the nature of our relationships with our brothers and sisters does not escape the Lord's watchful eye. It is good to have a God that cares about every aspect of our lives, including how we are treated.

Today's Song: "My Lord, What a Morning," #40

Journal Notes Very wonderful that God is always in my corner. How I'm blessed each day w/ his presance. I pray that I can put all my mischief behind me, and pray, Live, forgive, Respect, Love and prosper with the understand that God will always Be there once I do my part.

October 5

Who Can Accept It?

When many of his disciples heard it, they said,
"This teaching is difficult; who can accept it?"
JOHN 6:60-61

Today's Prayer

Holy One, I acknowledge that you are beyond my understanding. Your ways are so far beyond me that I can not hope to comprehend them. But I trust in you, that you are able to do what seems impossible in my sight. For Christ's sake, amen.

Today's Reflection

Jesus' words are often hard to understand and difficult to take. That is the nature of the gospel. After all, we profess a faith that requires us to eat the flesh and drink the blood of our founder, to love those who hate us, to pray for our enemies, to turn the other cheek, and to believe that all things—even the most inconceivable things are possible. These instructions defy human comprehension, forcing us to accept them solely by faith.

But if we look back over our lives, I am sure that we each can testify about the seemingly implausible blessings God has granted for us. Because we have access to God, who can raise the dead, why should we be limited to thinking in terms of what is humanly possible. As we go into the world today, let us live as if the implausible is possible because we have faith in a God who defies human reason.

Today's Song: "Let Us Break Bread Together," #123

Journal Notes Opening ones mind to believing that any thing is possible with God. I need to stay strong in faith with Gods health. begin to open any thought act, posibilitie that God and his son Jesus can make happend. Amen

October 6

An Ally among Adversaries

*"But a Pharisee in the council named Gamaliel, a teacher of
the law, respected by all the people, stood up and ordered
the men to be put outside for a short time."*
ACTS 5:34

Today's Prayer

Holy One, I am thankful that I can depend on you to provide a way of escape in my time of trouble. As I go forth today, help me to be bold in my witness regardless of the consequences. If I meet opposition from those opposed to your will, raise up a Gamaliel to speak a wise word on my behalf. In Christ's name, amen.

Today's Reflection

In Acts 5, Peter and the apostles were facing likely death at the hands of the Sanhedrin for preaching the gospel of Jesus Christ. It is at that moment that Gamaliel, the Pharisee who taught the apostle Paul (Acts 22:3), rose to intercede on behalf of the imperiled followers of Jesus. God used Gamaliel's wise words to convince the Sanhedrin to deal leniently with the apostles.

We can learn from the apostles' boldness as they spoke God's word without regard for their own lives. Their faith made them vulnerable, but their God shielded them from harm. The Lord raised up a Gamaliel to say a wise word and intercede on their behalf. Do not fear what the world can do to you because you have taken a stand for Christ, for God will raise up a Gamaliel in your life when the odds seem stacked against you, too.

Today's Song: "Lift Him Up," #227

Journal Notes Don't be afraid of things that raise up and odds stacked against me. God is there even when there seem to be little hope left in myself, but I must be strong to conquer these accurances with God and His Son Jesus Christ and the Holy spirit Amen.

October 7

Be an Example

*"Let no one despise your youth, but set the believers an example
in speech and conduct, in love, in faith, in purity."*
1 TIMOTHY 4:12

Today's Prayer

Holy One, I thank you for examples of Christian living. You set in my life models of Spirit-filled living that I followed to your cross, and I found salvation. Help me to be an example, too, so that some lost soul can see in me the light of your love, and follow it home. For Christ's sake. Amen.

Today's Reflection

I am struck by how frequently I hear that our young people lack positive role models. In our passage, the apostle challenged Timothy to be "an example in speech and conduct, in love, in faith, in purity." By this he would save himself and others.

As Christians, we have been called to set the standard by allowing Christ to live in us. In this way, the Christ in us will define righteous living for the world, and people young and not-so-young can see our speech, conduct, love, faith, and purity shining like a beacon. By this we may be coworkers with Christ saving the many daughters and sons of our community who are lost because they never saw anyone living for Christ. Let the life you live have an impact on others.

Today's Song: "Have You Got Good Religion?" #113

Journal Notes Must Apply myself better so I may be a good inspiration for God my father Christ Jesus, and Holy spirit, and The people or youth that is lost, With God's help I can achiev This Amen!

October 8

Love a Stranger Today

"You shall love the stranger."
DEUTERONOMY 10:19

Today's Prayer

Dear Lord, on my job, in my home, and at church help me to love people who are strangers to me. Amen.

Today's Reflection

Let's think back to the last time we were in a business meeting or church conference when people were discussing the bad background, wardrobe, speech, traditions, food, or hairstyles of a new person in the group. Are these discussions of God? Today, thousands of people have starved to death from malnutrition in the world. Thousands have been raped, tortured, or mutilated. Does God really care about clothing, hairstyles, and tradition?

Like the Israelites, we were once strangers in this land. We know either personally or through our ancestors how damaging it is to be excluded or criticized for being different. If we look to the life of Jesus, we find that love does not try to re-create another person that God has already fashioned in a unique way. Love accepts the variety that is humankind. Each flower is differently clothed and dances differently in the spring wind. Likewise, each human being is different. Let us strive to love humans who are strange to us.

Today's Song: "Lord, I Want to Be a Christian," #234

Journal Notes _____

_____

_____

_____

October 9

Living with Destruction

*". . . he left no one remaining, but utterly destroyed all that
breathed as the LORD God of Israel commanded."*

JOSHUA 10:40

Today's Prayer

Help me, Lord. I do not understand the destructive forces in this world, or why
you have allowed them. Amen.

Today's Reflection

How could Joshua do this? How could a loving God allow Joshua (and later
David) to kill like this? We should beware of easy answers. There are none. However,
it may help to note that the Bible does not prohibit killing. The Old Testament is
in Hebrew, and the Hebrew terms for *kill* and *murder* are different. The Sixth
Commandment is literally, "You shall not murder."

This does not answer any questions about under what circumstances killing may
be justified. What all this means is that there is no basis for using Scripture to argue
that *murder* and *killing* are always the same. The Bible says that only God can weigh
a person's heart. Beyond recognizing the difference between murder and killing,
there is not a whole lot we can say with certainty about these issues except this . . .
when it comes to malice, Jesus taught us a more excellent way.

Today's Song: "Give Me a Clean Heart," #216

Journal Notes _____

_____

_____

_____

October 10

God Is Transforming Our Grief

And I say, "It is my grief that the
right hand of the Most High has changed."
PSALM 77:10

Today's Prayer

Dear God, in the day of trouble I stretch my hand out to you. Amen.

Today's Reflection

The psalmist is struggling with an issue that causes nighttime agony. Sleep escapes the psalmist, and no comfort is found (77:2). Eventually, however, the psalmist's mourning and agony is transformed to rejoicing.

A transformation like this does not happen overnight. Yet be assured, when we struggle in the nighttime, a change will come. In sad times, it is tempting to think only of all the sad things in the past and present, but the psalmist takes the time to reflect upon what God has already done. At that moment. the psalmist recognizes that the Most High has changed grief to joy in the past—it will be done again. In hard times, recount the good deeds of God in your life.

Today's Song: "There Is a Balm in Gilead," #185

Journal Notes _____

_____

_____

_____

None Can Change God's Plan

"For the LORD *of Hosts has planned, and who will annul it?*
His hand is stretched out, and who will turn it back?"
ISAIAH 24:27

Today's Prayer

O Holy One of Israel, you showed me your way. You gave me a vision. Grant me, O God, the faith to trust that you will fulfill all that you have led me to do and be. Amen.

Today's Reflection

Isaiah is speaking to the Israelites during a period of oppression by the Assyrians. The prophet promises that deliverance is on the way because God has planned it. These words are meant to encourage those in captivity, and they has meaning for us today also.

Whatever the situation in your life, be assured that if God has planned deliverance, no boss, no spouse, no friend, no pastor, no prison guard, and no politician can turn it back.

Today's Song: "How Lovely on the Mountains," #99

Journal Notes _____

_____

_____

_____

Staying Strong in the Faith

"Do not judge by appearances, but judge with right judgment."
JOHN 7:24

Today's Prayer

Lord God, help me to remember that you do not judge as humans judge. I may not act like other Christians, but I love you just as much. Amen.

Today's Reflection

In the book of John we find some of the harshest criticisms of Jesus' ministry. Specifically, in chapter 7 we see that people had big doubts about Jesus' claims to be the Messiah. Have you ever noticed how people of the same faith question each other about claims to the faith. Remember, Jesus was a Jew being challenged by Jewish brothers and sisters. Modern-day Christians do this, too. You know the familiar refrain: "He is not saved" or "She is not saved."

The temptation to judge by appearances is great. Sometimes you may be judged because you drink socially; sometimes you may be judged because you wear make-up; sometimes you may be judged because you missed a few Sundays of church. Whatever the case may be, don't take these criticisms to heart. Your refusal to make faith decisions based on legalistic attitudes is in keeping with Jesus' way. Stay strong in your faith. God does not judge by appearances, and Jesus is instructing us not to judge by appearances either.

Today's Song: "I, the Lord of Sea and Sky," #230

Journal Notes _____

_____

_____

_____

The Importance of Waiting on Tables

*"It is not right that we should neglect the word of God
in order to wait on tables."*

ACTS 6:2

Today's Prayer

Lord God, please help me to appreciate the importance of different kinds of service to your kingdom. Amen.

Today's Reflection

In this passage, we learn that the apostles were unable to fulfill their duty to the widows while making sure the gospel was preached at the same time. They needed help. So seven men were chosen to assist them.

The body of Christ is made up of people with different gifts who help the whole body function well. Without those who preach, those who wait on tables would be serving in vain. And without those who wait on tables, those who preach would look like hypocrites because the Word would go forth, but the "weightier matters" would be neglected. Your gifts are important to the body, whether waiting tables or preaching, keep on serving!

Today's Song: "Let Us Talents and Tongues Employ," #232

Journal Notes _____

_____

_____

_____

October 14

Keeping Ourselves Pure

". . . and do not participate in the sins of others;
keep yourself pure."
1 TIMOTHY 5:22

Today's Prayer

Dear God, wash me, purify me this day from my sins. May I never take your Grace for granted. Amen.

Today's Reflection

In the book of 1 Timothy, Paul or one of his disciples, is laying out practical guidelines for believing communities. The key verse today encourages us not to be caught up in the sinful behavior of others, and to keep ourselves right in the sight of God.

We are often tempted to do what others are doing. Some Christians are temporarily lost. They make excuses and they try to convince us that a sin is not sin at all. The Bible instructs us to keep ourselves pure. This means that people who are not healthy influences on us will have to be removed from our inner lives, at least for a while, until we are strong enough to influence them. This is one of many ways to keep ourselves pure. It does not mean we are condemning anyone, we are simply doing our best to please God.

Today's Song: "Would You Be Free," #76

Journal Notes _____

_____

_____

_____

A Godly Conversation

*"Teach them to your children, talking about them
when you are at home and when you are away,
when you lie down and when you rise."*

DEUTERONOMY 11:19

Today's Prayer

Giver of the Holy Word, I thank you today for the blessing of your promises, your teachings, and your commandments. You speak to me so that I will know that you love me and that you want to guide me along life's pathways. Open my heart more fully to your word, so that I may both hear your voice and do your will throughout this day. Amen.

Today's Reflection

Too much small talk is not a good thing. Too much chatter results in worthless conversations. Today, I am determined to elevate my conversations. Today, I will be careful as I use my voice. Today, I will open God's word and listen to what God is saying to me. When I do speak, my words will reflect something good and true that I have heard from the Lord. Today, my words will be a blessing.

Today's Song: "In My Life, Lord, Be Glorified," #248

Journal Notes _____

_____

_____

_____

October 16

A Place of Mercy

Say to the Israelites, "Appoint the cities of refuge,
of which I spoke to you through Moses."
JOSHUA 20:2

Today's Prayer

God of Justice, in your wisdom you continue to teach me how to be merciful. Forgive the unfair judgments that I have made toward people in my life. Continue to challenge me with the stories of how your grace has entered the world. Show me today what I must do in my community to show your love. Amen.

Today's Reflection

How surprised I am to learn that God has always set apart places of protection for people who need to escape from those who seek revenge. God's justice is very different from the emotional rage of hurting human hearts. Today I examine my own life, thanking God for the safe places that were available to me when I did wrong to others, and praying that I might show the same kind of mercy to someone I find in need.

Today's Song: "God Forgave My Sin in Jesus' Name," #187

Journal Notes _____

_____

_____

_____

October 17

All Things Are Possible

*"O that my people would listen to me,
that Israel would walk in my ways!"*
PSALM 81:13

Today's Prayer

God of Infinite Power, all things are possible through you. Forgive my stubborn resistance to your invitation to me to live a new life. I am overwhelmed by your patient love. Fill me with a strong desire to know you and love you more deeply and to serve you more completely. Give me ears to hear your voice and a will to go wherever your Spirit is leading me today. Amen.

Today's Reflection

When the word of God tells me about my potential, my response is often unsure and confused. Nevertheless, God keeps pleading with me to trust the words of scripture that tell me who I really am and what I can become. I am challenged even more to believe in my community's potential. Today, no matter what the television and newspapers say, I will rejoice in God's assurance that if my people would only follow where God wants to lead us, we would find peace and joy and true greatness beyond our wildest dreams.

Today's Song: "Where Charity and Love Prevail," #84

Journal Notes _____

_____

_____

_____

Getting through the Bad Times

"In the streets they bind on sackcloth; on the housetops and in the squares everyone wails and melts in tears."
ISAIAH 15:3

Today's Prayer

God of Consolation, you remain present with me when times are good and when they are bad. Sometimes I feel discouraged, and I think that all my faith and hope is in vain. Thank you for the refreshment of your Holy Spirit that comforts me and restores my soul. Give me the strength today to comfort those around me who are sad and in despair. Use me to remind them of your faithfulness. Amen.

Today's Reflection

I cannot live in denial of life's suffering. Nothing can remove the reality of pain, destruction, and violence in the world. Even Jesus could not escape the hard and difficult days of his own suffering, humiliation, and death. Perhaps I have the opportunity today to reach out to someone who is going through bad times. I believe that when burdens are shared, they do become lighter. May God use me to bring comfort to someone who is hurting.

Today's Song: "Guide My Feet," #153

Journal Notes _____

_____

_____

_____

October 19

If Everyone Followed Me

*"Let anyone among you who is without sin
be the first to throw a stone at her."*
JOHN 8:7

Today's Prayer

Gracious God, I praise you today for the power of your love in my life. You know all of my faults and failures, yet you continue to reach out to me and call me your own. You reveal the depth of your love in so many ways. Give me a thankful heart today, and make me willing to extend the love I have found in you into the lives of people everywhere. Amen.

Today's Reflection

If everyone followed me, would the world be a better place? There is so much power in this question. It forces me to stop all of my casual criticism of people who live in the public eye, scrutinized constantly by the media, and easily condemned when they make mistakes. God reminds me today to be careful with my condemnations of others. If everyone followed me, would we all throw stones, or would we all show more love toward those who need it most?

Today's Song: "Oh, How He Loves You and Me," #82

Journal Notes _____

_____

_____

_____

The Gift of Leaders

*"God will raise up a prophet for you from your
own people as he raised me up."*

ACTS 7:37

Today's Prayer

God of Divine Inspiration, you are the source of every good and perfect gift. I praise you today for the gift of leaders made know in every generation. I remember with thanksgiving the great women and men you called upon in days past and filled with wisdom and courage. Give me the wisdom to appreciate and support the leaders of today who are instruments of your justice and your peace. Amen.

Today's Reflection

Who are the modern prophets? Where are the true leaders? I must never let the news media answer this question for me. I must not allow gossip and reckless speculation to confuse and mislead me. God has promised to keep lifting up ordinary people to do extraordinary things, people who are moved to speak and act with courage and wisdom and faith. The prophets are here. Today I am determined to recognize some of them and respond to their word from the Lord.

Today's Song: "When Israel Was in Egypt's Land," #87

Journal Notes _____

_____

_____

_____

Doing the Best that I Can Do

*"For we brought nothing into the world,
so that we can take nothing out of it."*
1 TIMOTHY 6:7

Today's Prayer

God of beginnings and endings, you are both the path that I walk and the destination that I seek. You surround me with the gifts of your presence. Give me the wisdom today to recognize the work that you have called me to accomplish this day. Let me be neither foolish nor fearful, but rather encourage my spirit so that I will use my life to honor you and serve my community with all that I am and all that I have. Amen.

Today's Reflection

Why am I here? What does God want me to do with my time and talents and possessions? What I have is not who I am. I am a child of God with a divine destiny to fulfill. If I am too concerned about the material things that I desire or already own, I will never turn my attention toward the mystery of God's purpose for my life. Today, I will seek to better understand that divine purpose, so that I will do the best that I can do with this precious gift called life.

Today's Song: "Have Thine Own Way, Lord," #152

Journal Notes _____

_____

_____

_____

October 22

Being in the House

" . . . but as for me and my household, we will serve the Lord."
JOSHUA 24:15b

Today's Prayer

Lord, help me to be quick to confess and model my faith. Help me to stand true to my convictions so that I will not hesitate to be counted among those who are in the "house" serving you. Amen.

Today's Reflection

When it is time to make most decisions, there often are competing factors to consider. Most choices involve complex components and multi-dimensional consequences, so it is not easy to choose.

When making decisions, we want to serve God, but we forget to align ourselves with God's purposes. We want to experience God's blessings, but we find it hard to obey God's command. However, we can find courage and strength in the testimonies of our elders and leaders who have already decided to serve God. Often the answers to some choices are discerned in our relationship with others.

Today's Song: "I Surrender All," #235

Journal Notes _____

_____

_____

_____

A Lost Generation

*"Moreover, that whole generation was gathered to their ancestors,
and another generation grew up after them, who did not know
the LORD or the work that he had done for Israel."*
JUDGES 2:10

Today's Prayer

Lord of ages past, I thank you for my foreparents who knew you. I thank you that you have already been present and active in the lives of those who came before me. Your history with them reminds me of my future with you. Help me to know and celebrate the great exploits that you accomplished through them. Help me to embrace their story as my own. Amen.

Today's Reflection

When we are surrounded by so many new innovations and technological advancements, the challenge is for us to truly appreciate the past, even as we envision the future. However, we sometimes forget that the energy that it took to achieve those accomplishments is the same devotion it takes to succeed in the future. Our knowledge of the past ensures our destiny. Hence, we are called to tell our trials and triumphs to future generations so that they might continue to know God.

Today's Song: "Bind Us Together, Lord," #217

Journal Notes _____

_____

_____

_____

Connected

*But Hannah answered, "No, my Lord, I am a woman
deeply troubled; I have drunk neither wine nor strong drink,
but I have been pouring out my soul before the Lord."*
1 SAMUEL 1:15

Today's Prayer

God, when I cry out to you from the depths of my being, please hear me. When words cannot express my anguish, disappointment, or even my dreams, hear the moans of my soul and answer me. Please surround me with people who understand me, and can support me in my pursuit of you. Amen.

Today's Reflection

It is no secret that desperate situations demand that we try some different tactics or techniques. When we cannot seem to get our needs met or our desires fulfilled, we can be propelled in a prayer whose intensity resembles the inebriation of others. So focused are we that our circumstances numb us to any other agenda. In fact, onlookers can confuse our devotion with fanaticism or error. But we must be careful to remember that God does honor our consistent supplication. God honors the prayers that ring from our soul.

Today's Song: "For All the Faithful Women," #219

Journal Notes _____

_____

_____

_____

October 25

A Spoken Word

"O God, do not keep silence; do not hold your peace or be still
O God . . . Let them know that you alone whose name is
the Lord, are the Most High over all the earth."

PSALM 83:1, 18

Today's Prayer

When I need you to speak, Lord, let your will and way be made known. Do not let my enemies or the nay-sayers make a mockery of you. Be glorified among them. Amen.

Today's Reflection

Every now and again, we desperately desire to see the power and majesty of God. We want God to openly confirm God's promises and plans for us. We need to be personally reminded that our God is the only true deity. We are afraid that God cannot be trusted. We don't want others to think too lowly of our God; we want non-believers to know that God is the Most High. So when God seems silent, we can begin to doubt God's ability is as if we think that God must prove God's worth to us.

Today's Song: "How Lovely on the Mountains," #99

Journal Notes _____

_____

_____

_____

October 26

On Turning Back

*"Because of this many of his disciples turned back
and no longer went about with him."*
JOHN 9:66

Today's Prayer

Lord, your words give my life meaning and direction. Help me to continue to follow you, even when your words are challenging and not easily understood. When I don't understand you, please help me to still follow you. When I want to turn back, help me to continue on the journey. Amen.

Today's Reflection

It is easy to go along with people when they say what we want and do what we expect. Yes, we find comfort when things go our way. But there are moments when God says a thing that challenges all that we have known. There are times when the voice of Jesus does not utter calming affirmation but challenging declaration instead. And we want to give up or give in. It becomes a lot of work for us to believe, to trust, to act. However, those who stay with Jesus, hear the words of eternal life.

Today's Song: "Will Your Anchor Hold," #255

Journal Notes _____

_____

_____

_____

Scattered Saints

*"Now those who were scattered went from place
to place, proclaiming the word."*
ACTS 8:4

Today's Prayer

Thank you for the many places and times that you allow me to share your good news. Help me to notice the opportunities that you create for me to give witness to how good you have been in my life. Give me strength and wisdom so that wherever I go, I show you to others. Amen.

Today's Reflection

Familiar places and people bring comfort to our lives. When we are among that which we know, we do not have to stretch or to grow. We can remain the same. But not only do we fail to mature, but also our effectiveness does not expand. It is often along the scattered places that we develop new skills, and perfect former gifts. If we find ourselves off the beaten path, it may be that God has sent us there so that we can impact others and so that we ourselves can grow.

Today's Song: "Let Us Talents and Tongues Employ," #232

Journal Notes _____

_____

_____

_____

October 28

On Being Ordinary

*"In a large house there are utensils not only of gold and silver
but also of wood and clay, some for special use, some for ordinary."*
2 TIMOTHY 2:20

Today's Prayer

Lord, I thank you that you don't require me to be anyone except myself. I praise you that you have a plan and purpose for my life that is not dependent on what others are doing. When I am frustrated or discouraged, please remind me that you use ordinary people for special projects. Amen.

Today's Reflection

It is often natural for us to gaze upon those people who are superstars or public spokespeople. Regretfully, their lives of glamour and privilege seem to become our secret aspirations. But the biblical record suggests that value is ascribed by our willingness to be used by God, regardless of our station in life. God has a purpose for what seems ordinary. Our obedience to God can change the ordinary into the extraordinary.

Today's Song: "I'm So Glad Jesus Lifted Me," #191

Journal Notes _____

_____

_____

_____

October 29

Doing Our Job

*"And they were left to the Israelites to see whether they
would obey the LORD's commandments."*
JUDGES 3:4

Today's Prayer

Dear Lord, forgive me for those times I've taken the easy way out. Please forgive the times I did not love my neighbor as myself, the times I horded my abundance and ignored those who were hungry and wanting, the times I was too busy to offer you praise. I want to be worthy. Help me walk in your commands this day. Amen.

Today's Reflection

We are constantly challenged. God provides us with challenges so we have the opportunity to grow both personally and spiritually. What challenge is in your life? What part of you is being tested? Is it possible that God has placed this challenge in your path to show you where you're not following what God mandates?

The good news is we serve a God of second, third, or even chances that number 70 times 7—that's how much we are loved. Each day the Lord provides is a chance to begin again.

Today's Song: "I Will Trust in the Lord," #256

Journal Notes _____

_____

_____

_____

Even the Children

"But Samuel ministered before the Lord, *even as a child."*
1 SAMUEL 2:18

Today's Prayer

Precious Lord, I thank you for our children. I thank you for sons, daughters, nieces, nephews, cousins, and grandchildren. I thank you for their innocence, their possibility, their energy, their questions, and their outrageous answers, for they are truly a gift from above. Give me the vision to see them as ones fit and capable to serve you. Amen.

Today's Reflection

It was a corrupt time. Eli was a priest and judge of Israel for 40 years, even his own sons abused their power and were immoral. Eli himself could not stop this. The hope emerged from a boy in Eli's house, Samuel, whose mother had dedicated him to God and he grew to be one Israel's greatest judges. What mighty deeds could be achieved is we dedicated more of our children to God's service?

Today's Song: "Jesus Loves Me," #249

Journal Notes _____

_____

_____

_____

Grace-filled Wait

"The LORD will give grace and glory;
no good thing will be withheld from them
that walk uprightly."
PSALM 84:11

Today's Prayer

God of all creation, you are with me when I don't even know it. You care for me when I have no concern for myself. You love me, even in those times I don't deserve it. Keep me focused on honoring your commands, and trusting your promise. In Christ's name, I pray. Amen.

Today's Reflection

We live in perilous times, corporate downsizing, family break-ups, and handgun violence. The Israelites also lived in perilous times. They were threatened many times by military attack, but they were delivered time and time again. They experienced firsthand the joy of living in the presence and under the protection of God. God required of them, what is required of you. Walk upright, act justly, love mercy, and in doing so honoring God. Do this with the assurance that no good thing will be withheld from you.

Today's Song: "Halle, Halle, Hallelujah," #25

Journal Notes _____

_____

_____

_____

November 1

Misplaced Malignant Anger

"Whom have you reproached and blasphemed,
against who have you raised your voices . . .
against the Holy One of Israel."
ISAIAH 37:23

Today's Prayer

Most merciful, most gracious God, I come today asking for strength to stand for righteousness, for power to be a voice for the voiceless. Fortify me, Lord. Empower me to stand, to do your will, for how will they know your works, your will, your promises if I don't witness for you. This I can do with God's help. Amen.

Today's Reflection

The early Christians were persecuted, and even today we may face persecution when we stand for what God requires of us. Sometimes when we are under attack, it is not about us, but about the God we serve. If you risk standing against racism, classism, sexism, or homophobia, you may find yourself under attack. Know today, that being on the side of God may make you a target, but God has your back.

Today's Song: "Some Folk Would Rather Have Houses," #236

Journal Notes _____

_____

_____

_____

Trusting God

*"I am the good Shepherd, the good Shepherd
lays down his life for his sheep."*
JOHN 10:1-21

Today's Prayer

Recite Psalm 23:1:4:

"The LORD is my shepherd, I shall not want. He makes me lie down in green pastures; he leads me beside still waters; he restores my soul. He leads me in paths of righteousness for his name's sake. Even thou I walk through the valley of the shadow of death, I will fear not evil." Amen.

Today's Reflection

We need not move in the spirit of fear. Know that we operate under God's protection. What dark places are you walking through? What enemy is constantly lurking—loneliness, depression, jealously, financial lack, or family strife? Trust God. There is no place, no circumstance where God is not. Remember today where God has brought you. Remember today the holy price paid for you.

Today's Song: "I Believe I'll Testify," #225

Journal Notes _____

_____

_____

_____

November 3

With God's Guidance

He replied, "How can I, unless someone guides me?"
ACTS 8:31

Today's Prayer

Thank you, God, for sending those into my life that led me to you. Help me to offer that encouragement and guidance to another. Open my eyes to all the gifts of opportunity to be helpful to others. Turn me from indifference to faithfulness. I enlist myself this day, to be a source of hope to all those I meet. This I can do with your help. Amen.

Today's Reflection

Think about where God has placed you. So often we think teaching is for educators, healing is for doctors, and preaching is for pastors and deacons. Consider today where God has placed you to give a word of encouragement, a healing embrace, or to set a Christian example. We all are equipped to uniquely serve God. We all can help guide another to the correct path.

Today's Song: "Lead Me, Guide Me," #70

Journal Notes _____

_____

_____

_____

Daring to Share

*"And the things that you have heard from me among
many witnesses, commit those to faithful people who will
be able to teach others also."*

2 TIMOTHY 2:2

Today's Prayer

Lord, I praise you. Lord, I thank you for all you've done in my life. Grant me the courage to tell how good you've been to me. Give me the words and a triumphant spirit that I may be a witness for you. Today my constant prayer is that the "words of my mouth and the meditation of my heart be acceptable to thee." In Christ I pray. Amen.

Today's Reflection

Paul provides a biblical description of mentoring in 2 Timothy 2. Paul helped Timothy develop, and then challenged Timothy to go and do the same for others. This is a biblical mandate that each one teach one. Find someone today who would welcome your knowledge and expertise. Dare to share yourself with someone. If we join forces as a community passing on our life's lessons, we will all gain.

Today's Song: "Just a Closer Walk with Thee," #253

Journal Notes _____

_____

_____

_____

A Womanist in a Time of Wonder

"At that time Deborah, a prophetess,
wife of Lappidoth, was judging Israel."
JUDGES 4:4

Today's Prayer

Blessed Lord, give me the insight to understand the difficult things in human behavior. Amen.

Today's Reflection

This text in Judges raises some very difficult questions for the modern reader. The words tell of a violent clash and brutal death. They evoke feelings of dismay and horror. Some, in modernity, struggle with human violence. Whether through interpersonal relationships or state-condoned executions, our inclination is that violence toward one another is not condoned by God. But the cruel oppression of King Jabin was met with surprising leadership from an unlikely sector of the Israelite community. This "good news/bad news" narrative illustrates that God chose to use women in this decisive battle in the early stages of development of the faith community. Regardless of gender, God will use those who are willing and able to serve, even if the task is unpleasant.

Today's Song: "Pass Me Not, O Gentle Savior," #150

Journal Notes _____

_____

_____

_____

Growing Up with God

"As Samuel grew up, the LORD was with him and let
none of his words fall to the ground."
1 SAMUEL 3:19

Today's Prayer

Lord, let your words, your ways, and your will guide and shape my life. Amen.

Today's Reflection

There was a sign in a common work area that indicated that change will happen your involvement is up to you. The reality of this sign was like blunt force trauma to my soul. I knew it was true. At the same time I resented the implications of my powerlessness. The narrative in this chapter of 1 Samuel offers some insight as to how Eli and Samuel made adjustments to life's every changing ebb and flow. God is not to be taken lightly trust God to lead you through the changes that life presents.

Today's Song: "I, the Lord of Sea and Sky," #230

Journal Notes _____

_____

_____

_____

November 7

Vector of Justice

"Faithfulness will spring up from the ground,
and righteousness will look down from the sky."
PSALM 85:11

Today's Prayer

God of the universe, help me in my human frailty to understand your divine ways. Amen.

Today's Reflection

Metaphor, allegory, simile, and parable are manners of speech or writing that give boundaries to the expression of ideas that the speaker or writer might use in an effort to give clarity in expression. Like the author of this psalm, we often look to the past works of God in our lives to make sense of our present situation. We have pleas and questions that rest in the hope of what God will do for us. It is the nature of God to be faithful, righteous, and steadfast in love. When humans share in the desires of God to be holy, there will be righteousness. In other words, when the human agenda follows God's divine will then, "Faithfulness will spring up from the ground, and righteousness will look down from the sky." This is a blessing waiting to happen.

Today's Song: "O Lord, Let Us See Your Kindness," #8

Journal Notes _____

_____

_____

_____

November 8

Holy Renewal

"But those who wait for the Lord shall renew their strength,
they shall mount up with wings like eagles, they shall run and not
be weary, they shall walk and not faint."

ISAIAH 40:31

Today's Prayer

Holy One, help me to lift up my eyes and see what you would reveal to me. And help me to receive your revelation. Amen.

Today's Reflection

During my early years of college I had a professor who said, "You will have to pay for your education." At that time, I thought that it was a message that pertained to tuition, books, and other fees. However, as life moved on and I matured, I realized this certainty applied to all that life had to disclose about the pleasant and unpleasant experiences of human existence. The ways of the world reveal that human rights and justice are often times disregarded. Power and privilege would appear to go hand in hand. However, Isaiah invites us to know that God is in control and what happens to us is not hidden from God. It is the nature of God to be just and knowing "he brings princes to naught and makes the rulers of the earth as nothing." The knowledge that God is just and powerful should empower us when we feel faint and powerless. Rest in the knowledge that God is just.

Today's Song: "His Eye Is on the Sparrow," #252

Journal Notes

November 9

Knowing the Right Voice

"My sheep hear my voice. I know them and they follow me."
JOHN 10:27

Today's Prayer

Lord, continue to speak to me so that in times of silence I will not go astray. Amen.

Today's Reflection

In a world of mass communication, television, and the Internet, there are competing voices that want to get your attention. They want to sell you on an idea. They want to lead you in a direction that they have chosen. This direction or path that has been designed and planned for you is most likely to suit the interest of those who are calling you to follow it. Hearing the voice of Jesus is not always easy. As a matter of fact, the competing voices can make it rather hard. Love, devotion and desire to please are very powerful attributes. Jesus knows that those who love, and desire to please God will hear his voice. They will recognize the family resemblance through words of love and deeds of power in their lives. This is God's path, and it has our best interest at heart.

Today's Song: "Savior, Like a Shepherd Lead Us," #254

Journal Notes _____

_____

_____

_____

A Chosen Instrument

But the Lord said to him, "Go, for he is an instrument whom
I have chosen to bring my name before Gentiles and
kings and before the people of Israel."
ACTS 9:15

Today's Prayer

Oh Lord, guide me in understanding that your ways are not the ways of human beings and your choices are designed to magnify your name and power to change the human heart. Amen.

Today's Reflection

The Lord continues to use the divine model of decision making to demonstrate and encourage humanity to believe. Paul's experiences, through the Lord's designs, within this chapter of Acts are beyond the comprehension of Paul and the members of the newfound Church. God chose the most unlikely character to carry out the divine agenda. This model is very similar to God's call on Moses life in the book of Exodus. These are clear illustrations that God does not adhere to human standards or qualifications to chose useful vessels for God's purpose. Be encouraged. If the Lord can use Paul who once persecuted the Church, then the Lord most certainly has use for us.

Today's Song: "God Forgave My Sin in Jesus' Name," #187

Journal Notes _____

_____

_____

_____

Pain and Reward

*"Indeed, all who want to live a godly life in
Christ Jesus will be persecuted."*
2 TIMOTHY. 3:12

Today's Prayer

Lord, in the name of Jesus I pray that you would allow my form of godliness to be a true reflection of your Holy Spirit that indwells in my heart and mind. Amen.

Today's Reflection

We often hear conversations that talk about the "last days." The words within this text will alert the perceptive, analytical Christian that he or she inhabits a world wherein many unflattering characteristics of human behavior are prevalent. Peer pressure and consensus are integral parts of our society. Paul reminds us that there are, other standards in place that we can look to in order to cope. The realization that suffering is often times part of Christianity does not appeal to our modern sensibilities. Nonetheless, there will come times when we will have to take an unpopular stand against consensus because of our faith. Know that God is with you for it was anticipated long ago.

Today's Song: "I, the Lord of Sea and Sky," #230

Journal Notes _____

_____

_____

_____

Serve God

"When the people offer themselves willingly."
JUDGES 5:2

Today's Prayer

Ever-present God, you have waited patiently on me to come into the knowledge of you. I surrender all to you. I ask that you help me to be as faithful to you as you have been to me. I love you and I thank you for your promise never to leave or forsake me. Amen.

Today's Reflection

It is amazing in the situations and circumstances where God can be found. Here we find God in the midst of a conflict. The people of God have tried God's patience and pressed on his last nerve by their disobedience and lack of faithfulness. In this case, however, the people obeyed God's directives through the prophet Deborah and went into battle. In the end, God gave them a victory. Life with God seems to work that way. While we are the people of God, we are not exempt from problems and may find ourselves in conflict. But if we are obedient and faithful to God, in the end we will get the victory.

Today's Song: "When Peace, Like a River," #194

Journal Notes _____

_____

_____

_____

November 13

When God Says Enough

"Why has the LORD put us to rout today before the Philistines?"
1 SAMUEL 4:3

Today's Prayer

Lord, forgive me for my sins, my selfishness, and my disobedience. Remember not my transgressions. Do not turn your face from me to take your Holy Spirit from me. I am sorry, and I ask you to give me a clean heart and to renew the right spirit within me. Amen.

Today's Reflection

The people of God had been living lives of peace. They even seemed pretty confident in themselves. However, they continued in religious and priestly disobedience against God's laws, the temple, and the offerings. Then they came under attack by the Philistines who were threatening to overtake the Israelites. The people of God seemed unaware of God's displeasure, and they immediately went out confidently to fight. But they lost the battle, along with the lives of 4,000 men. Then they cried out to the Lord, asking why he had let them lost the battle.

Isn't it just like us to blame others for our own predicaments? We seldom acknowledge the error of our own ways, the evil that we cause, or our own dishonor toward God. God can get our attention and make us reflect on our own actions—all the while staying close to us.

Today's Song: "Give Me a Clean Heart," #216

Journal Notes _____

_____

_____

_____

November 14

God Knows

"Have compassion on your servants."
PSALM 90:13

Today's Prayer

Most Merciful Creator, you have made all things great and small, including me. I have fallen short of your glory, Lord, but you know my heart and have mercy on me. Teach me your ways and fill me with your word. I thank you for the blessings you have given me, including those I have seen and those I have not seen. Amen.

Today's Reflection

When we think about the goodness of God in our lives, we should rejoice with a spirit of thanksgiving. Examining our lives with God shows us our own sinfulness and unworthiness. A life without God is a life without purpose, without wisdom, and without love, justice, and protection.

When looking at the characteristics of God, we are comforted in his unconditional and steadfast love. We can be intimate with God, who knows all about us. God doesn't hold grudges or keep lists of our wrong-doings. God is a God of equality and supplies us as we each have need.

Today's Song: "Blessed Assurance," #118

Journal Notes

November 15

Why You Can Smile

"Do not fear, for I am with you."
ISAIAH 41:10

Today's Prayer

Most powerful and all-knowing God, I thank you for your protection and for keeping me in your care. I am confident and trust in you. The situation in which I live is not hopeless, because you are here. And I am not helpless, because you have strengthened me in the truth of your being. With all of my love I praise your name. Amen.

Today's Reflection

Here we are permitted to observe a heroic trial. A trial in which Yahweh is up against the nations of the world with their gods. Yahweh has all power, whether they regard him or not. Then God assures Israel that they are chosen and will be saved. It is the same story repeated in our lives. The world is in a state of chaos. There are killings on all sides—parents killing children, and children killing parents. There are students killing teachers and teachers abusing students.

Everyone has someone to believe in—Yahweh, Jesus, Buddha, crystals, psychics, and themselves. But we who know God do not have to fear, for God is with us.

Today's Song: "I Can Hear My Savior Calling," #146

Journal Notes _____

_____

_____

_____

Walking in the Right Way

"I am the way, the truth, and the life."
JOHN 14:6

Today's Prayer

Heavenly Father, help me to grow in the knowledge of you and to get to know you better. Help me to follow your lead and to accept the abundant life you have so graciously provided to all believers. Amen.

Today's Reflection

We are all looking for the way to fulfillment. The journey, at times, appears to be an endlessly winding road filled with detours. Did you know that Jesus can provide the map that leads to the life we seek?

Jesus reveals the truth of who God really is in the life of people, and dispels the idea that God's holiness keeps God distant from us. Christ shows us that God is relational, personal, and near us.

Jesus tells us that he is the way to God, who is the giver, the provider, and the supplier of all of our needs. It is God who protects and keeps us. It is God who heals us from all infirmities. And it is God who sent us the Holy Spirit, who comforts and will never leave us.

Today's Song: "There's a Sweet, Sweet Spirit in This Place," #102

Journal Notes _____

_____

_____

_____

November 17

Defeating Discrimination

"I truly understand that God shows no partiality."
ACTS 10:34

Today's Prayer

Most loving God, creator of all things and of every good and perfect gift. My heart overflows with love and joy when I think about the grace and mercy you've shown me. I thank you for being a God of instruction and correction. I praise you for making me and loving me, just as I am. Amen.

Today's Reflection

The United States was founded on the principle of religious freedom. Even our money is imprinted with the words "In God We Trust." Yet this nation was built on prejudice as well. In our society, people experience prejudice because of their race, gender, sexual orientation, ethnicity, and economic and academic status. Prejudices can divide, demean, and destroy us.

Like Peter, many of us practiced prejudice as a basis of acceptable societal tradition. But God showed Peter that God shows no partiality. Everything God made good is good. Everything God made clean is clean.And we do not have authority to make it or call it any different. As children of the most High God, we are challenged not to go along to get along. We are empowered by the Holy Spirit to take a stand and to make a difference in our world.

Today's Song: "Satan, We're Going to Tear Your Kingdom Down," #207

Journal Notes _____

_____

_____

_____

If Called, Then Preach

"Preach the word, be urgent in season and out of season."
2 TIMOTHY 4

Today's Prayer

Heavenly Father, your love for me has helped me to share your word with those who are poverty-stricken, suffering from serious diseases like HIV and AIDS, beaten down by domestic violence, and hungering for righteousness. I thank you for the fire that burns in my soul to share the good news to all who would hear it. Amen.

Today's Reflection

As followers of Christ, we understand that our whole life is a high calling of God. We know firsthand that the Christian message builds self-esteem and unity. It gives hope, it offers encouragement, it embraces us with unconditional love as witnessed in Jesus Christ, the Word who became flesh and dwelled among us. It's a message that changes us, strengthens us, and prospers us. It's a message to share and to spread. It can transform the world in which we live.

Today's Song: "Go Tell It on the Mountain," #52

Journal Notes _____

_____

_____

_____

Trouble for God's People?

"But sir, if the LORD is with us,
why then has all this happened to us?"
JUDGES 6:13

Today's Prayer

God of all creation, please help my faith to grow. Help me to understand that human models of evaluating and measuring my relationship with you will not always work. You, O Lord, have seen all the past, present, and future of all life, while I sometimes struggle with my life alone. Be patient with me and teach me to be patient with others. Amen.

Today's Reflection

Gideon had to beat out the grains of wheat in concealment because the Midianites were oppressive adversaries. They used food deprivation as a method to control the Israelites growth and expansion. Gideon, like many of us, questioned the dissimilarity in the promises of the Lord and the reality of his situation. Interestingly enough, neither the angel nor the Lord ever focuses on the past. The only part of the past that was important was the community's covenant relationship with the Lord. The focus is on relationships, faith, obedience, and the future. The Lord's concern was moving on with the divine plan. Gideon had no idea of the role Israel would play in the history of the world. The Lord wanted to take Gideon and the community to places that were unimaginable.

Today's Song: "Precious Lord, Take My Hand," #193

Journal Notes

November 20

Falling Idols

*"When the people of Ashdod rose early on the next day, there was
Dagon, fallen on his face to the ground before the ark of the
Lord. So they took Dagon and put him back in his place."*

1 SAMUEL 5:3

Today's Prayer

Lord of heaven and of the earth, guide me through the snares of life. Allow me to focus on you continually. Help me to keep my priorities in order, with you always being first. Amen.

Today's Reflection

It has been said, "One's god is what one holds near and dear in their heart and relies on in times of trouble." In ancient Israel, the Ark of the Covenant was representative of the presence of the Lord. It is believed that it was a box that contained the Torah that Moses received on Mount Sinai. The elders of Israel had sought to use the Ark of the Covenant to ensure a victory. This was not the Lord's plan. It was of human origin and of human design. The Philistines captured the Ark of the Covenant in battle and housed it with Dagon, the human-made god of the Philistines. The end results were disastrous for the Philistines as well as for Israelites. The Lord refused to be used and manipulated by the human agenda and at the same time made it clear that there was no equating the presence of the Lord with a human-made god. This lesson was tough for the Philistines and for the Israelites. False gods will ultimately fall on their faces.

Today's Song: "In the Name of Jesus," #265

Journal Notes

_____

_____

_____

_____

November 21

Just Call Me

*"When they call to me, I will answer them; I will be with them
in trouble, I will rescue them and honor them."*

PSALM 91:15

Today's Prayer

Blessed Lord, I thank you for your promises, for the hope of a future even when
trouble surrounds me, for you are my God in whom I trust. Amen.

Today's Reflection

The psalmist begins this meditation by setting a set of parameters. It is a meditation of those who consider the Lord to be "My refuge and my fortress; my God, in
whom I trust." Many within our modern world are perplexed by such words of faith.
It challenges the very notion of "common sense" to place one's trust in someone
whom you cannot see, feel, touch, or smell. But faith in God does just that;
challenges the notion of physical and material resources as the only source of guidance and help! It takes a great deal of faith to pray to, and rely upon God. God
makes a statement about this kind of trust. "When they call to me I will answer
them; I will be with them in trouble." God does not say that trouble is not going
to come: as a matter of fact, it's implied that it will. God's promise is to be with us
during that time and pull us through it.

Today's Song: "Victory Is Mine," #266

Journal Notes _____

_____

_____

_____

Once Chosen Once Delivered

*"Here is my servant, whom I uphold, my chosen,
in whom my soul delights; I have put my spirit upon him;
he will bring forth justice to the nations."*

ISAIAH 42:1

Today's Prayer

Lord, I thank you for your faithfulness and for your infinite wisdom. Grant me the ability to understand your love for humanity and allow me to share that message and your love with others. Amen.

Today's Reflection

This particular portion of Isaiah has been termed as the first of the "Servant Songs." These Servant Songs appear in several places between chapters 40 and 55 in the book of Isaiah. The Servant Songs are crucial in the Christian understanding of who Christ is. According to Christian interpretation, they describe in great detail the attributes that the Messiah will possess.

They were written some five-hundred years before Jesus walked the face of the earth as a man. These Servant Songs not only tell the community of the faithful what to look for in the Christ, but they tell of an inclusive message of salvation that the Christ will bring to all humanity. The ability of God to disclose the attributes of the Messiah is amazing. Not only this, but God's faithfulness and reliability is certain. Only God has the power to deliver on promises that are more than 500 years old. Live in awe of God!

Today's Song: "How Lovely on the Mountains," #99

Journal Notes _____

_____

_____

_____

A Loving Parent

"I will not leave you orphaned."
JOHN 14:18a

Today's Prayer

Loving Jesus, you took on human flesh and human suffering to bring hope and new life to the world. You entered into our suffering. The hope of your return strengthens my faith and sustains me in trying times. Amen.

Today's Reflection

Betrayal and abandonment are two of the most devastating emotions humans can endure. In the midst of his own suffering Jesus' concern and love is for the twelve. He promises the disciples that he would not abandon them. Humans are prone to change their dispositions toward each other in the midst of trying times. The nature of God is revealed in Jesus—that is, knowing that he was about to be betrayed, he still remained faithful. The words of Christ are given to us as blessed assurances and comfort. Even when humans abandon us or betray our trust, God remains faithful.

Today's Song: "All Hail the Power of Jesus' Name," #267

Journal Notes _____

_____

_____

_____

November 24

A Pause That Saves

*When they heard this they were silenced. And they praised God,
saying, "Then God has given even to the Gentiles the
repentance that leads to life."*

ACTS 11:18

Today's Prayer

My God, creator of all life, I pray that you would allow me to understand the
changes that will continue throughout my life. Be with me and guide me through
those changes. Amen.

Today's Reflection

This particular chapter of Acts is one of transition. Dietary restrictions were a way
of life for the early Hebrews. The Jewish community practiced these laws during the
time of the apostles as well. The Lord was moving in a different direction. It was the
Lord's intention that the gospel message should be preached to all humanity. Those
who believed in Christ would receive the Holy Spirit. This message had to cut across
all cultural boundaries. God gave Peter a clear sign that the old customs were an
impediment to the spreading of the gospel. God's plan was not understood at first
but as the Jewish leaders listened to Peter's revelation, they came to understand.

Today's Song: "Praise Him! Jesus, Blessed Savior," #285

Journal Notes _____

_____

_____

_____

When the Trials Are Over

*"In this you rejoice, even if now for a little while
you have to suffer various trials."*
1 PETER 1:6

Today's Prayer

Loving Jesus, you took on human flesh and human suffering to bring hope and new life to the world. You entered into our suffering. May the hope of your return strengthen my faith and sustain me during periods of suffering. In your precious name I pray. Amen.

Today's Reflection

This is a message of hope to the Christians who were being persecuted for their faith. The message comes with words of encouragement to hold onto faith in the midst of suffering and distress with the promise of an eternal future in God's kingdom. Suffering is still a part of the human condition. And so, this message of hope holds true for Christians today as well.

The message is simple: "Hold on, in faith, to the one who suffered for you." This was a word of hope delivered in the middle of injustice and oppression. That hope is still alive. Rejoice!

Today's Song: "Great Is Thy Faithfulness," #283

Journal Notes _____

_____

_____

_____

Reading Warning Labels

"Now then, hearken to their voice; only,
you shall solemnly warn them, and show them
the ways of the king who shall reign over them."
1 SAMUEL 8:9

Today's Prayer

Give me wisdom, Father, to ask for what is pleasing to your will. Let me discern your leadership.throughout the days of my life. Amen.

Today's Reflection

A warning label should come on every bottle of ambition: "Proceed with caution. Ambition may be hazardous to your salvation." There is absolutely nothing wrong with a little ambition, but remember that ambition can drown out words of wisdom and make us slaves to it. Blind ambition for a king put the children of Israel at risk with their relationship with God.

God knew the pitfalls of following a king who may or may not have their best interest at heart. We know that God has our best interest at heart. He also is like the benevolent parent who wants us to have the desires of our hearts just as long as we go with him and not our ambition. Take inventory of your ambition and make sure that it is the Holy One who leads and inspires.

Today's Song: "Guide My Feet," #153

Journal Notes _____

_____

_____

_____

Supporting One Another

"Now may the LORD show steadfast love and faithfulness to you!
And I will do good to you because you have done this thing."

2 SAMUEL 2:6

Today's Prayer

Gracious Lord, wrap me in your inspiring love. Increase my faith in you and your plans for me. Amen.

Today's Reflection

When arguments and fights would ensue between cousins, eventually one of us would run to grandmother screaming at the injustice of a situation. My grandmother's response to that child would be, "What did you do?" She wanted us to be responsible for our actions even if the other person was wrong.

Such was the case concerning the relationship between David and King Saul. After a terse and devastating relationship with King Saul, David now had to mend fences and heal broken hearts. Even though Saul had caused much despair in his quest to kill David, when the smoke cleared David saw that many acted honorable toward the slain king. God calls for us to act honorably at all times—even when we're right and someone else is wrong!

Today's Song: "Give Me a Clean Heart," #216

Journal Notes · _____

_____

_____

_____

November 28

Time Out for God

*"A Psalm. A Song for the Sabbath. It is good to give
thanks to the LORD, to sing praises to thy name, O Most High."*
PSALM 92:1

Today's Prayer

Lord, every day of my life is dedicated to you, but the Sabbath is our time together for renewal and fellowship. Let me sing praises on this day to your glory. Amen.

Today's Reflection

Weeks on the road had made getting to church on Sunday virtually impossible. So it was a comfort to be sitting with friends and family enjoying the songs and the message of the day. This is heaven, she thought. How could I have gone so long without this?

David gave each of us bits of heaven through his psalms of praise to God. He lifted up God's magnificence and it has reached across the millennium to remind us today that the Sabbath is still the most important day in our lives. Sing praises and rejoice!

Today's Song: "Praise Him! Jesus, Blessed Savior," #285

Journal Notes

Expunged Record

*"I am He who blots out your transgressions for my own sake,
and I will not remember your sins."*

ISAIAH 43:25

Today's Prayer

O Lord, your grace abounds. Through my struggles to get it right, you have not abandoned me. I am grateful for your mercies. Amen.

Today's Reflection

The mother stood over her daughter's bed, watching each breath, wanting to breathe for her. The good news was that her daughter would live. For that she was grateful. The knife had missed her heart by mere inches. For months the mother and the daughter were embroiled in a contest of wills. Adolescence was hard on both of them. Now, observing both the monitors and her daughter, the mother only thought about her daughter's healing and recovery.

Like this mother, God is often put through misery and pain over our actions and decisions. In the end, God only wants our healing and recovery. It comes through God's unique brand of forgiveness—forgiveness so strong that it expunges our records of sin so that the healing can begin.

Today's Song: "The Blood that Jesus Shed for Me," #201

Journal Notes _____

_____

_____

_____

November 30

The Good Time News

*The angel replied, "I am Gabriel. I stand in
the presence of God, and I have been sent to speak to
you and to bring you this good news."*
LUKE 1:19

Today's Prayer

The good news, Lord, is that you and I together can get through anything. That's enough for me. Amen.

Today's Reflection

The day started off wrong for most people coming into the office. Along with traffic and a crowded parking lot, it was raining the proverbial cats and dogs and cold. Everyone who came through the door grumbled and complained. That was why it was so startling to see someone who was smiling.

"How are you?" the receptionist ventured.

The woman smiled broadly. "The good news is that I'm here safe and sound. Thank God."

Look for the good news. Even in the midst of a storm, there is good news in God.

Today's Song: "Great Is Thy Faithfulness," #283

Journal Notes _____

_____

_____

_____

December 1

Giving into God

*"If you keep my commandments, you will abide in my love,
just as I have kept my Father's commandments
and abide in his love."*
JOHN 15:10

Today's Prayer

Here they are, Lord. My heart and my soul, I give to you for safekeeping. With you at the helm of my life, I live your commandments in love. Amen.

Today's Reflection

On a wonderful sunny morning, the Sunday school class was filled with energetic teens. They looked like any other teenagers in any city, but these were young people who had been abused and neglected—discarded.

Bused to nearby church, they were in need of something that would help them get through the pain and hurt of separation. How do we answer the need?

Neglected and abused children need to know that Jesus is the answer, that he showed us the way. He restored individuals to communities through healing the mind, body, and spirit. We, too, can do this. The commandment to love one another means living the example that Jesus set for us. When we answer the need, we restore individuals not only to community but also to God.

Today's Song: "We Praise Thee, O God," #100

Journal Notes _____

_____

_____

_____

Same Today, Forever

"But the word of the Lord abides for ever.
That word is the good news which was preached to you."
1 PETER 1:25

Today's Prayer

Help me in my studies of your word, Lord. Etch the meanings in my heart for my day to day living. Amen.

Today's Reflection

As a biblical storyteller, telling the stories of hope is more than simple entertainment. Like the griots in Africa, storytelling united communities. Biblical storytelling unites the Word of God with people. These stories remind us that our God is still an awesome God. Peter believed that God's word would endure through time. It has. The same God that Peter preached and shared is with us today. Through everything, God is still uniting. In telling the stories, we can rest assured, secure in the knowledge that our faith in him is not in vain.

Today's Song: "Come, Thou Fount of Every Blessing," #108

Journal Notes _____

_____

_____

_____

December 3

Sacred Secrets

Saul's uncle said, "Tell me what Samuel said to you."
Saul said to his uncle, "He told us that the donkeys had been
found." But about the matter of the kingship, of which Samuel had
spoken, he did not tell him anything.

1 SAMUEL 10:15-16

Today's Prayer

I thank you, O God, for sharing the thoughts of your heart. I praise you that I don't have to wonder what you want for me, but am able to hear your voice through your word, your servants, and your witnesses. Amen.

Today's Reflection

In this information age, words, numbers, and theories flourish amongst our emails, pagers, and cellular phones. However, there are some times when the lack of information is just as critical. That is, some revelations are for our personal use, and others are for corporate consumption. We must use our wisdom on deciding what things we should share and what we should not. Often God will whisper something to us that is for us to hide in our hearts until the appropriate moment. Success and longevity are dependent on our ability to speak or be silent at the right time.

Today's Song: "Time Is Filled with Swift Transition," #231

Journal Notes

December 4

Heightened Perception

*"Then David perceived that the Lord had established him
king over Israel, and that he had exalted his kingdom
for the sake of his people Israel."*

2 SAMUEL 5:12

Today's Prayer

For the many ways you order my steps, I give you thanks. For the varied times you have allowed me to serve you and others, I give you praise. For the opportunity to give witness to your name, I offer thanksgiving. Amen.

Today's Reflection

Sometimes God blesses us or commands us to do something and we begin without being fully aware of what the assignment entails. We can be sincere in our commitment and devout in our duty, without really comprehending the significance of our service. Indeed, we do not perceive that our calling is connected to the fulfillment and realization of the kingdom. We forget or don't realize that we are part of a bigger cosmic plan. And that God is calling us and using our personal gifts for the benefit of God's divine agenda. Hence, we must remember that our seemingly small contribution is for the sake of God's people.

Today's Song: "Shine, Jesus, Shine," #64

Journal Notes _____

_____

_____

_____

Kin with a King

*"The Lord is king, he is robed in majesty; the LORD is robed,
he is girded with strength. He has established the
world, it shall not be moved."*

PSALM 93:1

Today's Prayer

God, you are King above every king. Thank you for the privilege of being in relationship with royalty. Because of my hope in you, I am grafted into the bloodline of destiny. I praise you for who you are and thank you for who I am in you. Amen.

Today's Reflection

The hallmarks of royalty are easily noted: expensive jewelry, elaborate haberdashery, eloquent service, and exquisite finery. To be sure, fairy tales and fantasy thrive because of the wonder and the glamour of kingdoms, old and contemporary, fictional and real. However, we who are not biologically born from the seed of a king and queen are not excluded from the benefits of being a prince or princess. Indeed, our parent is commander in chief of an eternal kingdom. Our God is not limited by the perishable accouterments of linens, but is robed with majesty, draped in glory and covered in strength.

Today's Song: "Blessed Assurance," #118

Journal Notes

_____

_____

_____

_____

Intentionally Dark and Elusive Light

*"I form light and create darkness. I make weal and
create woe. I the LORD do all these things."*

ISAIAH 45:7

Today's Prayer

God of day and night, ruler of joy and sorrow, I exalt you as king. I celebrate your power. I extol your glory. I celebrate your sovereignty. I am grateful to be called one of your children. I am awed by your commitment to me and the generations that will follow. Amen.

Today's Reflection

When horrible things happen to decent people and good things happen to horrible people, we are often quick to accuse the devil or question God. We rather easily behave as if God is not ultimately in control of the happenings in the earth and as if Satan has unlimited rule. However, the biblical text reminds us that God is creator of everything, and is aware of the good and the bad, the light and the dark. God is Lord of everything, and allows all according to God's perfect pleasure and plan.

Today's Song: "Guide My Feet," #153

Journal Notes _____

_____

_____

_____

Surprise and Servanthood

Then Mary said, "Here am I the servant of the Lord;
let it be with me according to your word."
Then the angel departed from her.
LUKE 1:38

Today's Prayer

In the midst of fear and confusion, give me strength to follow. When your word challenges my thinking and confuses my understanding, give me courage to believe. When your promise seems too spectacular to embrace, grant me patience to stand. In Jesus' name. Amen.

Today's Reflection

Often our response to God's invitation to service is outright query or subconscious refusal. We can be hesitant to concur with God's agenda, especially when God's intent both defies our understanding and challenges societal norms of acceptance and protocol. It is relatively easier to obey God when God follows the rules. But God is accustomed to working with divine paradigms and according to heavenly timing. As such, we are called to respond as servants awaiting our master's request. When we respond quickly, and in a posture of humble obedience, God can, and will, bring forth the birth of new destinies. Yes. Surprises can be God's invitation to servanthood.

Today's Song: "I Can Hear My Savior Calling," #146

Journal Notes _____

_____

_____

_____

December 8

Chosen

*"But you are a chosen race, a royal priesthood, a holy nation,
God's own people, in order that you may proclaim the mighty acts of
him who called you out of darkness into his marvelous light."*
1 PETER 2:9

Today's Prayer

When I was in darkness, you called me. When others disowned and disregarded me, you chose me. When I was wandering and wondering, you claimed me. Thank you for being attentive to and vested in me. Amen.

Today's Reflection

When God intentionally invited us into personal and intimate relationship, God slapped luck, chance, and accident in the face. We don't have to hope that we are valuable and were created to make a difference: we know it. God, through Christ Jesus, knitted together the scattered pieces of broken lives, making a spiritual quilt that heralds the diversity of the kingdom. In fact, we can no longer be confused with spiritual nomads or confessional vagabonds. We have a home and a God. Those of us who believe are not just any group of people, but God's own people—called to serve, celebrate, and stand on God's promises.

Today's Song: "I Heard an Old, Old Story," #97

Journal Notes

December 9

Spirit-Sense

*"When the Spirit of truth comes, he will guide you into all the truth;
for he will not speak on his own, but will speak whatever he hears,
and he will declare to you the things that are to come."*

JOHN 16:13

Today's Prayer

As I search after truth, O God, help me to sense your direction and perceive your will. As I seek after understanding, tune my ears to the frequency of heaven. As I hunger for you, cause me to understand your way. Come Holy Spirit, come. Amen.

Today's Reflection

Magazines or newspapers cannot contain the volumes of truth that flow from the Spirit. While such mass media help us to better understand the world and the issues that face us as human beings on a decaying planet, they only report what people have perceived via the natural senses. However, the Holy Spirit, the promised Comforter and Advocate, speaks that which comes from God the Creator and glorifies the Son. The Spirit is as the singular reliable source for the past, present, and future, the Holy Spirit guides us past the normal and natural to the realm of the supernatural and eternal.

Today's Song: "Spirit of the Living God," #101

Journal Notes _____

_____

_____

_____

December 10

God's Sight

"For the LORD does not see as mortals see;
they look on the outward appearance,
the Lord looks on the heart."

1 SAMUEL 16:7c

Today's Prayer

Gracious God, we judge ourselves and others by such superficialities. Outward appearance may make us recognizable, but it has little to do with integrity, character, or the kind of person you would have us be. Racism and sexism bar the reality of an individual's humanity. As I grow in your love, help me to grow in the depth of love for all people. Amen.

Today's Reflection

When the Lord rejects Saul as heir to the throne, the prophet Samuel, is sent to the home of Jesse in Bethlehem to choose a king. Seven of the sons of Jesse pass by Samuel. None of these are acceptable to the Lord. The eighth son, David the shepherd, is chosen and anointed by Samuel.

Today's Song: "We Praise Thee, O God," #100

Journal Notes _____

_____

_____

_____

Hearing God's Word through Others

"The Spirit of the LORD speaks through me,
his word is upon my tongue."

2 SAMUEL 23:2

Today's Prayer

Creator God, the words of David inspire me. I would want to live so closely with you that I would speak only your words. I am far from that kind of perfection. Let me grow in your grace, acceptable in your sight. In Jesus' name I pray. Amen.

Today's Reflection

David proclaims that God has made an everlasting covenant with him. He believes himself to be a just king. God is the only true judge for each of us. This is why the understanding of a savior who pleads on our behalf is so acceptable.

Jesus Christ is the model of perfection, the example of complete love. He stands in our stead and is God's instrument of our redemption. Praise God! Praise Jesus Christ! Praise the Holy Spirit!

Today's Song: "Lord, I Want to Be a Christian," #234

Journal Notes _____

_____

_____

_____

Singing Praises to God

"O come, let us sing to the LORD;
let us make a joyful noise to the rock of our salvation!"

PSALM 95:1

Today's Prayer

Creator God, praise is due you with every breath. It is by your hand that we are made. You are a great God, and we are called to worship and obey you. You are our God—guide us through the hard paths of this life. We look forward to the day of salvation. Amen.

Today's Reflection

When we look back over our lives and acknowledge the ways God has brought us through, we cannot praise God enough. At 81 years of age, I cherish each day and each experience. Yet I can hear my 102-year-old mother saying, "You come to the place where you know this world is not your home. My next move is to see Jesus. What a day of rejoicing!" I praise God for parents who were believers and for children who believe also! Praise to the rock of our salvation."

Today's Song: "Oh, When the Saints Go Marching In," #180

Journal Notes _____

_____

_____

_____

December 13

There Is Only God

"Declare and present your case; let them take counsel together!
Who told this long ago? Who declared it old? Was it not I, the Lord?
There is no other God besides me, a righteous God and a Savior;
there is no one besides me."

ISAIAH 45:21

Today's Prayer

Most gracious and all-wise God, there is no one beside you. There is no need for any other God. Your sovereignty is unquestionable. The longer I live, the surer I am that one lifetime is not enough to know all about you. Thank you for revealing yourself in Jesus Christ and covering us with your Spirit. Amen.

Today's Reflection

When God created humankind, God chose to love us, care for us, to show inexhaustible patience toward us. When God seeks our help, God doesn't really need us, but we need God and slowly and carefully God reshapes us in the image of God. When will we learn God's ways are past questioning? We need only to believe.

Today's Song: "I, the Lord of Sea and Sky," #230

Journal Notes _____

_____

_____

_____

December 14

A Growing Blessing

*"Elizabeth heard Mary's greeting the child leaped in her womb.
And Elizabeth was filled with the Holy Spirit, and exclaimed
with a loud cry, "Blessed are you among women and
blessed is the fruit of your womb."*
LUKE 1:41-42

Today's Prayer

Creator God, Mary was chosen for your great plan of salvation. Through a woman you have given to us your son. With millions of children without mothers today, this special relationship can be a choice of love. In the name of Jesus, I pray. Amen.

Today's Reflection

When Mary and her cousin Elizabeth meet, both are pregnant. Mary's song of praise, called the *Magnificat,* is one of the favorite biblical scriptures, especially for those of us who are blessed to have children. Mary's praise of God and all that God has done and will do sends chills of joy up my spine. Mary sings not only of her own blessedness but also of the justice of God toward all people. God has brought down the powerful and raised the lowly; filled the hungry with good things and sent the rich away empty. I don't want to wait till Christmastime to read these words of joy. I need them every day.

Today's Song: "My Soul Does Magnify the Lord," #168

Journal Notes _____

_____

_____

_____

A Holy Revelation

"For I want you to know, brothers and sisters, that the gospel that was proclaimed by me is not of human origin for I did not receive it from a human source, nor was I taught it, but I received it through a revelation of Jesus Christ."

GALATIANS 1:11-12

Today's Prayer

I thank God for another Christmas season. There is so much to celebrate. God's plan of salvation lifts my heart and encourages my spirit. The one that is to come is my Lord and Savior Jesus Christ. Amen.

Today's Reflection

Paul is one of the most unlikely miracles of God's choice for leadership in the church, but the Damascus Road experience with the risen Christ marks him as one to spread the good news of the gospel. He speaks and writes clearly and with certainty. God's revelation to Paul not only changed his life, but produced foundational documents of our faith.

Today's Song: "Go Tell It on the Mountain," #52

Journal Notes _____

_____

_____

_____

God's Seal

*"In him you also, when you had heard the word of truth,
the gospel of your salvation, and had believed in him, were marked
with the seal of the promised Holy Spirit. This is the pledge
of our inheritance toward redemption as God's own
people, to the praise of his glory."*

EPHESIANS 1:13-14

Today's Prayer

Dear Lord, thank you for those whom you called to follow you and to those to whom you revealed yourself and your message. As we study your word and share the faith, strengthen our witness by your power. In your name I pray. Amen.

Today's Reflection

For centuries, men and women have been "marked with the seal of the Holy Spirit" to become God's people in the world. As they proclaim the good news of the gospel of Jesus Christ may their lives be blessed by the constant assurance of God's love for them. May you continue to reveal your truths and make clear your call in their lives. Dear Lord, strengthen the church with inspired leadership.

Today's Song: "I Can Hear My Savior Calling," #146

Journal Notes

December 17

Holy Splendor: Worship the Lord

"Worship the LORD in holy splendor;
tremble before him, all the earth."
PSALM 96:9

Today's Prayer

May the brightness of our raiment declare the glory that is forever yours, O God, of our hope and our salvation. Amen.

Today's Reflection

We sing the splendor of God in song and all creation declares the wonder of God's work in the world. All peoples of the earth are called to know the salvation of God. And knowing the greatness of God, all people are called to worship.

In our contemporary world, worship, the worth we ascribe to someone or something, is often dependent on our sense of what's in it for me. What have you done for me lately? This question as a focus obscures the connection and focus we theologically understand, worship, of necessity must have. The emphasis in worship is on God. So then, why does the psalmist cry, "Worship the Lord in holy splendor"? What does what we put on have to do with God?

Everything we have, everything we are, everything we will become is God's gift of God's self to us. We are called by the psalmist to ascribe to God the worth that is God's by the adorning of ourselves in holy splendor.

Today's Song: "Give Me a Clean Heart," #216

Journal Notes _____

_____

_____

_____

December 18

Into God's Presence with Gladness

"Worship the LORD with gladness;
come into his presence with singing."
PSALM 100:2

Today's Prayer

Every day, Lord, may we find reason to give you thanks. For you are worthy of thanksgiving and blessing and honor whether or not we realize it. As you sustain this world by your loving kindness, sustain us also in the knowledge of your goodness and mercy as we give praise to you this day and all the days of our life. Amen.

Today's Reflection

Gladness. How does one know gladness? Is gladness a decision, a force of will? Can one decide within ones heart to be glad? Certainly the psalmist believes this to be the case. The psalmist commands that those who would worship the Lord do so with joy, with gladness.

But there are times when gladness seems impossible, and there are times when my soul is heavy. At such moments it seems there isn't much in life worth singing about. Is gladness like joy a state one can be in whether we're happy or sad? The psalmist seems to think this is the case. We can be glad because we know that the Lord is God, the creator of all that is. We can be glad because the love of the Lord for us lasts for always. God loves us. God loves this present generation as God has loved forever. God will be faithful in love with each and every generation.

Today's Song: "I Will Enter His Gates," #291

Journal Notes _____

_____

_____

_____

December 19

Look Up!

*"I lift up my eyes to the hills—from where will
my help come? My help comes from the* Lord*,
the maker of heaven and earth."*
PSALM 121:1-2

Today's Prayer

Lift us up, Lord God, creator of heaven and earth. Lift us up especially at those times in life when the shakiness of uncertainty plagues our coming and going. Then, trusting in the confidence that it is your will to protect souls everywhere always from every danger, as we raise our eyes to the hills in search of you, elevate our thoughts and imaginations to be in accord with your purpose for all creation. For you, O God, are worthy to be praised as one God Father, Son, and Holy Spirit, now and forever. Amen.

Today's Reflection

Sometimes life throws you nothing but curves. Sometimes life itself seems like nothing but a long unwieldy curve, difficult to navigate, impossible to predict. As a child I grew up in the flat lands of the urban jungle, Chicago. What passed for a hill there—would seem like nothing more than a bump in the road on the east coast where I've now lived most of my adult life.

As I've lived out this eastern sojourn in a number of places I've often looked to the hills for a sense of respite, assurance, and hope. Hills have reminded me of the need to go higher, to be close to God.

Today's Song: "I, the Lord of Sea and Sky," #230

Journal Notes _____

_____

_____

_____

What's in a Name?

*"For a child has been born for us, a son given to us; authority rests
upon his shoulders; and he is named Wonderful Counselor,
Mighty God, Everlasting Father, Prince of Peace."*

ISAIAH 9:6-7

Today's Prayer

As we call upon your name, O Lord, help us in the naming we employ with one
another to move the peoples of this planet closer to the transformation you desire for
all the world. Then may we hold you and one another as holy as we dare to acknowledge your name as Wonderful Counselor, Mighty God, Everlasting Father, Prince of
Peace. Amen.

Today's Reflection

Every child is a gift to the world, a gift to the child's loved ones, a gift to the
cosmos. This child, alluded to in the Christian use of a Hebrew prophecy, is the gift
of God, God's Son became incarnate for us and for all the world.

Today's Song: "I Will Call Upon the Lord," #277

Journal Notes _____

_____

_____

_____

In a Dream: A Resolution

*"But just when he had resolved to do this, an angel of the
Lord appeared to him in a dream and said, "Joseph, son of David,
do not be afraid to take Mary as your wife, for the child
conceived in her is from the Holy Spirit."*
MATTHEW 1:18-24

Today's Prayer

Emmanuel, God with us, you have revealed yourself to us in the birth of your
child, Jesus. As we celebrate this season of the Messiah's birth, may the conception
of your love born in us by means of a dream, make us forever accepting of all
children as gifts as ambassadors of your love and grace. Amen.

Today's Reflection

God acts. Instruction comes in a dream. The conscious of one who strives to
do God's will is troubled by his sense of propriety and his desire to do both what is
right and merciful. The resolve to quietly annul the marriage/engagement contract
between Mary and Joseph is a result of her seeming deception. To do what is right,
to demonstrate that his love for God is stronger than his love for anyone, Joseph
resolves to do what is right. But he also wishes to cause her no public humiliation.
In a dream Joseph is instructed by an angel that the child conceived in Mary is from
God. Joseph must accept the child as his own. By naming the child, Joseph demon-
strates his understanding that God's action requires our trust and our willingness to
act on that trust.

Today's Song: "I Will Trust in the Lord," #256

Journal Notes _____

_____

_____

_____

December 22

The Glory Shone Around

Then an angel of the Lord stood before them, and the glory of the
Lord shone around then, and they were terrified. But the angel said
to them, "Do not be afraid: for see—I am bringing you good
news of a great joy for all the people."
LUKE 2:8-20

Today's Prayer

Everlasting Father, Prince of Peace, we give glory to you even in the most trying of life's circumstances. Help us to see your glory where glory seems most to evade us. But help us always in all life's circumstances to see your glory in each other. Amen.

Today's Reflection

To all appearances there was nothing about the circumstances of this child's birth that would make me think of glory. At the time of delivery, Joseph and Mary are traveling so they may be properly counted in a census mandated by their Roman oppressors. They arrive in the ancestral homeland of Joseph and discover upon their arrival that there is no place for them to stay.

Our true home is found in relationships of belonging. The glory of God was manifest in creation that night as all the heavenly host praised God and surrounded this wondrous family with protection, even as they sing, "Glory to God." And the glory of God shone all around them. And the glory of God was everywhere in everyone. But, most certainly, the glory of God was in this child and in Mary and in Joseph.

Today's Song: "Glory to God," #24

Journal Notes _____

_____

_____

_____

December 23

Set Free

"For freedom Christ has set us free."
GALATIANS 5:1-6

Today's Prayer

Out of love you gave us freedom as one of your original gifts, Life-giving author of all creation, as we live our lives help us never to forsake the gift of liberty you have bestowed on us from the very beginning of creation's dawning. Amen.

Today's Reflection

During the days I served as Lutheran chaplain at Howard University, my office, located on the lower level of Andrew Rankin Memorial Chapel was privy to over-hearing the practice sessions of the Howard University Choir. More than once the smallness of the physical space granted me was enlarged by the greatness of the marvelous voices echoing through the building. On occasion I was present to hear the choir rehearse one of my favorite spirituals, "Oh, Freedom!" And as I heard the words of this spiritual resounding through the building, my soul and my spirit were not immune to the ponderous depths of the spiritual's refrain: "Oh, Freedom! Oh, Oh, Freedom! Oh, Freedom over me. And before I'll be a slave, I'll be buried in my grave and go home to my Lord, and be free!"

Those who remain in relationship with Christ Jesus are free in their souls, free in their minds, free in their very being. No one or no thing could keep them bound, keep them down, keep them from being who they were meant to be in God's sight or their own. God created us to live in freedom and for freedom Christ has set us free.

Today's Song: "Glory to God," #24

Journal Notes

Increase My Strength of Soul

*"On the day I called, you answered me,
you increased my strength of soul."*
PSALM 138

Today's Prayer

When we're at the end of our nerves and life's frayed ends disillusion us, we pray, O Lord our God, that you would increase the strength of our souls. Amen.

Today's Reflection

Good deeds are not always rewarded. I am counseled by one who advocates the idea of my caving in to the dominant materialist culture. Despite the urging to conform, I find it difficult to give in to the mediocrity of opportunism, and I am saddened, disillusioned and depressed by the morass of empty self-satisfaction I discover in those who are content with things in this world as they are.

How, I wonder, do they understand the call of God on them, on their lives, on their future? Or, do they even acknowledge there is a God whose love and care for us necessitates that we acknowledge in our lives that there is something far more important than the pursuit of materialist ends? Prayer reminds me that the gift of this season is known through God's giving of self for the sake of our well-being. Prayer links me with better times and with the generations of Christians who never forgot why we celebrate love, hope, and joy at year's end.

Today's Song: "Jesus, the Light of the World," #59

Journal Notes _____

_____

_____

_____

December 25

Fear or Wonder?

*" When King Herod heard this, he was frightened,
and all Jerusalem with him."*
MATTHEW 2:1-11

Today's Prayer

At the birth of the child, Jesus, heaven and earth witnessed your wondrous intervention for the healing of this cosmos as a new star rose to its zenith. So now, we pray, help us to remain steadfast and faithful without duplicity in giving honor to you and to your child, our savior, Jesus the Christ. Amen.

Today's Reflection

A new day is dawning. God is acting. In the seeming innocence of a child born in the dark of quiet night, whose imponderable depths were known only to a few human beings and those mysterious powers in the cosmos that were alert to the significance of this child, this rising star's cresting on the horizon, God was turning the world upside down. According to Matthew, this child—this incarnation of God, would have for a while remained hidden. Except that some wise men who were especially attuned to God's acting in the universe decided to do what is purely natural for those observant of God's work in the world, they sought the child to honor him, to acknowledge that in this child, God was doing something new.

Today's Song: "In the Morning When I Rise," #165

Journal Notes _____

_____

_____

_____

Herod's Nightmare / Joseph's Dream

*Now after they had left, an angel of the Lord appeared to Joseph
in a dream and said, "Get up, take the child and his mother, and flee
to Egypt, and remain there until I tell you; for Herod is about to
search for the child, to destroy him."*

MATTHEW 2:12-23

Today's Prayer

O Comforter, who gives us dreams both as a sign of warning and as sign of future fulfillment, give us courage to act pursuing only those dreams that accord with your will for our health and salvation. Amen.

Today's Reflection

In a dream comes a warning. Escape! There is danger in remaining in situations where the powerful have murderous intents. The threat Herod feels by the birth of Jesus will not cease until he has done whatever he can to eliminate the challenge this child represents to his power and privilege. To Herod, this child, Jesus, who is the fulfillment of Israel's dreams, is simply a nightmare.

In a dream, Joseph is warned—fly to Egypt. Stay there until you receive God's word "that those who seek the child's life are dead." As Israel found refuge and safety in Egypt at a time of calamity, so now, this child who is the new Israel finds solace with his family hidden out of harm's way in Egypt. The prophets had predicted God would release Israel to her homeland by calling his child out of that place. Herod's nightmare was Joseph's dream—and God's dream for us.

Today's Song: "Every Time I Feel the Spirit," #241

Journal Notes

_____

_____

_____

_____

December 27

Healing the Broken

The Lord has proclaimed to the end of the earth:
Say to daughter Zion, "See your salvation comes."
ISAIAH 62:10-12

Today's Prayer

When the hardships of life seem most bleak to us, Merciful and Compassionate One, help us to discern your caring presence. Do not be distant, O God, but draw ever nearer to us guiding us through life's wilderness and on life's journey. Amen.

Today's Reflection

Life, at times, may seem like one perilous battle after another. In the struggle to do what is right, to let justice prevail, to pay attention to that which is good, beautiful, and truthful, the victor often seems to be the one who cares nothing for virtue, only for what is self-promoting. Living, working, being in such a climate is toxic. It can feel like a personal experience of the torment of hell.

At such times, in such conditions, salvation comes only with God's help and the realization that God hurts when the wounded, suffering, or poor are neglected or ignored. God does not withhold compassion and mercy.

God desires healing for the nations, healing that begins with the broken hearts and restless spirits of people here, now.

The question for us is do we dare trust God to act? In the bleakness of days when the battles of life seem most dire we are asked to remember God will not abandon or forsake us.

Today's Song: "There Is a Balm in Gilead," #185

Journal Notes _____

_____

_____

_____

In Season and Out

*"For everything there is a season,
and a time for every matter under heaven."*

ECCLESIASTES 3:1-14

Today's Prayer

There is a time for every matter under heaven, but all too often we neglect sharing time with you, O Lord our God, so we pray, help us in the balance of our lives to spend our seasons of being with you, in the company of your loved ones. Amen.

Today's Reflection

Balance is required in this life and the paradox of opposites must remain juxtaposed in reality for life to be all that life is meant to be. The movement of life is like the seasons—there is a time for every matter, there is a time for every purpose under heaven.

Seasons change, seasons grow and evolve, and so do we. If we'd give more of our time and attention to the balance between doing and being, between making and becoming, we'd become more and more aware in the inner depths of our souls that God is present everywhere. God is in us and through us and all around us—all the time—in season and out.

Today's Song: "God Sent His Son," #93

Journal Notes _____

_____

_____

_____

What Makes for Wisdom

"Besides being wise, the Teacher also taught the people knowledge, weighing and studying and arranging many proverbs. The teacher sought to find pleasing words, and wrote words of truth plainly."
ECCLESIASTES 12:9-14

Today's Prayer

O Eternal Wisdom, you feed and nurture us from the well-spring of your being. Draw us ever nearer to you that we may never weary of the depths of your resources. Amen.

Today's Reflection

The teachers I remember most are those who shared with me their souls at the same time they were engaged in imparting learning. Some of my teachers were professional: those who taught me science and mathematics as well as the basics of the faith I possess. Others were mentors, friends, and family members.

My father, who for many years was as a teacher of emotionally and mentally disabled children, has taught me much on the journey of life, including this: first and foremost, do not let the circumstances of life diminish your sense of self. Your being consists of who you are—not necessarily, where you happen to find yourself. I believe he learned this from his parents as well as from my mother's parents, especially my maternal grandfather. Kindness, gentleness, generosity, and love were the characteristic marks of my grandfather. When you were in his presence you could feel the love. Love, it seems to me, is an essential aspect of teaching.

Today's Song: "When Peace, Like a River," #194

Journal Notes

_____

_____

_____

_____

December 30

Seeing Release

*"It had been revealed to him (Simeon) by the Holy Spirit that he
would not see death before he had seen the Lord's Messiah."*

LUKE 2:25-32

Today's Prayer

Fill us with your Holy Spirit, that we may be able to see in the present like Simeon
of old your future with us in the offering of our selves and the current generation to
accomplish your will, O God. Amen.

Today's Reflection

I grew up as one of those children who heard from my parents and grandparents
that opportunities were being given to the children in my generation that had here-
to-fore been unavailable to black children in the United States. Those who were the
elders in the time of my youth often longed and hoped for a more just and equitable
society. And they saw in the promise of their children, God's promise for release from
a racist and oppressive social order. I imagine Simeon to be an Israelite elder sharing
the same sorts of dreams and hopes for Israel that my elders held for the children of
my generation at the time of my youth.

Simeon, a devout and prayerful elder, filled with the Holy Spirit, was able to see
what passes beyond the eyes of most. In this child is Israel's redemption, but not only
Israel's redemption—in Israel's redemption is also the universal salvation of all
humankind.

Today's Song: "In the Name of Jesus," #265

Journal Notes

_____

_____

_____

_____

December 31

The Bright Morning

*"I am the Alpha and the Omega, the first and the last,
the beginning and the end."*
REVELATION 22:6-16

Today's Prayer

Eternal and Everlasting God, thank you for giving my life purpose and meaning. Lord God, you know my beginning and my end. I pray to trust you to guide me daily to worship and serve you with my life. Amen.

Today's Reflection

Jesus has seen our life from beginning to end. Jesus knows our past and future. Jesus describes himself as the first and the last. There is nothing outside of God's presence and power. All that exists comes before an eternal, everlasting God.

There is peace in knowing that our lives do not take God by surprise. Everything that touches us was part of God's plan in the life, death, and resurrection of Jesus Christ. God's plan to reconcile the world in Christ includes us and the events of our daily lives! As we go about our daily lives, experiencing the mundane and the unexpected, let us take courage in knowing that we worship an ever-present, eternal God.

Today's Song: "What a Fellowship, What a Joy Divine," #220

Journal Notes _____

_____

_____

_____

Contributors

The following people wrote daily devotions for *What Can Happen When We Pray*:

Maria Alma Copeland
Interim Pastor, Lebanon Lutheran Church (Evangelical Lutheran Church in America),
Lexington, North Carolina
February 26; March 4; August 20-26

Alise Barrymore
Campus Pastor, North Park University, Chicago, Illinois
April 30—May 6; June 11-17; October 22-28; December 3-9

Barbara Berry-Bailey
Senior Pastor, Trinity Lutheran Church (ELCA), Philadelphia, Pennsylvania
February 12-18; August 6-12

Ronald S. Bonner
Manager of Multicultural Resources, Augsburg Fortress, Minneapolis, Minnesota
September 24-30

Linda Boston
Pastor, Grace Lutheran Church (ELCA), San Jose, California
January 15-21; July 9-15

Diana Bradie-Timberlake
Battalion Chaplain, United States Army Reserve, and
Assistant Pastor, God Can Ministries (United Church of Christ)
May 21-27; November 12-18

Wyvetta Bullock
Co-Executive Director, Division of Congregational Ministries, ELCA,
Chicago, Illinois
December 31

Leslie Cannon
Senior Associate Minister, Peoples Congregational (UCC), Washington, D.C.
March 19-25; September 10-16

Joseph Donnella
Chaplain, Gettysburg College, Gettysburg, Pennsylvania
December 17-30

Barbara Essex
Coordinator, National Religious Leadership Project, and
Dean, Pacific School of Religion, Berekely, California
January 22-28; July 16-23

Michelle Hughes-Wade
Church program consultant and resource developer, living in Chicago, Illinois
May 7-13; October 29—November 4

Karl Johnson
Program Director, Mid-American Baptist Social Services, Minneapolis, Minnesota
May 14-20; November 5-11

Regina Johnson
Pastor, New Life Community Church (ELCA), Detroit, Michigan
March 12-18; September 3-9

Vera Johnson
Assistant Pastor, Shepherd, Hills Lutheran Church (ELCA),
Shoreview, Minnesota
May 28—June 3; November 19-25

Leotyne Kelly
Retired Bishop of the United Methodist Church, living in California
June 18-24; December 10-16

Walter May
Assistant to the Bishop, Southeastern Iowa Synod (ELCA), Iowa City, Iowa
March 5-11; August 27—September 2

P. K. McCary
Author and biblical storyteller, living in Houston, Texas
February 5-11; June 4-10; July 30—August 5; November 26—December 2

Madline Sadler
Executive Director, Exodus Foundation, Durham, North Carolina.
April 16-22; October 8-14

Rodney Sadler
Executive Director, Black Studies Program, Duke University,
Durham, North Carolina
April 9-15; October 1-7

Angela Shannon
Pastor and church administrator, living in Houston, Texas
April 3-8

Susan Smith
Senior Pastor, Advent (UCC), Columbus, Ohio
January 29—February 4; July 23-29

Gwen Snell
Pastor (ELCA), living in Cleveland, Ohio
March 26—April 2; September 17-23

Harvard Stephens
Lutheran Chaplain (ELCA), Howard University, Washington, D.C.
January 8-14; April 23-29; July 2-8; October 15-21

Joyce Thomas
Seminary student, Memphis Theological Seminary, Memphis, Tennessee.
February 19-25; August 13-19

Jacqueline Lewis Tillman
Project Consultant, The Alban Institute, Bethesda, Maryland.
January 1-7; June 25—July 1

Jeremiah A. Wright Jr.
Senior Pastor, Trinity (UCC), Chicago, Illinois.
Foreword